1984

THE CELLULOID SACRIFICE

THE CELLULOID SACRIFICE

ASPECTS OF SEX IN THE MOVIES

Alexander Walker

'The Cinema, that Temple of
Sex, with its Goddesses,
its Guardians, and its Victims.'

—*Jean Cocteau*

HAWTHORN BOOKS INC.,
Publishers New York City

 All inquiries should be addressed to Hawthorn Books, Inc., 70 Fifth Avenue, New York City 10011. Library of Congress Catalogue Card Number: 66-22309.

First American Edition
March, 1967

Printed in Great Britain

1118

For Father and Mother

CONTENTS

ILLUSTRATIONS

PREFACE

The theme of this book was suggested indirectly by a remark of Jean Cocteau's at the 1959 Cannes Festival. 'The cinema,' he said, 'that temple of sex, with its goddesses, its guardians and its victims.' I am aware that seven years later, written down, and in English, the words have a taste of preciousness about them. One really needs to have heard Cocteau pronounce them, in sing-song French, pointing his haggard lion's face carefully out to sea in the general direction of Egypt and, with his exhausted mane of grey hair, looking for a moment like France's own pet Sphynx. I have probably given his remark more Anglo-Saxon literalness than he intended. But it serves as a text for a book with three aims. The first is to enquire into the nature of female sexuality as it manifests itself on the screen and in the persons of over half-a-dozen stars. The second is to examine how the sex drive on the screen is controlled, and sometimes frustrated, by the censors who are the official guardians of public morality. The third is in the nature of an inquest, on the limited scale offered by the Italian and Hollywood sex comedies, into the way that male heroes on the screen have become the 'victims' of female domination. Overall, the book is an attempt to bring psychology, biography, film history and film criticism to bear on these aspects of sex in the movies.

It should be acknowledged at once that, with the exception of the Italian sex comedy and Marcello Mastroianni, the survey confines itself to Hollywood stars and films and Anglo-American censorship. One reason for this is the need to delimit the territory usefully – sex is a sprawling subject. Another reason is because the industry-centred films of Hollywood and Britain throw up sociological material more richly and directly than the cinema of Continental Europe which is, broadly spreaking, the product of individuals who impose their own view of life on society. A third reason is to enable some new and possibly controversial views to be presented of stars and films which the majority of people will be acquainted with, either from memory or from current filmgoing or TV viewing. The Italian sex comedy is included because of the close kinship it appears to have with the Hollywood *genre*.

Books about the movies generally ask 'How?' In the main, I have tried to ask 'Why?' Why such and such a star is, or was, so successful in projecting her sex appeal, rather than how she became the star she is, or was, in the purely biographical sense. Why the British censor permits more sexual leeway to some film-makers than to others; why his Hollywood counterparts take a far more repressive view of movie sex. And why, although the societies they spring from seem so very different, the Italian and Hollywood sex comedies both show the same declining graph of male supremacy.

It is scarcely necessary to say that in analysing the human personality there are no certainties, only subjective impressions. In the case of film stars, these impressions are made that much more treacherous by the 'myths' that surround the stars, falsifying one's view of their natures and achievements – sometimes greater achievements than they are given credit for, sometimes less. I have tried to make one aware of such 'myths' and the energising part they play in stardom. But I wish to stress that any conclusions I have reached about the appeal of the female sex stars are not put forward as categorical truths – simply as stimulating interpretations based on reasonable likelihood. My aim has been to ascribe a sexual identity to the artist in the way that, in other fields, one might furnish a character reference. It can be objected that a person's sexual identity is only a part, and perhaps not the major part, of his or her personality; and of course this is true. Nevertheless a moment's reflection shows that the dominant motif in the cinema has been sex appeal; and the stars chosen for study are those whose careers and lives off screen formed their characters in a way that assisted the peculiar kind of sex appeal associated with them on the screen. Some of them, of course, had this appeal deliberately created for them by others; and they then assimilated it into their performances and personalities. Often they regretted it: for the 'image' stuck to them and resisted change. If there is any theme, apart from the sexual, that runs through the first part of this book, it is the disorientating effect that stardom has on all but the most elemental wills.

The second section is not a history of censorship, but a commentary on the problems, again mainly sexual, which the British and American censors have had to face in recent years. The Hollywood 'morality crisis' of 1964–65 has probably changed the nature of American censorship as ruthlessly as the formation of the Legion of Decency created it during a similar morality crisis thirty years before. Similarly the involvement of the British censor in the artistic creation of films that he will later have to pass judgment on is changing the nature of *his* job. It is timely to examine both trends before subsequent events obscure them. Again the main aim is not to argue for or against censorship, but to enquire into *why* the current censors in both countries function as they do.

The 'Western' and the 'musical' are the two *genres* that Hollywood is generally given the credit for inventing; and each has a large body of critical writing devoted to it. Oddly neglected is the Hollywood sex comedy, both as a form of art and as a guide to the contemporary battle positions in the war of the sexes. Never has the sex comedy American-style thrown up more bizarre material for both kinds of study than it has done in recent years. The emasculation of the male by the female has now reached a pitch where it could be accommodated in some chapter of *Psychopathia Sexualis* more comfortably than in the review columns of a newspaper or periodical. Something similar may be observed in Italian films, especially in those being geared more and more to the needs of the international – i.e., American – market; and this phenomenon presents a chance to examine the paradox of an Italian sex symbol – male, this time – who is nevertheless as much a sacrificial victim of female domination as any American hero on whom the tender trap of matrimony has snapped.

I also wrote this book as a reaction to the pleasure, and sometimes the surprise, it gave me to see certain films which have only recently become generally available – either because they are part of film libraries which have been withheld from general distribution by film companies who have at last sold them to television, or, perhaps, because a once-underrated director like Josef von Sternberg has recently come in for re-appraisal and it is possible to see all his Marlene Dietrich films in sequence over a concentrated period. But a depressing experience of anyone engaged in film research is the ease with which films – not all of them old, silent ones – simply disappear, passing out of the producers' possession into that limbo land where their copyright becomes vague, prints have disintegrated by neglect and perhaps the only decent copies are owned by a handful of 'private collectors' who are probably doing more in their dimly legal way to preserve a part of cultural history than many a film company. Even as I write, I see a report that Orson Welles's *Citizen Kane* and *The Magnificent Ambersons*, John Ford's *The Informer*, the Marx Brothers' *Room Service*, among other 'classics', are to be withdrawn from public screening for periods of from one year to eighteen months. 'They are now at the end of the line,' their American distributor is quoted as saying, 'and we have come down to fifteen-dollar and 25-dollar bookings.' In other words, such films will be kept out of circulation until their rental values are enhanced. Would such a practice be tolerated in any other branch of the arts? If anything I have written about films, or their stars, stimulates interest in them or helps restore them to the screen, this alone will make me think that writing *The Celluloid Sacrifice* has been worth while.

One fact should be noted in advance: the date which appears after the first mention of each important film is the year when it was shown, not the date of its production, unless the two are the same.

A full list of acknowledgments, personal and general, appears at the end.

London, March, 1966.

Part One
THE GODDESSES

'I have gone through a long
apprenticeship. I have gone
through enough of being nobody.
I have decided that when I am
a star I will be every inch
and every moment the star.
Everyone from the studio gate-
man to the highest executive
will know it.'

– GLORIA SWANSON

CHAPTER ONE

STRANGE ROOTS, EARLY FRUITS: BARA, BOW AND THE 'FORGOTTEN' DE MILLE

Early Hollywood presents the same difficulty as Paradise before the Fall. It is hard to believe in it. Not on account of the absolute perfection it represented: no indeed. But because it is almost impossible to imagine that there actually was a time when sex did not exist there. Sex appeal, that is to say, as one now thinks of it, as the dominant element in the overwhelming majority of American films and as one of the most potent means of projecting a star's personality. The effort of imagination this requires is made no easier by the fact that Hollywood, as one now thinks of *it*, did not exist either. Not till 1913 did a section of Los Angeles which had been colonised by the movie producers from the East Coast get the separate name and identity of Hollywood. But Hollywood is, as has been remarked, a state of mind as well as real estate; and before the outbreak of World War One the state of mind was still innocent. Movies up to 1908, according to Lewis Jacobs, the doyen of American film historians, 'advanced from "sensation, grotesque humour and everyday life" to morality dramas, the early West, American history and literary adaptations.'* Film audiences were predominantly working-class: nor were they for the most part native Americans. It is often overlooked that if the movies had been born talking they might not have been so enormously popular right away. Their very voicelessness was their main appeal to people who did not know or could not speak English – the immigrants from Europe. Native-born or second-

* *The Rise of the American Film*, by Lewis Jacobs (Harcourt, Brace & Co.), p. 77.

generation Americans had the theatre and vaudeville to entertain them: the Pole, German, Slav or Italian turned to the silent movies. It is no accident that some of the best-known of the original Hollywood moguls were of the same ethnic stock as their paying patrons – men like William Fox and Adolph Zukor from Hungary, Samuel Goldwyn from Poland, Carl Laemmle from Germany, Louis B. Mayer from Russia. (One wonders, incidentally, how far Goldwyn's celebrated gaffes like 'Include me out', which were mostly invented and which he came to detest because they made him sound like a hick, had their origins in his early adventures with the English language.)

Being newcomers, the immigrant moviegoers were mostly poor as well. And the stories the films told from 1908 till 1914 offered them consolation for their social condition by showing them people whose life was just as tough as their own, but whose spiritual goodness, cheery optimism, Samuel Smiles type of self-improvement and love of God, country and family far outweighed their daily tribulations. Sex kept its head well down in this working-class milieu. There was a curious exception, though. This was a late eruption of films about prostitution and the white slave traffic which were based, loosely, on vice investigations in New York. The first of them, *Traffic in Souls* (1913), was advertised as 'a spectacle in 700 scenes with 800 players' and certainly established the immense value of sex to the box-office. Made for 5,700 dollars, it grossed over 450,000 dollars and was followed by a host of films with similar themes including *The Inside of White Slave Traffic* (1913) which, Terry Ramsaye noted drily, 'became the focus of considerable police action and various kinds of litigation which helped to establish precedents for the motion picture.'*

It is undeniable that these films popularised sex as a subject for the screen by exploiting its social abuses. But none of them projected sex in a way that would set social fashions. One good reason for this was that as yet there were no sex stars. Indeed before 1910 it was the practice of producers not to name any of the artists in their films, lest they got a false idea of their own importance and demanded more money. (How this unexpectedly

* *A Million and One Nights*, by Terry Ramsaye (Frank Cass & Co.), p. 618

assisted some future stars, who became an image with which audiences powerfully identified even before they became a name on the posters, will be apparent from Mary Pickford's career.) Carl Laemmle was the first producer to realise the drawing-power of star names and publicly identify his players by film credits, advertising campaigns and personal appearances. By 1913 most of the major companies had publicity departments to promote interest in their contract artists. Fan magazines, which started to appear in 1912, burnished the individual personalities of the stars still more brightly. The myth-making machine was getting into felicitous clank and the players' images began to assume superhuman importance to the twenty million or so regular moviegoers. Only the producers were disenchanted as they realised how wrong their fear had been that such promotion would give the actors a false sense of their own importance. For many actors for the first time got a true sense of their own importance – and demanded more money. The producers paid up; and so the potency of large sums of money became established as an essential, almost charismatic ingredient of the star's personality.

By 1914, therefore, all the apparatus existed and was ready for the idea of sex appeal, as one now understands it, to be incarnated on the screen and projected so forcefully that it would change the sort of expectations that people took with them to the nickelodeons and establish itself as the dominant theme of the American cinema. How this came about constitutes a freakish offshoot in the movement of ideas. For it is unlikely that the names of a Pre-Raphaelite painter and an English poet are among the first that spring to mind as the progenitors of Hollywood sex appeal.

* * *

In April, 1897, Philip Burne-Jones, the son of Sir Edward, showed a painting of a woman – pale, dark-eyed, magnetic, surreal – in the summer exhibition at the New Gallery, London. It was called 'The Vampire'. The woman was clad in white, on which played a ghastly green glow, and her male victim lay stretched out on a couch beside her, his chest bared and punctured and his body suitably bloodless-looking. It was intended to be one of those 'shock' pictures which are talked about widely; and in this it succeeded. The word most frequently heard was 'gruesome'. But what was much more appreciatively discussed was a poem, also called 'The Vampire', which Burne-Jones's kinsman, Rudyard Kipling, had contributed to the catalogue. It began

> A fool there was and he made his prayer
> (Even as you and I!)
> To a rag and a bone and a hank of hair
> (We called her the woman who did not care)
> But the fool he called her his lady fair –
> (Even as you and I!)

and continued with five more stanzas relating how the worthless but irresistible woman ruins her besotted lover. The poem, which Kipling had been inspired to write by sight of the painting, was widely circulated in the United States where Bram Stoker's novel, *Dracula*, had just appeared. The two events created a vogue for the vampire type of woman who sucks the love and life out of a man; and one Porter Emerson Browne successfully achieved another kind of extraction by turning the theme of the poem into a play (1906) and later a novel (1909), both with the title *A Fool There Was*. The play was staged in 1909 at New York's Liberty Theatre, where it was a popular hit. The ingredients were stock ones on Broadway before World War One: drink, debt, marital infidelity and their melodramatic effect on the home life and the career of the Fool, whom Browne made into a diplomat recalled by the President of the United States after disgracing himself with his lady fair. The difference was that in this play the stress was laid on the fascinating home-breaker. She was a sexually aggressive woman who took pleasure in her lover's destruction. People flocked to witness this; and the most frequently used word was 'gruesome'. Porter Emerson Browne had done his work faithfully.

Some time between 1910 and 1914 William Fox bought the screen rights. Fox was then a bustling independent producer and cinema-owner fighting the monopolistic tactics of his rivals and in search of lurid subjects to give his campaign edge. Upton Sinclair has recorded, almost verbatim, Fox's version of what happened next. Before filming the play, he consulted its Broadway producer and leading man, Robert Hilliard, who told him how actresses who played the villainess tended to let success go to their heads and were always having to be replaced. 'Put the girl you choose under contract,' he advised Fox, 'as the part will make her.'* This was to be extremely important advice. For when the film's director, Frank Powell, discovered an almost unknown girl to play the part, she was put under contract to Fox who had thus the strongest self-interest in promoting her career by an unprecedented barrage of publicity. She was of course Theda Bara: the first film vampire, or vamp, and the first star to have a screen personality specially fabricated for her. Fox excelled at this. He had two vital talents for it which sometimes are mistakenly regarded as the same. He could manipulate the public's will and anticipate the public's taste. (Is it only a coincidence that he, like some of his most powerful rivals, spent part of his early working life in the garment trade where success depended above all on creating new styles, then persuading people that they wanted them? Fox cut out suit linings, Goldwyn sold gloves, Zukor was a furrier, Laemmle's family had owned an outfitter's.)

When Theda Bara met him she was called Theodosia Goodman, a tailor's daughter from Cincinnati, and she looked, one is told, 'circumspect and demure'. Fox remoulded every part of her into the image of a sex siren, starting with her name. Because the name Theda Bara is an anagram of 'death Arab', it is generally believed to have been created for these sinisterly emotive associations. This is the story Fox stuck to later on, good showman that he was. But 'Theda' is a straightforward contraction of Theodosia, 'Bara' could have come from a relation named Barranger. The likelihood is that a nimble-minded employee of the Fox publicity department evolved 'Death Arab' out of Theda Bara, not *vice versa*, and let it suggest the rest of the campaign. For Fox recalls, 'we had every type of woman on the screen except an Arabian. Our publicity director felt that the public would like

* *Upton Sinclair Presents William Fox* (published by the author), p. 56–7.

an Arabian . . .'* So an atmosphere of exotic and totally ersatz mystery was built up around the girl. Having as yet no fame of her own as an artist, she was given fascination as a personality; and this has been Hollywood's technique ever since.

She was said to have been born in Egypt, in the Pyramids' shade, child of a sheik and a princess, weaned on serpents' blood, taught the secrets of love, given in mystic marriage to the Sphynx and fought over, for more practical ends, by the wild nomadic tribesmen. Her home pastimes were listed as distilling perfumes, predicting the future and, above all, driving men crazy with love for her. The emphasis was laid on her supernatural powers, lest any sceptics questioned her consistent run of success in mesmerising all-comers. A vamp could not afford to suffer one brush-off.

Every item of the props, costumes and make-up used in the publicity photographs was made sensually suggestive. Sometimes the poses Theda Bara strikes in these are pantomimic, obviously meant to impress the hicks. The most famous shows her squatting like a jackal beside the body of a victim and, consciously or not, it apes the Burne-Jones painting which, in due course, had gone to the United States: it was exhibited by Knoedler's in 1902. But Bara in this photograph has done more than slake her thirst like the Pre-Raphaelite vamp – her victim has been reduced to a skeleton. A carnivore, too? one wonders.

But occasionally the poses project a baleful eroticism – especially the ones done in the Hoover portrait studio. In particular they emphasise her arms, long, slender and generally bare to the shoulder, to suggest her flaunting and unchaste nature. She had naturally long wavy hair that reached below her knees. Sometimes it is piled cumulously round her face like a Sphynx, sometimes she is holding skeins of it high above her head like a Fury: it is as if these were both branches of the family. Her black and sulky-looking eyes are sunk in hungry cavities of shadow in the portraits: on the screen the effect was somewhat starker, since make-up was still a short-hand way of writing one's character on one's face. (The crude, blue-white arc lamps remained in force until the

* Ibid.

Talkies brought the silent, steady-burning incandescent lighting into general use and allowed more finesse and character shading in make-up.) Bara's costumes were often more erotic than many a studio would think prudent today. A couple of loosely spun spider's webs did duty for a bra, or else an asp curved snugly round the contours of each breast, while a few bead whorls appliquéd on to her hip bone by gum arabic looked like some satyr's erotic doodling. In the historical vamp roles she wore heavy jewellery and metal chains against the bare flesh in a way that carried an undertone of perversion. At this period, of course, films had no obligation to self-censorship. In any case, more licence was allowed costumes that were surreal or plausibly historical.

Bara's build-up continued on publicity tours. Wearing Arabian robes and pretending not to speak English, she gave audiences in canopied hotel suites sweltering with incense, thick with the perfume of lilies and roses, dimly illuminated by the same greenish radiance that suffuses the Burne-Jones painting. 'The newspaper men left that day,' Fox told Upton Sinclair about one such occasion in Chicago, 'and said that the Fox Film Corporation had discovered the greatest living actress in the world.' A moment later, the 'discovery' staggered to her feet, threw up the window and gasped, 'Gimme some air!' It is extremely doubtful if newspaper men were taken in by such a charade; but Fox had calculated exactly the degree of cheerful collusion that reporters in search of good copy could be persuaded to show. With a certain cynicism he also noticed that although at first Bara did not respond when addressed by her 'stage name' (sic), little by little the star personality settled round her. Some years later she confessed, 'Never have I liked being a vampire and never, of course, have I believed there was any "such animal", but since the public did and liked to see me as one, I agreed to become one. Naturally all sorts of wild rumours and weird stories about me sprang up and naturally the company exploited my . . . vampishness."*

* * *

A Fool There Was, released in January, 1915, was an instant sensation. Seen today, it is an incitement to laughter and derision.

* *Pictureshow*, October 2, 1920.

But it is not hard to understand its impact at the time on relatively unsophisticated audiences intrigued for months in advance by the manufactured news of Fox's hardly human discovery. The publicity campaign that preceded the film was really the exposition of the character Bara plays in it: for her mesmeric malevolence has neither rational nor supernatural motivation. What the critic of *The Stage* had to say about the vamp in Porter Emerson Browne's play at its London production, at the Queen's Theatre, 1911, applies in all but one respect to the vamp of Fox's film. 'She has no tone of the supernatural, as distinguished from the vulgar stage adventuress about her, except the mocking laugh supposed to be one of the characteristics of witches.'* In the silent era, of course, Bara had not even the laugh. The film's costumes and sets are all early twentieth century and drink is the only demon in sight. The scene in the vamp's salon shows inebriated couples waltzing together, club arm-chairs, fur coats lying where they were dropped, chandeliers and tapestries dimly depicting an orgy – liquor and cards are strewn around, but no skeletons.

Wearing Empire line dresses, and occasionally a diadem with a stiff tuft of feathers on it, Bara does not do much langorous dallying, but pursues her victims with energy and strikes poses of regal triumph when they grovel at her feet. Six months after taking up with the Fool, she has turned him into a groggy wreck, clawing his way to the whisky bottle like a man buffeted by ten-foot waves. Two scenes in the 'final degradation' sequence illustrate the way she snaps on her spell like a power switch. Hearing the Fool's wife is planning to return to him, Bara flings on a fur coat, forces her way back into the mansion and deflects the fallen husband from his wife's forgiving embrace with a kiss full on the mouth. He pats her cheek fondly and his wife runs distractedly out of the house. At the second attempt she brings along their little girl to woo father back; and she looks like succeeding till Bara is observed sidling downstairs in a muslin nighty, her hair cascading over her bare shoulders down to her waist. Instantly the father breaks out of his child's arms, clutches Bara round the

* *The Stage*, March 30, 1911.

bosom and pillows his head on it with an expression of profane bliss. As his tiny daughter is dragged away by her fainting mother, all the while pointing accusingly at her berserk papa, the vamp's eyes flash with victory like a sky sign. And up comes the Kipling-esque title:

The Fool Was Stripped
To His Foolish Hide.

Bara made about forty films over the next three years, averaging one a month. She was paid $75 a week for *A Fool There Was*: by the time she left Fox she was getting $4000 a week. *Eternal Sin, Purgatory, The Forbidden Path, Ivory Angel, The Serpent, She-Devil* are some of the titles between 1915 and 1918, redolent of damnation, transgression, fall from grace, profane worship and the rest of the foklore and topography of heaven and hell. This was the part of the vamp tradition that went back to the nineteenth century fascination with sinful love, salvation and fear of God, the flesh and the devil. The specific addition that Fox and Bara made to it was the modern notion of sex appeal – with the emphasis on the 'appeal' as something positive and perhaps pleasurable, at least until the final reckoning. The morality dramas before 1914 preached the homely virtues of the working classes: the trend that Theda Bara and her imitators set, however crudely, was to make screen sex fascinating to the growing middle-class audiences.

The characteristics of the historical vamps she played – Carmen, Du Barry, Camille, Salome, Cleopatra – were indolence, love of luxury, a copious desire for sexual gratification without the necessity of marriage. Middle-class morality might not be ready to recognise the attractiveness of these ideas, but they stimulated needs that were being felt if not expressed inside many middle-class households. The servants frequently seen in these films, fussing over the vamp's wardrobe and toilette, have an air of preparing her for the sex war on some grandiose scale. De Mille was to seize on this motif and domesticate it by making the bathroom, where the sexual charms are displayed, and the bedroom, where the sexual desires are fulfilled, into the popular focus of his early films. Mae West was to vulgarise it even further and strip it of its mystery by using her chuckling squad of Negro maids for sexy badinage before the looking-glass. 'Kiss me, my fool,' was a famous line in *A Fool There Was* which became a camp password to the romantic flippancy of the young at the turn of the 1920s. It is hardly a solemn way of summing up the pleasure principle which Theda Bara helped to make fashionable, but many social revolutionaries who achieve more in their time have to make do with duller memorials.

What killed the vamp was ridicule. She simply could not keep up with what she had started. Since the only reason for her existence was to make men suffer, she had to remain immutably evil. But as filmgoers became more sophisticated they demanded more subtle motives for the passions they saw on the screen. They may not have appreciated it then, but what they were looking for were neuroses as well as sex; and the answer to this was provided by the *femme fatale* the alluring, driven, fatalistic woman of the world who feels suffering herself as well as making others do their share. Beside her, the vamp looked a comic caricature of the libido.

There was another reason, too. Women who went to work in all the range of jobs that World War One threw open to them soon got disenchanted with the vamp – a creature without visible means of support yet under no obligation to earn her livelihood. More and more in the 1920s sex on the screen, and off it, too, went with a job – the kind that a store assistant or office girl could see herself in and identify with the girl on the screen. When it ceased to be a full-time pursuit in itself, screen sex got less portentous, more flirtatious. And the vamp who sucked men's blood gave way to the flapper girl whose only aim was to 'snap a trap on a sucker's bank-roll'.

When her contract ended, Theda Bara went on the stage, then returned to films at intervals in the 1920s, this time burlesquing the character she had once played for real. Her entry in the casting directories continued to list her as 'at liberty' up to her death in 1955; but she was in everything but the literal sense in captivity. As the first star to have her image entirely created for her by others, she was among the earliest to discover how fatally an image could stick. Although she nearly always played the vamp, actually the types of vamp she played were quite diverse in their social settings and historical periods. But throughout her long retirement she was continually meeting people who expressed astonishment at finding that she was 'human after all' – so well had William Fox established her supernatural pedigree and unnatural appetite for sex. 'Not all my films have been about vampires,' she was driven to protest. When asked to name the exceptions, she came out with, '*Under Two Flags* and *Kathleen Mavourneen*.' And she added with brightening optimism, 'I am glad to say that I am not known as a vampire at all where these two films have been shown. In Australia.' But this was in 1920. By now, no doubt, Australia has caught up with her.

* * *

Cecil B. de Mille's reputation has been unbalanced by time and his own predilection for being known as the man who brought the Ten Commandments to the motion picture screen. (Already mention of de Mille encourages one to write reverentially: 'Motion picture screen,' instead of 'the movies'. His influence is one to be resisted in matters of style as well as worship.) The sanctimonious credit he always took for this sometimes suggests that only an accident of time prevented his getting to the top of Mount Sinai first. Almost entirely forgotten by the general public is the part de Mille played between 1918 and 1922 in making a more secular article available to the masses, namely sex – sex in ever more tempting and permissive forms. The early post-war years in Hollywood were dominated by him and Erich von Stroheim. There is now no question which one of them was the greater director – obviously von Stroheim. But de Mille was the one who could have justly claimed that the films he made had the greater effect on the sexual mores of the public who saw them. Decadence and debauchery, princely in style and European in tone, were some of the distinguishing marks of the films of von Stroheim, an aristocrat by temper if not birth. But his mocking and cynical illustrations of corruption were, by their very nature, hard for middle-class American moviegoers to reproduce in their own homes and emulate in their daily life. For lessons in sexual pleasures and material comforts, they turned rather to de Mille. And he gladly preached what they wished to practise.

'(The producers) are in a state of panic and chaos and . . . they rush for the bedspring and the lingerie the moment the phantom of empty seats rises to clutch them,' he wrote in 1931 to a Jesuit priest with whom he was on intimate terms.* Except that he left out the bath-tub, this pious lament applies precisely to the type of film de Mille made from 1918 onwards.

The war had accelerated the changing national attitude to marriage. Ideas about virginity and faithfulness had to be revised when the country was sending its young men away to battle. Adultery was treated more sympathetically by judges, divorce evoked a more tolerant response in the community. Films naturally reflected the changing morality and, in doing so, quickened its pace even more. The war-time filmgoers came increasingly from the middle-classes, for it was part of the patriotic mood that the cinema was to be preferred to the theatre as a source of relaxation. (It had also become a means of escapism. Lewis Jacobs dates the notion of the movies as 'escapist entertainment' from this time and infers it was deliberate government policy to take people's minds off the war in this way.) Thus sex appeal on the screen was infiltrated by middle-class material values. De Mille scored an early popular success in this genre with *The Cheat* (1915), the story of a society woman who embezzles Red Cross funds, borrows 10,000 dollars from a rich Japanese, but then tries to pay him back in cash instead of as promised and gets branded on her shoulder blade as one of his possessions. This was praised for the realism of its players, Fannie Ward and Sessue Hayakawa, but the moral was scarcely American enough to set a vogue. It soon was.

'What the public demands today,' a Paramount publicity

* *The Autobiography of Cecil B. de Mille* (W. H. Allen & Co.), p. 276. The priest was Father Daniel A. Lord who, according to Ruth A. Inglis in *Freedom of the Movies,* was the man who did the 'actual writing' of the Hollywood Production Code.

executive in New York cabled to de Mille in Hollywood in 1918, 'is modern stuff with plenty of clothes, rich sets, and action. Nothing prior to the Civil War should be filmed . . .' And Jesse Lasky, his East Coast production chief, also advised him to 'get away from the spectacle stuff for one or two pictures and try to do modern stories of great human interest.'* De Mille cites this advice in his autobiography in a tone of touchy defensiveness, almost an apologia for the run of films he then embarked on. Starting with *Old Wives for New* (1918), he continued with *Don't Change Your Husband* (1919), *For Better For Worse* (1919), *Male and Female* (1919), *Why Change Your Wife* (1920) and other slyly titillating titles to *Manslaughter* (1922) and *Adam's Rib* (1923). It is one of the most sustained series of incitements to imitation that the silent cinema produced. What stands revealed is a socially cynical, morally permissive de Mille: an image wildly at variance with the evangelical righteousness he later cultivated so assiduously.

The frequent theme of these films is the need to continue romance after marriage, if not with one's own husband or wife, then with some other willing party. Sexual pleasure is necessary for happy married life, but marriage is an institution which is deadening to sexual pleasure; for it leads to dowdy wives and neglectful husbands, or else turns wives into tartars and husbands into boors. When Gloria Swanson's nagging drives her husband off with another woman in *Why Change Your Wife*, she instantly smartens herself up, orders a new outfit – 'Make it sleeveless, backless, skirtless – in short, go the limit. I won't be dressed like anyone's aunt!' – and so seduces him back. The remedy that de Mille often suggests is a reshuffle of marriage partners: the implication is that this brings on a real appreciation of the latent virtues of the ex-husband or ex-wife, and so reunites them. In *Don't Change Your Husband* the moral was clearly – do. Gloria Swanson runs off with a bishop's ne'er-do-well nephew, but comes swiftly back once she sees how her hitherto humdrum husband has improved himself now that his time is not all taken up with making money for her. It follows from this that divorce

* Ibid., p. 194.

must lose its reprehensible aspect, since it has become merely a practical means towards better sexual adjustment. In short, the best way to stay happily married is to act as if one is not married at all. According to the size of the audiences for these films, it must have been a highly attractive view. Of course it is not possible to assign to it any precise degree of responsibility for the breakdown of moral values in many areas of American life in the 1920s. But one can hardly doubt that it helped foster an atmosphere in which traditional values were being questioned and balanced against the alternatives of freedom and pleasure.

* * *

Naturally this was not how de Mille saw it. He justified making the films because (a) he was practically ordered to make them by the New York headquarters and (b) they were, in any case, highly moral sermons as he made them, commending wedlock and the mutual performance of marital duties. At times even his sophistry got a little strained. A lazy and slovenly wife can certainly do damage to her marriage; but this was hardly what made members of the audience at the sneak preview of *Old Wives for New* go out to telephone their friends to come on down and see what was happening on the screen. Similarly the famous bathroom, which was featured in this film for the first time, might make the point that cleanliness was of great importance to solid marriages. But, again, audiences did not relish the scenes set in it simply for sanitary instruction.

De Mille always conveniently ignored the fact that he placed the fascination on infidelity, graduated nudity, luxurious display and sexual appeal. Easy manners and relaxed morals were made all the more attractive to copy because his films depicted them so opulently. 'Establishing costume departments to fashion the latest styles in clothes for his players, he brought in hairdressers from New York and Paris, ordered the newest in shoes from manufacturers, and set up a staff to design lingerie, gowns, hats, furs, accessories. Under his influence . . . films began to be rated according to their sumptuousness and display.'* He also estab-

* Lewis Jacobs, op. cit., p. 340.

lished another, if minor, Hollywood characteristic: that of letting production qualities swamp dramatic relevance, so that Gloria Swanson in *For Better For Worse* is shown as a pleasure-loving woman living in a beautiful mansion and sitting down after dinner in a *haute couture* gown – to knit socks for soldiers.

Somewhere in many of these films a chance is found to show the characters scantily or lasciviously dressed, or in suggestive settings and vice-ridden times. The de Mille bathtub, with the camera's enquiring eye continually meeting the intervening towel or being unable to penetrate the coloured water in the tub, is the homely way of facilitating this kind of display. The other was the flashback to historical times, and even pre-history. In *Don't Change Your Husband* the bishop's blackguardly nephew seduces Miss Swanson by describing her as the Goddess of Pleasure, Wealth and Love. De Mille obliged with illustrations. In *Manslaughter*, the would-be cautionary story of a speed-crazy girl sent to jail for her own good by the D.A. who loves her, there were flashbacks to degenerate scenes in Rome: no doubt a telling parallel to the hedonism of the 1920s, though only tenuously relevant to road safety. Even J. M. Barrie's play *The Admirable Crichton* filmed as *Male and Female* did not escape. In order to let the butler make love with uninhibited ardour to Lady Mary whose charms he has only viewed from afar – actually through her bathroom key-hole earlier in the film – de Mille introduced a historical interlude inspired by W. E. Henley's lines, 'I was a King in Babylon / And you were a Christian Slave.' It certainly inverted the social order even more ruthlessly than Barrie intended.

As the 1920s advanced, de Mille moved smoothly from films that set standards of misconduct for the married middle-classes to films that championed the cause of rebellious youth. His ear was always well attuned to catch the tom-tom message of the box-office; and sensing the new young audience to be won, he made *Adam's Rib*, a story of a teenage flapper girl who saves her parents' marriage. In it the characters are transported back to prehistoric times and shown in revealing animal skins. The justification was still as curious as ever: 'to show that bare legs, short skirts, and feminine resourcefulness were nothing new'.* *Adam's Rib* took a drubbing from the critics for the bad example it set youth, so de Mille appealed over the critics' heads to the public for the theme of his next production. He was struck by the many suggestions for a religious story. The result was *The Ten Commandments* (1923). It was a tremendous success. And henceforth the energies de Mille had put into displaying sex in the name of marital adjustment were diverted into displaying sex for the purpose of divine retribution. Every Faith that patronised a box-office could be sure in future of hearing him blast the very 'immorality' that his films had helped popularise. The task was made all the sweeter to the convert by reason of the larger budgets that God's work required.

In course of time and with the advent of the Talkies, his social drama films became period pieces and fell into neglect, from which they have not yet been successfully rescued. De Mille himself seems to have buried them gratefully. Whenever a tactless interviewer quizzed him about sex, he would crisply identify it as something in the third chapter of Genesis, rather than in the misadventures of Gloria Swanson. All the same, he had formulated an attitude to sex that, whether or not he later regretted it, entered into the Hollywood system and still characterises the moral content and production values of a well-known class of Hollywood film. That in which fashionable settings, up-to-date attitudes, desirable standards of living and tempting standards of conduct are reflected in a self-consciously frank story that flaunts the fascination of illicit relationships and tries to condone them as more honest expressions of the sex drive, yet prudently safeguards itself from giving real offence by a gradual endorsement of the very moral values under attack and by the hypocrisy of its happy ending. Nearly forty-five years separate de Mille's *Old Wives for New* from a typical Hollywood sex drama like *The Chapman Report* (1962). But the latter film is simply a contemporary manifestation of the trend that Cecil B. de Mille established so permanently on the American screen.

* * *

* Cecil B. de Mille, op. cit., p. 228.

Theda Bara: one of the portraits which successfully projected the vamp's baleful eroticism in advance of her famous film, *A Fool There Was*.

The original Vamp. Philip Burne-Jones's painting, 'The Vampire', exhibited in London, 1897, was accounted a 'gruesome' success and brought the artist lucrative, if less dramatic, commissions in the United States. Meanwhile his kinsman Rudyard Kipling's poem, inspired by the painting, was preparing the American stage, and later the screen, for the kind of woman who drained a man of love, not blood.

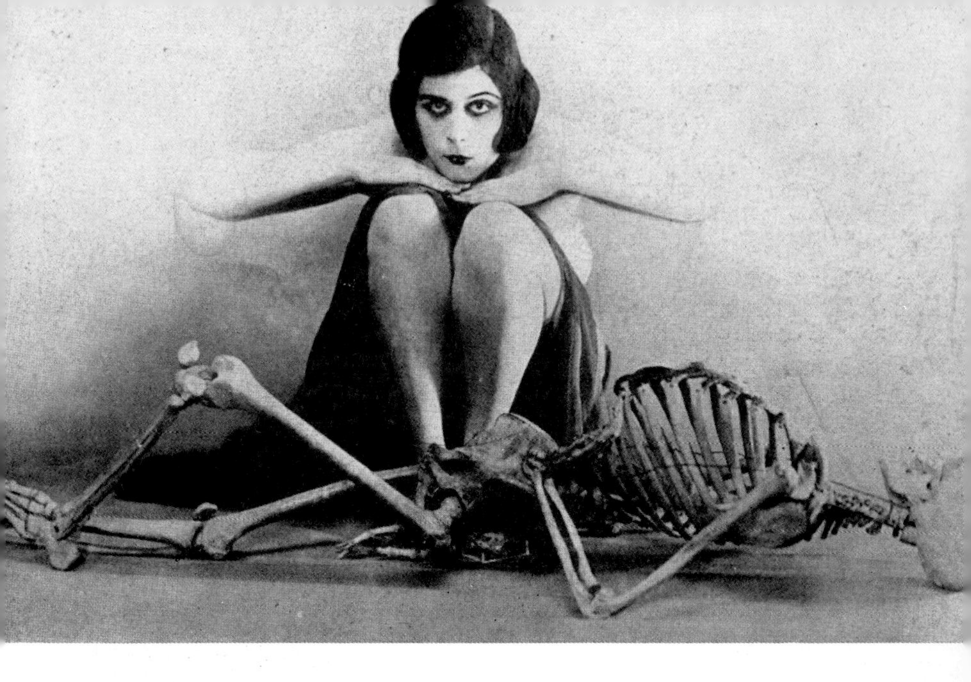

Above: Hollywood Vamp. Theda Bara and ex-lover. Meant to impress simple-natured filmgoers with the supernatural tastes of William Fox's new 'discovery', this publicity still did its work too well – Miss Bara later complained of people continually expressing surprise that she was a perfectly normal young woman. *Below:* Vamp at home. As this studio portrait shows, Theda Bara was also a strikingly handsome woman.

If the influence of Kipling and the Pre-Raphaelites on Hollywood sex appeal was well filtered by passing through other media, the impact of Elinor Glyn in the mid-1920s was felt directly and in person. Yet in its way it is just as bizarre. For it is extraordinary that this Englishwoman, born in 1864, reared in an atmosphere of good breeding and rigid social etiquette and taught to believe in the natural ascendancy of the aristocracy, should have developed into an arbitress of star quality in the American film studios and imposed her ideal of sex appeal on the screen and the career of her protégée, Clara Bow.

Nowadays Elinor Glyn is inadequately remembered as the authoress of *Three Weeks*, an audacious love story when published in 1907, and for her choice of a tiger skin upon which to sin – unless, as the verse had it, you prefer to err on some other fur. But the masterly biography by her grandson, Sir Anthony Glyn, reveals a much more psychologically complex person, a blend of Celtic dreamer and Gallic cynic, a reader of Arthurian romance and ribald French fiction, a genuine gentlewoman and a shrewd publicist whose life-long glorification of romantic love and passionate adventure may have been encouraged by her early and bitterly disillusioning discovery that her own marriage was going to provide her with neither. What Emily Post did for manners, Elinor Glyn did for love. In her novels and in works of practical advice, like *This Passion Called Love*, she explained and codified it. According to her biographer, she believed that 'a wife . . . should be elusive, mysterious, unpredictable so that her husband's hunting instinct would never be lulled to sleep, later to be reawakened by some new quarry.'* This was the de Mille ethic, but without the de Mille hypocrisy attached to it. By the early 1920s, it was being carried to extremes in films that preached a woman's right not only to keep her husband from taking her for granted, but also to shake him off altogether and live a fully independent sex life.

Elinor Glyn, along with other famous writers, was brought to Hollywood in 1920 by Paramount – to write and advise on films, she thought. She soon found it was only her name that was

* *Elinor Glyn*, Sir Anthony Glyn (Hutchinson), p. 75.

wanted, 'as a shield against the critics', and not till 1923, when she went to Metro-Goldwyn-Mayer, did she become a power in the studios. But she had already made her presence forcefully felt outside them: she used her talent to impinge directly on the American people's love-affair with love. She wrote *The Philosophy of Love* on how to make love last, which sold a quarter of a million copies in the first six months. She gave ten-minute talks on love for £500 a week. She used her celebrity in this sphere to establish herself as an authority on which film stars had what was needed to make them good screen lovers. And she was hard to please. 'I had not been long in Hollywood before I discovered that what I had always suspected was true. American men in those days could not make love. Not even the leading actors had any idea how to do it then. One after another screen tests of handsome young American film stars were shown me for approval, but in every case I considered that the performance was lamentable.'*

Madame Glyn, as she preferred to be known, made it her business to remedy these short-comings. Just as she had taught good deportment to Beverly Hills hostesses, she taught selected stars how to project themselves romantically. She is reputed to have supplied Valentino with his arch little trick of kissing the open palm of a lady's hand, instead of the back of it. She also began testing players for star quality, as her rules defined it. She first looked for the player's general 'outline'; and if this was intriguing, she concentrated on some individual feature, generally the eyes. 'The true test of a real film actor,' she called them in an interview.† She made the artists cover up the rest of their faces and express their emotions through their eyes alone. 'If they cannot do it, it means they are not thinking their parts and I have no further use for them.' She wrote about this personal magnetism in a novella published in 1927 in the magazine *Cosmopolitan*. It was called 'It'. In that slangy, trend-conscious era, 'It' was an idea of simple genius and beautiful generality.

* *Romantic Adventure*, The Autobiography of Elinor Glyn (Ivor Nicholson & Watson), p. 299.

† *Picturegoer*, April, 1930.

America was soon agog to know what 'It' was, who had 'It' and how to get 'It'. Madame Glyn readily obliged, and, in articles, talks, interviews and even short instructional films, she defined 'It' as 'a strange magnetism which attracts both sexes . . . there must be physical attraction, but beauty is unnecessary'. One thing that 'It' was not, she insisted over and over again, was sex appeal. 'To call "It" that is nonsense – why even a priest could have "It".'

But as frequently happens, the idea did not travel as well as the catch-phrase. Sex appeal was what 'It' connoted to Hollywood and millions of Americans. 'It' boomed with the financial independence of the young female wage-earner who wanted to acquire not social status, but sexual attractiveness to match her spending power. So when Paramount resolved to film 'It', which in its original form had been a romantically sombre story of a dynamic businessman and a store girl both of whom had 'It', the studio decided to change the mood into light comedy and to make the girl the only one possessing 'It'. But at least Elinor Glyn, by now well established as an exacting supervisor of the films made from her novels, could still authenticate which of the actresses considered for the part had the genuine 'It'. She gave her approval to Clara Bow who became, and has ever since remained, the 'It' Girl.

* * *

Why was Clara Bow selected? To say that Elinor Glyn felt she had 'It' is self-evident, but an insufficient explanation. And in the teasing absence of more precise reasons in the Glyn autobiography, *Romantic Adventure*, one must fall back on speculation. Between the romantic novelist of sixty-two and the flapper girl forty years younger there must certainly have been some affinity. Nearly all Elinor Glyn's heroines are projections of her own personality and fantasies; and she had taken great pains when M-G-M were filming *Three Weeks* (1924) to select an actress who resembled her closely in looks, allowing for their age differences, to play the passionate Lady of the book. There was at least one distinctive feature she shared with Clara Bow. Both of them had red hair. In Elinor's childhood, red hair had been considered rather vulgar for a girl and, according to her grandson's biography, had condemned her to play the comic roles in amateur theatricals. In compensation, it would seem, she bestowed red hair on several of her heroines, including the 'It' girl. Red-heads in the 1920s, on the other hand, were in fashion and thought to be highly sexed girls: just as black had denoted the vamp of the previous decade, and the sex symbol of the 1930s was to be the platinum blonde.

Some heroines in the Glyn romances had other characteristics of the flapper girl as played by Clara Bow, in particular the eponymous heroine of *The Vicissitudes of Evangeline*, written in 1906, and described by a critic as 'cat-like . . . amusing (with) a mixture of wisdom and cunning . . . innocence and precocity and calculated demureness'. This novel was later published in America under the title *Red Hair* – though it has nothing to do with the Clara Bow film of the same name written by Elinor Glyn the year after *It* (1927) which justified its title by a scene in early Technicolor.

But there is an even stranger anticipation of Clara Bow, in looks if not temperament, in the frontispiece of *Three Weeks*, representing the strange Lady who, on the rebound from a disappointing marriage, enjoys a romantic interlude with a young English aristocrat. The frontispiece is actually a painting of Elinor's daughter, Margot, now Lady Davson, who recalls it was done from a photograph, perhaps *upon* a photograph, of herself as a 'still rather chubby fourteen-year-old, posed and dressed in one of her mother's black chiffon frocks and decorated with emeralds – obedient, but, as one can rather gather, a little sulky!'* The painting illustrated one of Elinor Glyn's ideas about personal magnetism; and allowing for the differences in media and mood, the heart-shaped face, meticulously outlined mouth and especially the heavily accentuated eyes all prefigure the looks that Madame Glyn was to approve in Clara Bow twenty years later.

Moreover, Lady Davson states: 'It was always part of my Mother's personality-teaching that people emphasised their

* Margot, Lady Davson in a private letter.

character and its projection much more by keeping their heads low, and glancing up from under the eyebrows, than by "sticking their noses in the air".' The pose is perceptible in the *Three Weeks* frontispiece. But it is also a characteristic attitude of Clara Bow's, so common with her as to be almost a tic, except that what she projects is not the long, mesmerising look of romantic passion, but the enchanting *moue* of the flirtatious flapper.

Clara Bow was born in Brooklyn, in 1905, an only child whose parents were too poor to do more than dress her shabbily. 'The worst looking kid on the street,' she recalled,* and for this reason she avoided playing with the better-dressed little girls and, instead, joined in the boys' games – baseball, football, even boxing. It is possible that her boyish approach to life owes much to this early companionship. Her figure was boyish, too, slender and very flat-chested; and it is not surprising that the critics first noticed her when she was masquerading as a boy in boys' clothes in *Down to the Sea in Ships* (1923), a film in which she got a part because its miniscule budget meant it had to use relative unknowns. She also had a boy's restlessness. Even when she stood still she seemed to be in motion, as if the rhythm of the Jazz Age was galvanising her bones. 'She constantly dances and jiggles while waiting on customers,' Adolph Zukor wrote about her in *It*. 'There is seldom, if ever, a moment in the entire picture when she is in repose.'† Her hair was piled capriciously high but came down low on her face emphasising the boyish roundness to which her eyes were in intensely feminine opposition. Flirts' eyes. They revealed large areas of white which were increased by her habit of roguishly looking up at a man from under her brows, or back at him from over her shoulder.

But her highly individual way of projecting sexiness was by touch: she was always touching her man lightly and fleetingly, seldom lingering, as if she found it stimulating to break contact and come again. Through all her flirting runs a hint of playful

* Clara Bow, quoted by Rudy Behlmer, *Films in Review*, October, 1963.

† *The Public Is Never Wrong*, by Adolph Zukor (G. P. Putnam's Sons), p. 248.

boxing. It is characteristic of the impatient age she represented that she never went in for the long, premeditated embrace, but would pat a guy on the cheek, chuck him under the chin, fix his tie, brush an invisible speck off his lapel, or ferry a kiss from her lips to his on her finger-tips. For the really big moments, she would leap bodily on to the fellow's lap as if playing leap-frog. She has only to spot an unattached male 100 yards away and she starts freshening her make-up, patting her hair and giving her dress half a dozen more nips and tucks that in the course of a film took on an almost fetishist feeling.

Millions of girls copied her and Clara's roles made identification easy and attractive. After *Black Oxen* (1924), which had the gimmick of her playing a woman of sixty rejuvenated by the current craze of animal glands to look aged twenty, she significantly kept to roles within the average American girl's experience (and pay packet). She was a manicurist, usherette, waitress, cigarette girl, taxi dancer, swimming instructress and salesgirl generally found round the lingerie department. All were roles in the range of promiscuous but legal employment where a girl can flirt with an ever changing male clientele. In these films Clara is lifted out of a milieu familiar to her flapper fans and shown the shopgirl's dream world of high life and wild parties. There she snaps her garters for a reel or two with the cry that embodies the peculiar urge of the 1920s – 'So this is freedom!' – and having found it is nothing of the sort her natural goodness restores her to her sweetheart whom she recognises with the glad cry, 'Now I know what a real man is!' Except that she ends up making love to her boss on the giant anchor of his yacht, *It* is this sort of film. But it owes its fame, like *A Fool There Was* largely to the publicity that heralded it – and 'It'. (Madame Glyn even appears in it, explaining her invention to Clara's boss at a table in the Ritz.) The film is a good showcase for Clara to display her flirt's repertory; but it was really the part that made her. Simply being designated the 'It' Girl gave her a charmed reputation that put her out ahead of a large field of rival flapper types, including Colleen Moore of the Dutch Boy bob who could claim to be the original screen flapper and who was making $12,500 a week at this date compared with

Clara Bow's $2,500. Clara soared higher with the fame, but never did catch up on the pay.

For proof that Clara Bow had talent, as well as a highly publicised personality, one would not turn to *It*. *Mantrap*, directed by Victor Fleming in 1926, the year before *It*, shows her not only in the hands of a better director than Clarence Badger, but is a far less artificial film and reveals one astonishing aspect of her.

Mantrap is a log-hut community in the Canadian Rockies whose aging store-keeper takes off his apron and goes down to Minneapolis for the first time since 1903 on hearing that 'ankles ain't the half of what the girls are showin' now'. Finding Clara buffing the customers' nails in a barber's, he impulsively weds her and carries her back to Mantrap, whereupon she instantly begins making eyes at a smart divorce lawyer from New York who is on a hunting trip, and forces him to carry her back to civilisation in his canoe. 'Madam,' he says, with the caginess of his calling, 'you must look on me not as a man, but as a means of transportation.' The story was by Sinclair Lewis; Percy Marmont and Ernest Torrence play the lawyer and the husband, and Fleming's humour is fresh-squeezed and slightly acid at Clara's expense where she starts prettifying herself on spotting her husband chugging over the lake in pursuit – with a shotgun. She imposes her little teasing tics on the great outdoors as successfully as in her city slicker pictures, even going one better than catching a guy's eye with a wink – she uses her powder-compact mirror to deflect a love-beam from the sun full in his face.

But what one is not prepared for is a love scene in the fir forest when the runaway couple are exhausted. It is an isolated patch of seriousness and for once Clara Bow is directed to act with surprising naturalism. Her hair blowing back softly from a tired face shows a mature, nearly carnal beauty and for a moment or two she resembles a warmly desirable 1920 version of Patricia Neal. For the first time one understands Elinor Glyn's cryptic reference in her autobiography to a tragic side to Clara Bow's talents as an actress. One bitterly regrets not seeing it more frequently employed: when the mood could be induced in her by a director like Fleming, who went on to make *Red Dust* (1932) with Jean Harlow and, of course, co-direct *Gone With The Wind* (1939), then she responded intuitively and with a sudden deepening of personality.

* * *

What ended Clara Bow's career was not simply the flat voice revealed by the Talkies. 'The unrestrained vitality which had been her great asset was now a curious handicap,' Adolph Zukor's memoirs record. 'The technicians had not learned to use the microphones as skilfully as they do today, and the players had to manage to stay near one of them, which was likely to be concealed in a bouquet of flowers, without giving the impression that the voice was being aimed into it. Clara was too restless. She would be all over the set, and then, finding that the microphone was not picking up her voice she would sometimes stand and curse it.'* Moreover the Depression quickly chased her flapper type off the screen; and when she tried a comeback in *Hoopla* (1933) it was as a hard-boiled Mae West type. But with the real Mae West around, anyone else was a two-minute egg at most.

What finished her off decisively was the immaturity of her own personality. Everything happened too quickly for her and she never really got on top of being the 'It' Girl sex symbol, so that her words on finally quitting the screen in 1933 sound like those of a run-down clockwork doll: 'I've had enough. It wasn't ever like I thought it was going to be. It was always a disappointment.' She had lived a life off screen that aped the flapper girl's fantasies on it; but the publicity value of wild parties, love affairs with stars like Gary Cooper, fast cars and her seven red chows dyed to match her hair, turned sour and injurious when she sued her secretary, one Daisy De Voe, for embezzling over 15,000 dollars and heard it alleged by the defence that the money was used to supply her with drink, drugs and gigolos. Her secretary was convicted, but the charge hit hard at Clara's popularity, exacerbated her health worries and led to a breakdown. Like many of her tribe, her emotional immaturity seems to have been matched by extreme mental sensitivity and she spent long spells of her later life in a sanatorium.

* Adolph Zukor, op. cit., p. 184.

But not long before her death, in 1965, time and the sight of other sex symbols who had come to more tragic ends, had cheered her up sufficiently to look back on her career and offer a revised opinion. 'We had individuality,' she said. 'We did as we pleased. We stayed up late. We dressed the way we wanted. Today, stars are sensible and end up with better health. But *we* had more fun.' Even Elinor Glyn herself would hardly have put it more passionately.

CHAPTER TWO

YOUNG BUT NOT INNOCENT: PICKFORD

If mass popularity is the divinising power that makes a star into a modern immortal, as the French critic Edgar Morin postulates, then Mary Pickford is certainly a screen goddess. But can we, by any stretch of syntax, speak of her also as a sex goddess? To do so would seem like wilful assault on popular legend – a rape of screen innocence. Vamps, virgins and sweethearts are the archetypal trinity of the silent cinema; and oral tradition has enshrined Mary Pickford, *intacta*, in the last two categories and kept her strictly away from the first, like a child instructed not to go near suspect neighbours. Fans remember her with accentuated affection as Innocence in Rags, or Little Mary of the Ringlets: titles that today convey to people who have never seen a Pickford film the idea of a Portrait of the Year in some Royal Academy of Sentimentality, or else a minor saint in a saccharine hagiography. But neither view would survive a retrospective screening of the many films she made from 1909 onwards.

For it is precisely because Mary Pickford's films are little known, seldom shown, poorly preserved in many national archives, inaccurately remembered and oddly neglected even by film historians, that the popular myth has been allowed to perpetuate the idea of America's Sweetheart, with her famous curls haloed in light, playing the sexual innocent in so many High Victorian weepies populated by blind cripples, sadistic foster-parents, or persecuted orphans. People generally remember not what they see on the screen, but what they wish to remember – and this, in turn, dictates what they wish to see. Hence images form and legend accretes. To an astonishing degree Mary Pickford was the victim of the sentimentalising legend in her own working lifetime. And it helped shorten this life-time and restrict her talent – one may think tragically.

She suffered a fate that would have interested Pirandello. She became in large measure a prisoner of her star personality: not necessarily as it was in many of her films, but as her adoring public wished it to be. In 1923, through the pages of *Photoplay* she appealed to filmgoers to tell her which roles they wished to see her play in future. What was she hoping for? The evidence will suggest that it was a release, or, at least, a respite, from playing the kind of parts that her fans obsessively associated with her. She wanted freedom from parts that were supercharged with rags, curls, sunny tempers and innocent spirituality, but necessarily short on sex appeal. Back came the replies in due course: Cinderella, Anne of Green Gables, Heidi, Alice in Wonderland. They would be dispiriting to any child of normal sensitivity: to Mary Pickford they must have been additionally disturbing. For at this time she was aged thirty-two. And remember that this was in the middle of the jazz era, when the go-getter creed flourished, the materialist ethic prevailed, family life in its sense of pre-war solidarity had become devalued, conventions were being increasingly ignored and the crazes of the day were short skirts, rolled stockings, beauty treatments, speed, youth and pep. It is vital to be aware of this contemporary social counterpoint to the Pickford myth, for the nineteenth-century hangover that envelops many of the stories in her films is powerfully hypnotic. After a few reels one can well imagine that Dickens had a hand in the screenplay and Lewis Carroll supervised the production. Moreover, Mary Pickford was certainly assisted to stardom by the same idolising of prepubertal girlhood which is so persistent, and at times sinister, a strain in Victorian popular sentiment. Her first director was a Tennysonian romantic. Her first fans were still nineteenth century working-class folk. In spite of all of which, she and her career are more modern and far less sentimental than the myth makes out. And innocence, sexual and otherwise, does not begin to explain either.

* * *

The Pickford family were Canadians called Smith when Mary was born in Toronto in 1893; and she was baptised Gladys. It was David Belasco, the New York impresario, who re-christened her as she is now known. She was born without, but speedily acquired, what were to become the central things in the Pickford myth – namely the Pickford curls. They are the emblem and the source of the spell she threw over America, yet their significance in Mary's life and career has seldom been examined. Scattered through her autobiography are clues to their importance, but it is hard to tell if she appreciated these when she was writing, dictating or collaborating on the book. Nevertheless they must be followed if one seeks to discover why she became the star she did.

Her infancy followed the fairly normal pattern of a little girl who is deeply attached to her father, slightly less so to her mother: yet her way of showing she was 'Daddy's girl' is already noteworthy. Once she recalls rubbing the tassels of a yellow silk scarf draped round a 'monstrous sketch' of her father so as to make them more like her own golden ringlets. They simply lost their lustre, but it was an irony that certainly escaped her at that age. Then, when she was five, her father was killed in an accident at work. Of the grief that filled the house on this terrible occasion, she recalls one detail in her memoirs with extraordinary vividness. Tip-toeing downstairs, she saw her mother beating her forehead bloodily against the wall; and she noticed, and remembered fifty-eight years later, how the distracted woman's hair covered her face and streamed down round her waist. Now hair is frequently an inseparable part of the image – generally erotic – which female stars project: one thinks of the incendiary glow of Jean Harlow's platinum hair, or the way Bardot wears hers in lewd dishevelment. But in Mary Pickford's case hair is associated with childhood and parenthood – that is to say, with the states of dependence and protectiveness. And these are precisely the emotions that her mass public enjoyed vicariously in the two kinds of role they preferred to see her play and remember her in – the orphaned waif and the little mother.

Mary could act both with passionate conviction because they were the roles that the Pickford family fortunes thrust her into.

With her husband's death, Mrs Pickford rented rooms to touring players and gradually let herself and her family be drawn into stage appearances with her paying guests. All the while Mary acted as deputy mother to her brother Jack and sister Lottie and eventually became the principal breadwinner for the whole family. This may help explain the curious predilection of her films – especially the stories which Mary chose – for showing children burdened with parental responsibilities, being made into little mothers or substitute fathers. What is more disturbing to observe is how, when the cast of the films includes a father, or a father figure, he often frustrates his little girl's independence to pick and flirt with a boy-friend of her own age, or thereabouts. Apart from the physical handicaps of blindness or crippled limbs – which were common shorthand aids to dramatic exposition as well as easy sympathy-getters in many silent movies – it is the loneliness and deprivation which particularly characterise a Pickford film and, of course, intensify the good humour and resilience that Mary shows in the face of such adversity. 'I never had any young companions my age, except my brother and sister,' she wrote in her autobiography. '. . . All this matured me very early, I suppose, but it cheated me of my childhood.'*

The hardships prepared the way for formidable compensations, however. Although she only tasted childhood briefly, she got the chance to play the child in films instead. And she went on playing it. When over thirty she could – and did – act the little girl of thirteen or fourteen in films. Her own small stature helped. She was just over five feet in height and sometimes proportions were falsified in the décor, or extra-tall supporting players used. But she possessed more intuitive equipment, too. Growing up for Mary Pickford was like being in rehearsal. She got accustomed to observing small children, one guesses, from looking after her brother and sister from the age of five. This is what may have developed her talent for miming children which gives her silent screen acting its amazing delicacy and charm. It was her own idea when she came to play a little mother in *Stella Maris* (1918) that

* *Sunshine and Shadow: The Autobiography of Mary Pickford* (Heinemann), p. 47.

she should have one shoulder drooping and one too high from having carried younger children on the other hip in her formative years. This is the kind of 'study from the life' that gives variety to almost every juvenile role she played. But the sentimentalising Pickford myth makes one lose sight of such an achievement by running the distinctive age groups which she played in many films into the single muzzy-eyed category of 'sweetheart'.

She knew when it paid to be a child off screen, too. For though Mary got a quick reputation as a hard bargainer, she went about it in a soft-tempered way, rarely making blunt demands if contemporary evidence is to be believed, but using the wiles of a small child, with many coquettish hints, to obtain more money out of David Belasco or, later, Adolph Zukor. Only in films like *Daddy-Long-Legs* (1919) did Mary have trouble identifying her generous benefactor.

* * *

She grew up a shrewd, tough and conscientious child: so conscientious that in later life she once found herself spontaneously apologising for her acting in a film being previewed at a Pasadena theatre because she felt it was not up to her best. By the age of thirteen she had made up her mind to land on Broadway: by the age of fourteen, she did so, bursting in on Belasco and giving him to understand that her life depended on his seeing her. When the impresario asked the tiny girl why she was so desperate to audition for him, Mary answered, 'Mother says I should aim high or not at all.' Mother was Mrs Charlotte Pickford, a steel-willed, ambitious woman who first chaperoned and then managed Mary and stayed in charge of the bank till her death. She headed the band of formidable women – they included scriptwriter Frances Marion and Cora Carrington Wilkenning, an agent sent out on reconnaissance to talk figures with rival bidders for Mary's services – whom Mary relied on to bring up the heavy armour after she had sighted the target. She could do her own scouting, too, when a star. She used to order her chauffeur to stop at a picture palace while she bought a ticket and inspected the house. It did not need to be a Pickford film showing. A small audience for a rival actress helped Mary argue just as eloquently for her own worth to be adjusted accordingly.

But there may be another reason for the vigilance Mary always displayed where her own interests were concerned: one that has nothing to do with her mother's ambitions for her. Her first director was D. W. Griffith, who later made *The Birth of a Nation* (1915), that spectacular blend of national pride, Southern chivalry and racial bigotry. At heart, Griffith was a sentimentalist: at work, he could be a rather malicious disciplinarian, especially towards the winsome adolescent girls whom he hired in his apprentice days at Biograph. His way of bringing them to emotional pitch was to make them intensely jealous of each other; and it is very likely that her smarting experience of Griffith's moody favouritism made Mary adept at a very early age at looking out for herself in the film industry.

What did Griffith see in this sixteen-year-old girl from the Belasco touring companies to make him want to engage her for Biograph films? One is so conditioned by the Pickford myth that one imagines Mary's qualities must have been blindingly evident right from the start. This does not appear to be the case. According to Mary Pickford, the director said to her when they met in a corridor at the Biograph studio, 'You're too little and too fat, but I may give you a job. My name is Griffith. What's yours?'* (Belasco had changed Gladys Smith into 'Mary Pickford', using one of her first names along with one of the names in her family.) While this account hardly flatters the 'sweetheart' myth, it still gives the impression that Mary Pickford was hired at her first attempt to break into films. One must now doubt this. Two studios, Essanay and Biograph, are said to have refused her work before she ran into Griffith at Biograph, where the front office had turned her away for the second time.† Moreover it was not just to a chance encounter in a corridor that she owed her job on this occasion, but to something much rarer still – an accident of temperament. Griffith's temperament.

* Ibid., p. 105.

† James Card, of George Eastman House, is, as far as I know, the only film historian to mention this. *Image*, December, 1959. Vol. 8, No. 4.

Griffith was a Kentuckian reared in the courtly Southern tradition of treating women as the innocent and maidenly objects of male politeness and devotion. The readings of works by the Victorian poets which his father used to give after supper only reinforced this attitude. In the course of a penetrating analysis of Griffith's films, Lewis Jacobs makes this observation about his character: '(His) romanticism determined not only his choice of subject matter but his choice of players . . . All his heroines . . . were, at least in Griffith's eyes, the pale, helpless, slim-bodied heroines of the nineteenth-century English poets.'* One of Griffith's most cherished projects was a film of Browning's verse drama, *Pippa Passes*. In spring, 1909, at precisely the time he was on the look out for a cast of perfect players for this film, what happened? – Pickford passed. They may indeed have met in the corridor, but according to Linda Arvidson (Mrs D. W. Griffith), the director *first* spotted her among the workless extras lining the studio perimeter. 'Don't you think she would be good for Pippa?' he asked Miss Arvidson. 'Ideal,' she answered.† And Mary Pickford was engaged by Biograph. It should be recorded that when the film was made, in mid-September, 1909, she did not play the part of Pippa. Griffith had decided she had grown too fat.

* * *

Mary Pickford also profited by the historical accident of launching her film career at exactly the right moment to catch the tide. Movies in 1909 were already a mass production business: they were about to become a mammoth industry with the concentration of capital. America had nearly 10,000 nickelodeons, many changing programmes daily, some twice daily. Films were made in a day or two, but competition among the companies was improving the quality and soon Adolph Zukor was to demonstrate that films could run for an hour, or longer, without the audience collapsing from exhaustion. His policy of 'Famous (Stage) Players in Famous Plays' was also an attempt to raise the status of film actors: it did so, but paradoxically at the expense of the famous stage names who discovered that film acting was a

* Lewis Jacobs, op. cit., p. 96–7.

† *When the Movies Were Young*, by Mrs D. W. Griffith (E. P. Dutton), p. 99.

Left: In 1907, Elinor Glyn's famous romantic novel, *Three Weeks*, appeared with this miniature reproduced as the frontispiece. Painted by the authoress on a photograph of her daughter Margot, then aged about 14, it illustrated Madame Glyn's ideal of the sexually attractive and fascinating Lady of the novel. (*Actual size, 3 ins. approximately.*) *Below:* in 1927, allowing for the difference in media and mood, a similar image and the same kind of personality projection are apparent in this portrait of Clara Bow whom Madame Glyn selected to play the girl's role in the film version of her novella, *It*.

Elinor Glyn referred cryptically to Clara Bow's potential as a tragic actress. Lost in the fir forests in this sequence from Victor Fleming's film, *Mantrap*, the 'It' Girl reveals a sombre and touching side to her usual flirtatious personality, more like Patricia Neal or the young Judy Garland. (*Frame enlargement.*)

different art altogether. In 1909 film actors were looked down on professionally, so that Mrs Pickford virtually had to ask Mary if she could demean herself enough to seek film work. At the same time, public curiosity in film actors was mounting – and what stimulated it was the very anonymity of the magnified faces that mesmerised the nickelodeon audiences.

Since film companies at that date did not risk inflating their artists' salary demands by naming them in the cast, the way people identified their screen favourites was by some striking physical feature or personal characteristic. It was a curious reversion to the practice of primitive societies where names evolved from how members of the tribe looked or what they did; and it had also a characteristic of primitive magic. For with its reappearance in each film its nameless owner made, this feature tended to become charged with the potency of a totem – a focus for the loyalty, emotions and fantasies of the mass of moviegoers. In Mary Pickford's case, this feature was her curls. Before she became known to them by name, people recognised her by her cascade of ringlets. They were the first things that made her talked about. She literally got a head start in her career. Cinema managers, eavesdropping in the way of business on patrons as they came out, appear to have evolved a rough and ready 'star system' before the film studios adopted it as a means to stabilise and encourage cinema attendances. And they featured 'The Girl With the Curls' on their advertising bills. At the same time, as Terry Ramsaye mentions in *A Million and One Nights*, Griffith occasionally referred to 'Mary' or 'Little Mary' – note the early use of the sentimentalising epithet – in the scene-linking titles he wrote for his films. 'Mary' is the commonest of names and perhaps Griffith never intended to identify one particular Mary. At any rate in the public mind 'Mary' was soon associated with curls, and 'curls' with Mary. The feature of hers that was already emotionally charged with childhood experiences had become that dangerous thing – public property.

But one surprising episode – which contradicts the myth – suggests that Mary Pickford was either ignorant of her growing fame, or else did not think it would last. In 1913 she quit the screen in a huff. The reason is illuminating. Griffith, in one of his *pour enrager les autres* moods, had given the star part in *The Sands of Dee* to Mae Marsh, a department-store girl, untrained by Mary's stage standards, who nevertheless appeared to act excellently in the finished film. Mary was dismayed to see a performance created where none ought to have been–which is evidence of the time lag before it was recognised that acting for the stage and the screen are separate crafts – and despising this mendacious medium she headed back to Belasco, took his offer of a leading role on Broadway and confided to him 'it would make me very happy if he would add $25 to my weekly earnings'. Yet a year later she was back in films. Why? Nostalgia? Money? Ambition? James Card has suggested, and one must agree with him, that Mary Pickford had the nature of her fame and future brought home to her for the first time by the audiences who came to the theatre to see not a Belasco leading lady, but a Biograph film star.

A few figures. In 1909 she got $40 a week from Biograph; in 1910, $175 a week from Carl Laemmle's IMP Co.; in 1911, $275 a week from Majestic; in 1912, $500 a week from Adolph Zukor's Famous Players Co., doubled to $1000 a week in February, 1914, doubled again to $2000 a week in November, 1914, doubled yet again to $4000 a week in March, 1915 – at which point she was the only Famous Players artist really known to exhibitors and filmgoers. Now began in deadly earnest a great series of bargaining matches for her services in this booming industry. Vanity as well as profit fed Mary's unsentimental attitude to money. She was determined not to come second to Chaplin, then getting three times what she was paid. 'Whoever emerged from the situation in possession of a contract with Mary Pickford was going to hold the whip hand in the whole industry.'* In June, 1916, she signed with Zukor for $10,000 a week, drawable on Mondays, with a $300,000 bonus, and various sops to her pride like star billing, free transport and a New York studio 'to be known as the Mary Pickford Studio, in which no other pictures could be made'. This well-publicised contract did more than anything else at the time to give the public a taste of the growing

* Terry Ramsaye, op. cit., p. 750.

glamour, wealth *and extravagance* of the movies. But in 1917 even it was topped, Zukor was outbid, and Mary left 'that dear, dear man' to make her pictures for First National – at $350,000 *each*. For her 'good offices and good wishes', Mrs Pickford picked up a useful $50,000.

* * *

Her tremendous popularity and economic power gave Mary Pickford full control over her films from early on. Cecil B. de Mille records, with the asperity of a slighted autocrat, that for the films shot in the New York studio, Zukor gave Mary the privilege of choosing the writer, approving the script and 'in other ways exercising the authority that belongs strictly to the producer and director'.*

In the period before 1914 when American films in general moralised about the working classes who were their principal patrons, inspiring, consoling and entertaining them in that order, Mary Pickford had the shrewdness to see the commercial value of humour and optimism without overt sermonising. And the nickelodeon patrons were as quick to accept her as their bantam-weight champion in the daily struggle. She aimed her first films at the family audiences, at mothers and children who might be expected to enjoy the antics of the children she played so brilliantly. The fun and zest she put into these parts are as fresh today as when she played them. And it is important to emphasise that though the humour in the film is scaled down to the size of household pranks, it is often quite destructive, very rarely indeed is it sentimentalised. In *Pollyanna* (1920: when she was aged twenty-seven), for example, she plays a child of twelve who sticks flypaper squares to her boots, so as not to muddy her aunt's carpets, and clumps upstairs as if on snowshoes – all the while a strand of wool adhering to the fly-paper is unravelling the aunt's new knitting. In *Through the Back Door* (1921: aged twenty-eight) she ties scrubbing brushes on to her feet and skates exhilaratingly over the soapy-water puddles on the kitchen floor. And in *Daddy-Long-Legs* (1919: aged twenty-six) she gets herself and

* Cecil B. de Mille, op. cit., p. 164.

another orphanage kid drunk on a jar of hooch, swings with inebriated brio on the playground trapeze like a pig-tailed Tarzan and is only sobered up by seeing the orphanage dog, also sloshed, trying to walk in a straight line on its hind legs.

As well as staying within the body of a child – marvellously well, considering her actual age at the time – she stays within its understanding. Compare her with Shirley Temple who gives the impression of a miniaturised child-adult, wiser than grown-ups, dressed for cuteness, a little manageress of her guardians' fortunes or her parents' love life, who exchanges a wink of collusion with the divorce court judge before the reconciliation of mother and father. A more sophisticated moppet than Mary Pickford, she is also the more sentimentalised one. Mary extracted an unpampered realism from her own curtailed childhood – and her equally underprivileged fans sympathised with it intuitively. Margaret Case Harriman once remarked of this aspect of her: ' "Good will prevail," her charming mouth will tell you, while something in her wise, uncompromising face adds silently that it damn well better.'

But these child roles are almost the only ones conceived and played in total innocence of the facts of life. Move on to the gawky adolescent girl aged fourteen to sixteen, which is the next Pickford *persona* and something unexpected appears on the screen. Not aggressive sexuality, certainly. But a tough little sweetheart appeal that looks very much alive to the offer of love and not at all blind to the risks of sex. The eyes of this Mary Pickford can veil their spirituality and glare forth plain jealousy if her boy friend looks too long at another girl. Her sweet mouth can pount sulkily. She can toss the famous curls as disdainfully as a jilted coquette already stalking her next quarry. This is the forgotten aspect of Mary Pickford, effaced from many memories by the more famous child roles she played and by the sentimental myth of sexless girlhood. One sees it in flashes in many films, but most vividly perhaps in *Heart of the Hills* (1919), when she does a jitterbugging barn dance, makes eyes that would not have disgraced Clara Bow at a country beau played by the young John Gilbert, and is plainly itching to scratch out his girl friend's hair 'an' raise h – – l generally', as the title puts it. In fact she tries to do just this, and turns into a fighting h – – lcat who shows her teeth even when she is forced to apologise.

Rags (1915) reveals her in patched overalls and a tattered blouse suddenly becoming a Tobacco Road spitfire when given the brush-off by her boy friend whom she then coaxes flirtatiously into bestowing a forgiving kiss on her. In some films she is downright militant, taking a pitchfork to the owner of a baby farm in *Sparrows* (1926), donning Ku Klux Klan robes to administer mountainy justice in *Heart of the Hills* and erupting into a saloon in *Rags* to give her drunken father a severe dressing down and to repulse a barfly who has dared rumple her curls. Beneath the maudlin elements of many of the stories lies a sexual realism that, especially in the early films, was not unfamiliar or offensive to audiences accustomed to it in their own overcrowded, back-street communities. Remember this was also the period that saw the outburst of early 'public interest' films like the cycle of white slave traffic 'investigations', or the uplifting abortion dramas described laconically by Terry Ramsaye as 'idylls of interrupted gestation'. In several films Mary feigns pregnancy in order to save others from the consequences of their sin (*Tess of the Storm Country*: 1914) or simply to get the man she loves to marry her (*A Romance of the Redwoods*: 1917). In *Hearts Adrift* (1914) she plays a Latin-looking girl who is shipwrecked on an island and has a baby by another castaway; in *Fate's Interception* (1912) she is a Mexican girl apparently living with the man she is in love with; while *Amarilly of Clothesline Alley* (1918) showed her to have a fiancé who is human enough to consider visiting a brothel.

Even where the one she loves is no longer a boy but a mature admirer, there are surprises. *Daddy-Long-Legs*, for instance, ends on a shot of Mary's young legs kicking joyfully from the lap of a wing chair into which her elderly guardian has pulled her. The skill she showed in jettisoning her gingham pinafore and 'growing up' in the film into a young lady in her mid-teens no doubt allayed the unease of any moviegoers who pondered on such a match. The Pickford teenager is certainly not an obsessive flirt; but neither is she a passionless virgin. 'If ever you strike me again,' the outlaw in *The Eagle's Nest* (1914) growls at her, 'I'll either beat you or kiss you to death.' One is left in no doubt about which fate Mary would have picked.

* * *

This, then, is the mystery. Why do the later Pickford films not express this intermittent sexuality more openly in more mature roles? Mary Pickford herself was a woman of spirit: a love life mattered to her. She disobeyed her mother to elope with and secretly marry one of her fellow Biograph actors, Owen Moore. When this marriage foundered on her husband's addiction to alcohol, she risked besmirching her own image in the public's eye by divorcing him and marrying Douglas Fairbanks Sr who proved both a bad husband and, as will be seen, a worse influence on her career. Whatever Mary Pickford's marital sorrows, she lived a fully adult emotional life that could have been a great reservoir of feeling for her acting to draw on, given the right kind of roles.

The evidence suggests that, more and more throughout the 1920s, this is what she was seeking to do – but could not manage it. Her film roles, her public statements and one momentous decision that she made are all expressions of her increasing dissatisfaction at being known, or, rather venerated, as America's Sweetheart: a personality, not an actress, a child, not an adult. Taken by itself, her fondness for dual roles in her films might seem just a ruse for adding to her popularity, or giving her favourite photographer, the brilliant Charles Rosher, a chance for some exceptionally convincing trick photography. But taken with the other evidence, it is a psychologically relevant trend: a reaction against her public image which would give her the relief she sought in a wider range of characters, yet not carry any risk of destroying her image too abruptly. So in *Stella Maris* she played both the angelic cripple, Stella, and the twisted little skivvy who worships her. It was the first time she had played an ugly little girl. 'I could end one of the characters unhappily,' she wrote later in *Photoplay*, 'and not sacrifice the desired happy ending.' Similarly *Little Lord Fauntleroy* (1922) allowed her to play the adult role of Fauntleroy's mother while continuing to please her public by doubling as the eponymous infant peer – not forgetting the curls. This dualism continued off screen as well: only here it was not a means of artistic liberation, but an increasingly inconvenient necessity to preserve her child image. Though a young woman of nearly thirty, she was obliged to keep on switching into children's clothes to be photographed with distinguished visitors to the studio. Adolph Zukor has recalled that 'in Mary's public appearances her mother was always in evidence, but her husband, Owen Moore, hardly ever . . . If the public did not recollect that Mary was a wife, no harm was done . . . While Mary was not asked to appear in curls and pinafore off the screen, we did, frankly, want her to seem a teenager. It was understandable that Mary wished to dress her age and in the height of fashion, but neither of us could afford it.'*

But Mary's need to do just this was increasing. In 1923 she planned a film of the historical drama *Dorothy Vernon of Hadden Hall* to give her promotion to young womanhood on the screen for good – and to young *modern* womanhood, too. 'It wedded together yesterday and today,' she later wrote of the film. 'Against the feudal background of Elizabeth's court, it offered the portrayal of a modern-minded girl.'† Ernst Lubitsch was engaged to direct it as his first Hollywood film. But he found fault with the story and instead directed her as the gypsy heroine of *Rosita* (1923). She did not make *Dorothy Vernon* till 1924. Lubitsch's method of directing his players made it hard to light Mary as well as usual. Her concern was translated, literally, to Lubitsch: it was one thing to lose one's childhood years, quite another to lose one's looks. Thereafter her lighting improved, but relations with her director deteriorated.‡ Both *Rosita* and *Dorothy Vernon* did so badly that Mary felt it was a judgment on her presumptuousness at daring to grow up on the screen, and she plunged contritely into *Little Annie Rooney* (1925: aged thirty-two) in which she played a slum kid of twelve. She gave a brilliant, tough, feisty performance: but it was back to the junior league again. In

* Adolph Zukor, op. cit., p. 175.

† *Photoplay*, June, 1925.

‡ Information supplied by Charles Rosher.

an odd way, too, the film seems to personify her professional dilemma: for in it she has a boy friend who is in love with her, while at the same time her dependence on her policeman father keeps her from growing up emotionally.

Under the sweet reasonableness of her appeal to *Photoplay* readers for suggestions for new roles, one senses this mood of frustration. Back came some 20,000 replies: 'the majority was overwhelmingly in favour of roles depicting childhood,' with Cinderella the top favourite, although it was a part she had already played. The prize-winning letter came from a woman who implored her not to shatter 'an illusion that there are such little girls and that we have one before us: an illusion that you are a little girl in spite of the fact that we know you are a grown-up woman.'* Mary's curls must have felt as heavy as lead.

Although she prudently assured *Photoplay* readers that she meant to continue on the way of sweetness and youth, she was dispirited enough to declare publicly in an interview in London in 1928. 'I am sick of Cinderella parts, of wearing rags and tatters. I want to wear smart clothes and play the lover (sic) . . . I created a certain type of character and now, I think, it is practically finished.' It was indeed. The social and moral revolt of the 1920s had infiltrated every part of the screen except this backwater of Victorian melodrama featuring a heroine whose sex appeal only got released intermittently in the stock situations of the *genre*. Almost everywhere else, as Lewis Jacobs noted, 'sex appeal became the ultimate criterion of personality.' Resentment at not being able to participate in this now seems to have played the preponderant part in dictating Mary Pickford's actions. Another factor was the death of her mother, in 1928, which afflicted her grievously, yet maybe emboldened her to take the step she did not contemplate in her mother's lifetime. Declaring to her hairdresser that 'my curls have become a stumbling block to the future of my career', she had them cut off. Separated from her personality, they appropriately became quasi-sacred relics: two of them now repose in the Museum of San Diego, two in the Los Angeles Museum and two at her home, Pickfair. She declared that the shingling

* *Photoplay*, October, 1925.

gave her a novel sense of independence: little mother seemed all set to become a modern miss.

She then made *Coquette* (1929), her first talkie, the first film she acted in with shingled hair and the first to let her play an explicitly 'vampish' role. But in all other respects it was dismayingly like the mixture as before. She appeared as a girl torn between love for a boy and devotion to her father who ultimately kills the boy and then kills himself. During the shooting of the film she reprimanded the cameraman who had automatically stopped filming when a shadow accidentally fell across her face – sincerity, not looks, were what mattered now. But the new realism she went after in her acting was fatally obscured by the old melodrama of the story. The reaction was ominous. Her voice passed the sound tests, though the Southern accent she used for the role irritated some people. But exhibitors complained of poor business on the film's release and some audiences in Britain are reported to have booed it. Her performance won her an Academy Award, but not the satisfaction of appealing to a new public in a new role. It seemed that by cutting off her curls she had broken the enchantment without lifting the curse.

After this, one senses a failure of the spirit. Against her will she made *The Taming of the Shrew* (1929) with her husband, Douglas Fairbanks Sr. She found him a trying co-star. He would show up late on the set, forget his lines, insist on doing re-takes of the scenes he was displeased with but deny his wife the chance of re-shooting her own scenes. (Fairbanks's athletic pep on the screen seems to have been the positive charge of an acutely neurotic, even melancholic personality in private life.) 'The making of that film,' she wrote in her memoirs, 'was my finish. My confidence was completely shattered and I was never again at ease before the camera or microphone.'* The finished film dispirited her even more by showing how the years she had spent repressing her adult personality on the screen had diminished her power to play a vigorously sensual heroine like Katharine. 'Instead of being a forceful tiger-cat, I was a spitting little kitten.'† She

* Mary Pickford, op. cit., p. 312.
† Ibid., p. 311.

abandoned her next film, *Secrets*, at a cost of 300,000 dollars. It is noteworthy that it was to show her for the first time as aging from a young frontier wife through the stage of mature womanhood and ending up as an old, wrinkled woman. Now it was a case of adding on the years, not subtracting them. *Secrets* finally got made in 1933, with Leslie Howard as her co-star rather miscast as a rugged pioneer. Coming out at the peak of the Depression, it was received unsensationally though at least more warmly than the film which had preceded it. *Kiki* (1931) bears all the signs of desperation in the abrupt casting of Mary Pickford as a volatile French chorus girl trying to woo a husband over from his unfaithful wife. Critics conceded she had energy, but was short on conviction.

After *Secrets* she opted for retirement in an afterglow of worldwide affection and a third and this time extremely happy marriage to the actor Charles Rogers. She had bought up her early films to protect herself against their commercial re-release by someone else; but in 1931 she announced that she had determined to have them destroyed at her death. 'I would rather be a beautiful memory in the minds of people, than a horrible example on celluloid,' she stated.* Fortunately she was prevailed on to reprieve them: yet it looks like a harsh sentence passed by some part of her on her film childhood. No one seeing those performances today could doubt that she was an actress of manifest talent and imagination – and exciting but unrealised potential. One bitterly regrets that she never met the right director or found the right story at the same time as she was trying to impress the other part of the Pickford personality, the sexual awareness and worldly toughness, more clearly and uncompromisingly into her performances. The power of the myth which preserves her affectionately in people's memories today also made her the prisoner of their sentimental predilections in her working lifetime. 'We did, frankly, want her to seem a teenager,' Adolph Zukor says, generously overstating the terms on which the mass public gave Mary their loyalty. They, frankly, wanted her to seem a little girl. And this is the view of her that still prevails,

* *Photoplay*, May, 1931.

although one is now accustomed to films that adapt their themes swiftly, and sometimes worthily, to take advantage of the earlier and earlier onset of puberty in the young. The oversexed teenager nowadays seems the norm on the screen, while the sexually promiscuous infant is regarded as merely tomorrow's trend-setter. Perhaps this is the reason – or one of the reasons – for the persistence of the Pickford myth. It represents the possibility of innocence. Perhaps the more commonplace we find Baby Doll and Lolita becoming, the more we resist the thought that Mary Pickford could have been anything else but America's Sweetheart.

CHAPTER THREE

ITS FUNNY HEAD: MAE WEST

When she was a child of eleven, as she tells it, she was already a woman to look at. And the boys in Brooklyn, where she had been born in 1892, used to fight over her in street gangs. Thus was fixed, early and gratifyingly, the pattern of Mae West's lifelong relations with the male sex. Throughout her career she never deviated from this attitude of provocative sexuality which often did not require her to do anything – but just stand there. When George Jean Nathan saw her posed in *Vanity Fair* as the Statue of Liberty freeing her fellow Americans from their moral inhibitions, he remarked, 'She looks more like the Statue of Libido.' Of course over the years she refined and complicated this image until a quite bizarre personality took bold shape. It was one imbued with such a natural charge of sex that it could hardly help making the most innocuous gestures and lines of dialogue appear highly suggestive: at the same time it also made them extraordinarily funny. Sex rampant and unrepentant, yet redeemingly self-satirising, is what Mae West represents: a sex goddess who mocks the very qualities she dangles before the public. No one who has once seen her snaking perambulations outside the circus tent to whet the customers' appetites in *I'm No Angel* (1933) ever forgets the disdainful exit she makes through the flap with a muttered, 'Suckers!' In film terms she was an almost entirely self-made sex symbol whose handling of the illusion she knew her public wanted to enjoy was performed with a talent for the comic-erotic that has been very much underrated. It is time to try and prove her artistic claims.

How did she learn to make the most of herself, and then add some more? First of all, that anatomy helped. Her father was an Irish prize-fighter, her mother was Franco-German; and from such stock she probably got her earliest asset. Actually, she was no Amazon, being under five feet three inches in height, a fact she adroitly concealed by extra-high heels and trailing gowns. But when photographed, she gave the effect of well-weighted flesh and bursting ripeness – the anti-dietary kind of buxom health that might have inspired Rubens. Her walk was a curious contradiction of what is meant by sensuousness, for Mae West lumbered – if the truth must be told, she slouched. Yet again the effect when seen on the screen was startling, for it appeared as if the action had been slowed down. And slow motion, in films at any rate, is the essence of eroticism. It can make a plain handshake in a reception line look like an intermeshing of quite carnal intention; and the illusion of it in Mae West's heavy limbs invested her walk with the suspicion that perhaps she had learnt it through trampling over men. 'I'm a fast-movin' girl that likes 'em slow,' she sang. In fact, the truth was very much the opposite and posed one of the earliest problems when she entered films. On the stage she was used to having the actors round her work faster than herself; but her first film, *Night After Night* (1932), was being directed in a slow tempo, which meant she would have had to speed up her technique, or risk seeming slower than a funeral. Instead, she virtually took over the direction of her scenes and restored the illusion that she moved under sail – not steam.

Unlike the later sex symbols, she emphasised her hips rather than her bust. They were padded out and sometimes additionally accentuated by the wearing of six-shooters on them. When she moved they acted as stabilisers; when she was at rest, they served to take the weight off her hands. Her hair was invariably platinum blonde, close but waved above a full-moon face – a slightly lazy face. The eyes under the enormous false lashes did their hardest work of the day or night when they travelled unhurriedly up and down the length of a man evaluating his virility: they very nearly closed completely when she began purring out her innuendoes. Her voice – that was unforgettable! It was like a kazooka blown through steel wool: the kind of siren song only a Popeye would have needed to tie himself to the mast in order to resist. But it was perfect for the flip ribaldries she stored up in her mouth, like gum.

And when really attracted to an available male, she dropped register into a languorous drawl punctuated at intervals by the oddest sound of all, a sort of clucking as she sized him up, a nasal 'huh-huh' of approval, a rutting note uttered very softly and very close to him. Her love call.

Considered separately, every item of Mae West's physical personality is a caricature of sexiness. The overall effect ought to be grotesque. At times one even suspects the presence of a female impersonator behind the performance; and it is perhaps significant that in her zestfully written autobiography she makes a point of recalling that Julian Eltinge was the best known artist in that branch of vaudeville when she was an impressionable child trouper on the same stage. And yet the effect is *not* grotesque – or not quite. What redeems it is a surprising degree of propriety. Though her view of sex was healthily post-Freudian, and she saw it as a commodity to be enjoyed without guilt, her code of manners was eminently Victorian. On screen and off it she insisted on all the social courtesies due her sex. Men must take off their hats to her, stand up when she entered a room, never smoke in her presence. (Tobacco smoke held the unpleasant reminder of being kissed by her father after he had finished one of his long black cheroots.) When she behaves vulgarly in her films we notice it immediately, for it happens very seldom and then usually with justification. The woman in *I'm No Angel* who gets a jigger of raw liquor chucked between her bare shoulder blades happens to be jesting about Miss West's lack of breeding at the time. A little later the same snobbish socialite unwisely offers Mae West money to keep away from her fiancé, and gets bounced abruptly out of the apartment. Whereupon the offended party recovers her aplomb and shrugs off the low incident in the most imperious (and celebrated) instruction ever given to a domestic servant. 'Beulah,' she orders her coloured maid, 'peel me a grape.' Mae West brazenly advertised that she was no angel: she would never have dreamed of calling a film I'm No Lady.

* * *

From an early age she was highly conscious of her anatomy: but it took longer for her to grow aware of her talent for using it.

From amateur-night appearances she graduated into stock-company roles; and at first sight the parts she played, ranging from the neglected babe in *Ten Nights in a Bar Room* to an innocent princeling in *Richard III*, hardly seem like a rehearsal for *Diamond Lil*. In fact learning her lines literally at her mother's knee gave her one of her most seductive mannerisms: the slow way that she would savour the rhythm of a line or a word that her mother was drilling into her. This is probably why her handling of dialogue puts one in mind of the old-fashioned type of infants' primer where the hard words are divided up for easier comprehension. Sex comes out of Mae West's mouth broken into syllables: e.g. 'You're no oil paintin', but you're a fas-cin-at-in' monster.' About 1910 she was singing and dancing on the vaudeville stage. In contrast to the preachy tone of the American cinema at that date, vaudeville was conducted with brio, licence and vulgarity, though its folk tradition made it respectable enough on occasion for a Bernhardt or a Maurice Barrymore to appear on it in excerpts from the classics. The song with heavily stressed *double entendre* was then the vogue, so were jokes with innuendoes: which reminds one that the form of humour that Mae West made into her speciality really dates from this earlier period, although the screen in the 1930s had wisecracks being snapped out all over it. In almost every way, her style was set early.

The main precaution that vaudeville artists had to take was to reconnoitre the local tastes and taboos before opening their act in each community. It was in these touring companies that Mae West learned how to be a judge of every township's degree of sexual sophistication, how to adapt her effrontery, elide an innuendo or risk a blue joke, and otherwise trim her act to the moral atmosphere 'out front' as well as to the rise and fall of the clapping and laughter. The necessity to feel out an audience in this way is what gave her film style a range of nuances that latter-day comedians playing to audiences for whom anything goes often fail to develop when they take to the screen. Prevailing morality is always a keener test of a humourist than an applause meter. Mae West's finesse and projection of herself needed no adjusting when she arrived in Hollywood, and she soon made her films take their timing from her, too. Her personality was so powerfully developed that her stage techniques only increase her screen impact, yet do not leave her films looking 'stagey'. This paradox becomes clear in the account she gives in her memoirs of how she 'stage-managed' a scene in *Night After Night*. In this Prohibition-era story she has to check her wrap with a cloakroom lady who cries, 'Goodness, what lovely diamonds.' 'Goodness has nothing to do with it,' drawls Mae West. Then, instead of the film cutting directly into the next scene on a roar of audience laughter, as the director, Archie Mayo, had intended, the camera at Mae West's suggestion was held on her like the eye of a watcher in the stalls as she sashayed her way up the grand staircase into George Raft's speakeasy. 'I don't have to wait for laughs,' she told Mayo. 'I just roll with the punch – the punch line.'* The punch line in this case had been a mockery of morality: the 'roll' was a parody of carnality that topped it.

Nor was Mae West significantly in debt to her screenplay writers. Her memoirs show her continually dissatisfied with any story or dialogue that she did not write herself, or at least improve on. This atttitude also derived from her *having* to write her own patter and songs in vaudeville. Her source material was already to hand. It was the same lewd, laconic, unsentimental environment she worked in and on which she imposed her own vivid sexuality. (In the same way, and for the same reason, Mary Pickford's choice of stories for her films remained stubbornly influenced by the sentimental melodramas favoured by the Belasco touring companies and their audiences. This was a pity: for Mary Pickford's film art derived from an already debased form, Mae West's from one that still had a vulgar vitality flowing through it like an induction coil.) When she arrived on the New York variety stage she continued to borrow elements from her immediate environment. She adapted the shimmy for her act: this was a dance consisting of a strenuous series of lascivious bumps and grinds hitherto confined to Harlem Negroes. It was a minor border raid into sociological territory that she soon staked a claim to in a

* *Goodness Had Nothing to Do With It*; *The Autobiography of Mae West* (W. H. Allen), p. 130.

Mary Pickford as she is remembered: an aura of back lighting and innocence, pendant ringlets, angelic posy and soulful gaze. The sentimental image of this portrait is the one that dominated and even distorted her screen career and has been inherited by people who have never laid eyes on a film of hers.

ary Pickford as she could be: e curls are still visible, but a f-reliant realism replaces the ntimentality. ' "Good will preil," her charming mouth will l you, while something in her se, uncompromising face adds ently that it damn well tter.' She was in her early 30s nen she played this child in *ttle Annie Rooney*. (*Frame argement*.)

Mary Pickford as she tried to be: the excitable French chorus girl in her last film but one, *Kiki*, who – as a contemporary reviewer put it – 'wins over a husband' from his unfaithful wife. To her regret, this change of role was rejected by her public. The same reviewer called the film 'the biggest mistake Mary Pickford ever made in her career'.

series of 'showcase' plays for herself that she wrote about the New York underworld of pimps, prostitutes, racketeers and even perverts. The first was a melodrama about a sailor who is seduced by the girl whom he has brought the gift of a bird of paradise. It was crudely constructed. But its castration theme, with the male losing the feathered token of his masculinity, apparently gained in erotic vigour when Mae West read it aloud to the successful Broadway director Edward Elsner. Elsner, who had worked with John Barrymore, agreed to stage it.

He did more. He analysed why her performance, as she read the script, had appealed to him. 'You have a sexual quality, gay and unrepressed,' she recalls him saying. 'It even mocks you personally.' In the career of most successful artists there is a generating moment of self-awareness, and for Mae West there can be no doubt that it was then, in that remark, 'It even mocks you personally.' For it not only sharpened her self-awareness, but under Elsner's direction, it showed her the way she could reconcile her inflammatory personality with the demands of public decency. She later wrote: 'I learned . . . that I could say almost anything, do almost anything on a stage if I smiled and was properly ironic in delivering my dialogue.'*

* * *

At first, though, the spell fell utterly flat. She had called the play *Sex* (1926), putting the word in solo boldness for the first time on a Broadway theatre marquee, though it was commonplace in the titles of the flood of films reflecting the hedonism of the 1920s now issuing from Hollywood. Society answered Mae West's audacity with a morals charge, a fine, and a ten-day jail sentence. She got three days off for good conduct and the notoriety did her no harm at all. But while she assiduously cultivated her aura of ill fame, she typically did not let it spoil business. Noticing that men made up eighty per cent of the audiences for *Sex*, she set her next play in the 1890s, so that its extravagant costumes would bring in the women. It was called *Diamond Lil* (1928).

* Ibid., p. 94.

Yet one suspects that Diamond Lil owes her existence in Mae West's imagination to deeper compulsions than the pulling power of period finery. For in this bejewelled, ribald, emancipated Bowery bawd, Mae West fully developed the character she was to exploit for the rest of her life under different names in different films. She has stated that she got the idea from a night porter's reminiscences of the old Bowery. He remembered the real-life character well; and he also suggested the setting for her in the taverns that had found a loophole in the Raines Law and added bedrooms upstairs so as to pass for 'hotels' and be able to sell liquor more freely. This evidence of an era still within easy memory is what makes Mae West's play, in spite of its melodrama, feel like a realistic reconstruction of Bowery night-life at that date. But when she got down to elaborating the character of Diamond Lil, Mae West looked nearer home. The name was derived from her father's affectionate nick-name for her mother – Champagne Lil. The change of epithet may be taken to indicate the daughter's discovery that there are more lasting investments than wine-bubbles. Now the emotional tie between mother and daughter in the West home was much more intimate than that between Mae and her father. 'For some time I had become conscious of a growing resentment in me towards Father . . . I was crazy about Mother, but I found myself not liking my father, and Freud wasn't there to explain it to me.'* As a child her mother had dressed her in the same kind of clothes and fabrics that she herself wore. The identification of mother and daughter was so close that when the former died, while the daughter was on tour with Diamond Lil, Mae lost her power of speech for three days; and her grief was intensified because her lack of any spiritual convictions denied her the consolation of looking forward to seeing her mother again in some after-life. It may have been some comfort to her, however, to feel close to her mother through the character of Diamond Lil. For it is significant that most of the films made by Mae West at the height of her fame are set in the 1890s, the formative period of her childhood but also the time when her mother was in the prime of life and the deep attachment

* Ibid., p. 14.

of mother and daughter was forming. Diamond Lil is a mother image on whose idealised endowments the daughter has superimposed her own post-Freudian sexual freedom and enjoyment.

It may be objected that Diamond Lil has more of the madam in her make-up than the mama. But this leaves out one consideration. 'Because I portray sex with humour and good nature instead of as something shameful,' Mae West has said, 'I think my portrayals are accepted in the spirit in which I play them. I have excited and stimulated, but *I have never demoralised*.'* This is the truth about Diamond Lil, too. She does not corrupt anyone. She is much too busy enjoying sex to stop and organise it for profit. She may be a kept woman – she frequently is – but she is a lone agent who does not keep other women in her employ. In some films where Mae West has a young protégée in tow, she shows a warmly maternal concern for the girl's well-being and happiness. This was just the sort of girlhood Mae West had enjoyed herself, from a mother about whom, she also records, 'there was a power and vitality . . . that made a man melt before her glance.'† Her autobiography carries the laconically affectionate dedication: 'In loving memory of my MOTHER without whom I might have been someone else.' Diamond Lil was a part that provided her with the means to be 'someone else' – and without breaking the umbilical cord.

* * *

When the Depression was hitting hard at Broadway theatre receipts, in 1932, she decided it was timely to switch to the larger box-office of the movies. A Paramount executive, Jesse Lasky, had at one time written sketches for her variety act, and it was to this studio she went. Her reputation, which travelled well, had preceded her; and old Hollywood residents who thought the name Diamond Lil looked common on a calling card quickly changed their minds when she proved her money-making power on the screen. In a very short time she was in a position to construct films around her so that they projected her sex appeal to the maximum. She began, naturally enough, with her leading men.

* Ibid., p. 217. Italics mine.
† Ibid., p. 2.

She picked them first for muscle. This was a highly visible way of recharging her own batteries from the virility of the adjacent males. (The techniques used by stars at Press interviews have not yet received the serious anthropological study they merit; but when they do, Mae West's habit of feeling a reporter's biceps with clucking approval may be judged as much representative of her and her era as the snapping shoulder-strap of today's frailer goddesses.) After muscle, what she valued was class, breeding, gentlemanly deportment. This was the Victorian side of her outlook. She spotted and instantly recruited Cary Grant while he was doing press-ups just after blowing into Hollywood to try his luck. But it was for his polished performances that she kept him on as her co-star, playing the well set-up detective in Salvation Army disguise who falls for her in *She Done Him Wrong* (1933) and the Social Registerite for whom she makes a play in *I'm No Angel*. Rough diamonds were all right to have as cash customers, but a cop or a 'silk-hat type' as an escort was a tribute to her discrimination – as well as the power of sex to subvert the Law and jump class barriers.

Her films frequently open with a consummately skilful build-up for her first entrance. This is absolutely theatrical in origin, yet when well done it achieves the effect of good cinema: a sense of things mounting pictorially to a climax. *She Done Him Wrong* – the title under which *Diamond Lil* was filmed – opens with a quick series of little scenes in dissolve, establishing the rowdy vitality of the Bowery in the 1890s. Then we pause on a bar-room painting of a nude, hear the men boast that 'she's the swellest girl that ever came down the Bowery,' pick up a hint of the jealous passions she arouses – 'What would you do if you found her with another man?' her saloon proprietor-protector is asked, and answers, 'Nothin' mebbe – to her.' – and finally we see her rolling up in an open carriage, parasol lofted, drawing glares from the ladies and bows from the men. 'A fine woman,' one admirer says, and gets the ambiguous reply, 'One of the finest women that ever walked the streets.' Her sex appeal, her pedigree and her potential for causing tragedy have all been established with flamboyance *and* with fluent economy. In *I'm No Angel* she cries her own wares, parading along the show-tent ramp, displaying the goods, sardonically quipping 'Penny for your thoughts' at the gawking men, lifting and lowering her long gown with the provocative query 'Am I makin' myself clear, boys?' before belting out the song They Call Me Sister Honky-Tonk and sidling off with that *sotto voce* 'Suckers!' As it was meant to, it leaves us begging for more.

The appeal she projects can be broken down into its elements without any fear of dissipating the allure of the total effect. First, her sexiness is presented as something as natural as drawing breath. 'You were born in August,' a circus-tent astrologer observes. 'Yeah,' she answers, 'one of the hot months.' To Cary Grant, as he is about to fit the handcuffs on her, she says, 'Are those strictly necessary? You know I wasn't born with them.' Comes the laconic reply, 'A lot of men would have been safer if you had.' Coupled with this is her ever-readiness to be a good sport, which is likewise conveyed in ribald wisecracks that moderate into comedy what would otherwise be a raging case of nymphomania. 'Haven't you ever met a man who can make you happy?' she is asked, and she turns the spirituality of the word 'happy' inside out with the pert admission, 'Sure I have, lots of times.' A client boasts to her, 'I've been places and seen things,' but she caps that with 'I've been things and seen places – guess that evens us up.' And of course there is her own celebrated gloss on the meaning of promiscuity, which turns the dictionary definition into a personal credo – 'It's not the men in my life, but the life in my men.'

Mae West's innuendoes are the oblique side of the same comic candour. They depend less on slickness of phrasing than on the tone of voice in which they are uttered. Which is why the most famous of the lot – 'Come up and see me some time' – has endured to become a catch-phrase. For like all catch-phrases that can be traced back to an individual personality, it invites the mynah bird that lurks in us all to mimic the original speaker as well as attempt to transfer the magnetism of his or her personality to ourselves by repeating the actual words. Curiously, however, this catch-phrase is not to be heard in the precise form in which it became world famous anywhere on the sound track of *She Done*

Him Wrong. One can hear, 'Why don't you come up again some time, I'm home every evening?' And also, 'Come up again, some time.' And even, 'Come up again, any time.' But not 'Come up and see me some time.' It is rather like the dismaying discovery everyone makes sooner or later that Conan Doyle nowhere in fact wrote the words, 'Elementary, my dear Watson,' in that precise order.

In the art of innuendo Mae West has no equal: she can break the Ten Commandments with every inflection of her voice. What she implies is sometimes so subtly lewd that it is missed. At the end of *I'm No Angel* the judge who has winked as well as nodded over Mae West's breach of promise action against Cary Grant is seen taking leave of her in her apartment. He has clearly not come up just to hear her say thank you. The courtly old fellow reaches out to take her hand and kiss it – and he fumbles slightly. 'See you've trouble with your hand, too, judge,' she flashes at him. And what a charge of suggestiveness is contained in that one word, 'too'.

Her films do not shrink from showing her making money out of sex. The act is pleasurable, and if it can be made to show a profit, too – then take it. She excels in scenes showing the seductive shake-down she gives customers. Traditionally in such transactions, the client calls the tune. In one case it is Mae West who literally pre-selects it, softening up her man with mood music from a range of discs labelled with an eye for alternative choices, Nobody Loves You Like That Dallas/Frisco/Chicago Man. Otherwise the old commercial relationship is strictly maintained by her and a satisfied caller who tells her, 'You've given me the time of my life, honey,' puts her instantly on guard against the word 'given'.

Perhaps because it evolved from vaudeville and the stage, her screen personality is accompanied by a richer selection of erotic props and set-pieces than that of any of the other sex goddesses in the 1930s. One recurring scene is her morning levee, with its parody undertones of Pompadour luxury, as coloured maids jubilantly go about the ritual of dressing her in outrageous creations, manicuring her, and feeding her lines to draw flip retorts from her about her current lovers. Another is the harem scene with the sex roles reversed and Mae West queening it over a pack of humiliated ex-lovers like the witnesses against her in the breach of promise suit whom she discredits by enquiring if they got value for their money, or otherwise servile males like the convicts in the cells she parades past in *She Done Him Wrong*. Catherine the Great was one of her later stage roles: she played her like a sexually bountiful Diamond Lil with more men under her command. And one suspects the part appealed to her precisely because of the Empress's reputed predilection for surrounding herself, at all hours of the day or night, with the tallest and most obedient guardsmen in her army. Even the law of the jungle was bent to her will. In one of her films she plays a circus artist who whips the king of beasts into submission; and when she played Eve in a radio sketch in 1937 she shocked listeners across the nation by coolly seducing the Serpent. Not that there was ever anything morbid in her appeal, unlike that of the old-time vamp. For her, sex reared its funny head – sometimes in the unlikeliest places. In several of her movies there is featured, with blatant immodesty, a golden bed built to Babylonian specifications, all swans' necks and cupids' heads. A couch of Eros constructed in the atelier of some master satyr. And on it lolls madame, clad in a gown that would shatter the steadfastness of St Anthony himself. There is only one item out of place. A tiny item, but it purposely sends up the whole voluptuous tableau. What Mae West is reading is the *Police Gazette*.

* * *

By the end of 1934, however, not quite three years after she had arrived in Hollywood, Mae West was well on the way to becoming a ruined woman. She was being made the principal target of a purity campaign of unprecedented ferocity. The Motion Picture Production Code had been devised in 1930 as an earnest of the film industry's intentions to be on good moral behaviour in future, after the excesses shown in Hollywood films and in the private lives of Hollywood stars during the 1920s. But the Code had not silenced the critics of the lax behaviour and sagging standards they still detected in films. What producers righteously upheld in public, they dishonoured with the utmost impenitence in the studio. In word and gesture Mae West was the living mockery of all the Code's pieties. But Hollywood made her welcome for one excellent reason: her early films were enormous money-makers. At one time she could command as much money for a film as Garbo. It is true that *She Done Him Wrong* was shorn of its white slavery sequences before it was released, but these sequences had nothing directly to do with her part in the film. So this bow to censorship scarcely mitigated the shock of the moralists when they saw the flamboyant way she conducted herself. And after *I'm No Angel* was released, many critics said that censorship had become a farce.

Then in April, 1934, a ginger group of Roman Catholic clerics and laymen formed the Legion of Decency, with the aim of advertising the moral dangers to Catholics in seeing certain films. Protestant and Jewish bodies resolved that their faithful should not want for protection, either. Hollywood might have successfully staved off federal legislation enforcing rigid censorship; but the Legion of Decency's threat could be clamped on to the box-office of any allegedly corrupting film in just as short a time as it took for the word to be circulated in a parish. Speed was the great weapon in the Legion's campaign, coupled with the psychological advantage that the film industry, which is one of the most worldly outfits on earth, was, and still is, unnaturally frightened of incurring the disapproval of spiritual bodies. The American Depression also assisted the Legion. For film studios who were already facing a sharp decline in receipts were in a low state of morale. To have Mammon desert them and then find God coming up on their flank was too horrid to contemplate. They capitulated and promised not to distribute or exhibit any film not sanctified by a seal of approval – showing it conformed to the principles of the Production Code. The purity zealots now moved into the film studios and set themselves to reform Mae West. In the end, of course, they done her wrong. By November, 1934, the title of her new film *It Ain't No Sin* had become *Belle of the Nineties*. Her studio was reported to be considering re-making it completely in accordance with the eye-tooth imperative of the

Code that 'the sympathy of the audience shall never be thrown to the side of crime, wrong-doing, evil or sin.' Where that would have left Mae West suspended it is hard to imagine. But she undertook her own purification with exquisite cynicism by importing into the film a Negro choir of ninety singers to chant antiseptic spirituals.

All the same, censorship quickly made a changed woman of her. Her scripts were bowdlerised and the character she played was cleaned up. And like most reformed characters, the later Mae West is hard to warm to on the screen, though one can exult in the sequences – usually early in the film – when she kicks against the short moral tether that the killjoys have fastened on to her. *Klondike Annie* (1936) opens with a lot of the old promissory build-up, establishing her sexy reputation as the chief exhibit in a Chinese sporting house in Frisco. Nor is one disappointed when she appears sitting in front of a gong, wearing a head-dress in the style of Classical matriarchs like the Gorgon, playing a lute, and singing nasally, 'I'm an Occidental woman in an Oriental mood for love.' 'Languor becomes you, my beautiful one,' murmurs her Chinese protector, whom she very soon kills in self-defence while helping the characteristic ingénue girl escape from the brothel. She flees to the Klondike on Victor McLaglen's boat, and to escape the law at the other end she assumes the identity of a dead woman missionary. Up to then, her wisecracks have come fresh from the salt-barrel. 'If there's anything you want, just yell for it,' says skipper McLaglen. 'Do you have to yell for it?' she answers. But once the Quaker bonnet goes on her, she sprouts a conscience underneath it, begins to 'see things different', smugly advises a dance-hall hostess, 'Any time you take religion for a joke, the laugh's on you,' and exhorts a saloon full of miners to repentance with a pepped up blues hymn that would be amusing if one did not feel that Mae West had been 'got at,' nobbled, made to preach 'Be sure your sins will find you out,' instead of her usual 'Be sure your sins will find you in.' She ends the film afflicted by considerations that are unusual for her, like going back to face justice, doing the right thing, and making up for the past – all calculated to rouse loud hosannas from the Production Code vigilantes.

According to Adolph Zukor, quoted by the American critic Murray Schumach, 'at least one state, and many communities, opposed a portion of every movie that Mae West made for Paramount. In every case, he says, his company won a reversal of the censorship decree.'* But if censorship did not actually kill her, it left Mae West sadly debilitated.

There was another reason for her waning popularity. Her films never made fans out of the all important female audience. This continued to elude even her later and rather pathetic attempts to lay down bait for them by supplementing her stage shows with muscle-bulging males in leopard-skin briefs. It has been said that Mae West's films are the culmination of women's claim to lead a full love life of their own. Perhaps they are. But if so, women were not noticeably grateful. Alfred Hitchcock, although a connoisseur of a more enigmatic, svelte type of female, put the reason succinctly when he said, 'Women resent someone who steals their menfolk from them.'† When Mae West said, 'Come up and see me some time,' she was not talking to the ladies; and she could hardly complain if they picketed her doorway. Moreover her physical proportions, and even more the way she emphasised them, hardly made her a woman's woman. It is significant that the director who tried to coax Mae West out of retirement was Federico Fellini, a recurring characteristic of whose films is a zestful appreciation of actresses of abnormal measurements. This remains very much a male prerogative.

Not that Mae West is diminished artistically by being exaggerated statistically. She is one of the few, the very few film stars who owe their fame to no one but themselves – to no director, scriptwriter, make-up artist or lighting photographer. She was self-made and self-sustaining. She was a creative force in almost every department of her early movies. She was not for a minute fooled by her own act, but this did not stop her perfecting it to a pitch that left the field free of competitors. She was aged forty when she arrived in Hollywood, which is grotesquely late to

* *The Face on the Cutting Room Floor*, by Murray Schumach (William Morrow & Co.), p. 204.

† *Evening Standard* interview, March 24, 1965.

begin a film career; but she took command of the medium like one of those matriarchal figures who bossed the covered-wagon trains in an earlier America. Actually she had very few years at the top before censorship damped down her creative as well as her profane fire. But if one regrets this, consider that she could not have succeeded in Hollywood much before she did. For her brand of the comic-erotic depended upon her being heard as much as seen. And what would the caption in a silent film have done for her immortal invitation to 'Come up and see me some time'?

CHAPTER FOUR

AT HEART A GENTLEMAN: DIETRICH

In the case of Marlene Dietrich one might risk saying that home is where the art is. She was born in Berlin. Various dates have been given for the event. Some references say 1903, some 1906. The unkindest came from the Russians of East Berlin who discovered what they claimed was her birth certificate and ungallantly published the year written on it: 1901. Her family were comfortably off. Her father and subsequently her step-father were Prussian officer corps soldiers, severe disciplinarians who brought her up on lines of stern discipline and propriety. In particular they drilled into Maria Magdalene – names she later elided into 'Marlene' when applying for admission to Max Reinhardt's theatre school – that any display of temperament, any show of emotion even, was bad manners. Until she was about twenty and developed a wrist ailment, her mother intended her to be a violinist: a profession which encourages the student of it to keep her body still and her mouth shut. 'My mother,' she said later, 'made acting difficult for me. My whole upbringing was to mask my feelings.' The remark is noteworthy. For it shows poor insight into her screen personality and the nature of her appeal. It also implies that feelings ought to be a part of an actor's essential equipment, like lungs, tongue and lips; whereas the man who made Marlene Dietrich into a star considered them closer in kind to the nuciform sac or human appendix – an unnecessary organ, more likely to be a source of irritation, and better removed.

What compelled Josef von Sternberg to keep his eyes fixed on Dietrich as she leaned against the wings of the Komödie Theater one night in 1929 was her very lack of feeling, her impassiveness. 'Cold disdain,' is how he remembered it in his autobiography thirty-six years afterwards, though it is likely it was nothing as positive and he was simply attributing to her his own dislike of the insipid musical she was appearing in. One does not need to have been there on that occasion to know how she looked; for von Sternberg reproduced the pose in film after film, in different lights and against different supports. It seems to have had the clarity of an Epiphany for him. The indolent angle of her body sketches the patient waiting-game of the street-walker, or the poised confidence-sharing of the night-club chanteuse. It is that of a woman alone, who nevertheless intimates that men are in the vicinity, while something unmistakably confident about the relaxed posture adds that she meets them on equal terms. It is no accident that one night club where she sang commemorated the fact with a plaque on a pillar inscribed: 'Dietrich Rested Here.' Years later, von Sternberg was accused of using Dietrich as simply a decorative prop in his films. Untrue though that is, he certainly sensed right away the suggestive insolence emanating from her when propped up. Her lack of emotion only fortified that impression. Even in repose her features have a supremely independent allure centred on the flyaway eyebrows and the heavy lids that can flatten a presumptuous male with a single dismissive bat. She corresponded in every way to what von Sternberg demanded from his players – the obedient projection of his own attitude to life.

Born in Vienna in 1894, Josef Sternberg acquired his 'von' in Hollywood: it was put on the screen by a producer to preserve the symmetry of the credit titles; and when critics jeered at it, he belligerently adopted it. He won overnight fame with *The Salvation Hunters* (1925), a bleakly poetic dirge about human derelicts living beside a river dredger, which brought him Chaplin's patronage; then he originated the American gangster cycle with *Underworld* (1927) and was alternately revered and reviled by the studios according to the money his films made or lost. Every wound von Sternberg received as well as every scar he inflicted is precisely located and identified in his autobiography, *Fun in a Chinese Laundry*, a book written in a bitter, lancing style, in which he forgets little and forgives nothing. Its tone makes it unique among film memoirs – a not very polemical *genre* on the whole.

The book's theme is humiliation. Sexual humiliation like the indignities inflicted on the Vienna prostitutes by packs of fierce little children who tossed their skirts up; personal humiliation like the charity-chest clothes he had to wear as a boy; but especially artistic humiliation like the abasement of a film actor before his director. For von Sternberg, direction meant subjection: the quasi-slavery of the player's body, the suppression of any feelings he was not specifically instructed to show by his director, the surrender of his own ideas about playing the role, in short such minute manipulation of his body, brain, innards and viscera that it amounted to what von Sternberg called 'editing a human being'. By the time he came to Berlin to direct Emil Jannings's first talking film, *The Blue Angel* (1930), he had a satanic reputation among actors, and exulted in it. 'Affected by legends spread by some of those who worked for me, and in the expectation that something great, though horrifying, was in store, actors and actresses fainted in the anteroom of my office even before they were ushered into the lion's den.'* But one who did not was Dietrich.

When she discovered that von Sternberg was offering her the role of Lola Lola, the *femme fatale* of *The Blue Angel* who humiliates her infatuated lover, Dietrich's on-stage impassiveness was merely modulated into disinterest. She coolly told him she photographed badly. (She had already made a number of German films of fairly local distinction.) This unprecedented indifference intrigued von Sternberg. His autobiography suggests no reason for it; but a hint has recently been given by Louise Brooks, the American actress who played the part of Lulu the prostitute in G. W. Pabst's film *Pandora's Box* only the year before – 1928. She has related that she got the coveted part in preference to Dietrich whom Pabst was said to have considered too obvious – 'one sexy look and the picture would become a burlesque.'† Now Lola Lola in *The Blue Angel* was inspired by Lulu, even named after her by

* *Fun in a Chinese Laundry*, by Josef von Sternberg (The Macmillan Co., N.Y.), p. 114.

† Article by Louise Brooks, *Sight and Sound*, Summer, 1963.

von Sternberg, who does not appear to have been aware of Dietrich's rebuff by Pabst. Very likely she did not want to risk a second rebuff, especially as Lucie Mannheim was being widely tipped for the part. Hence her indifference.

In any case, concealing her feelings as she had been taught from childhood, she performed a screen test – she sang *You're the Cream in My Coffee* – with the unconcern of someone who felt it all a waste of time. According to von Sternberg, she did not even ask to see the test. It is easy to understand how a man who loathed his stars to have 'feelings' and who demanded their complete obedience must have found this kind of behaviour intensely intriguing and gratifying. As for Dietrich, one might say it simply shows how upbringing *will* out.

* * *

Garbo and Dietrich are the two stars who tempt writers into myth and metaphysics to explain their art. No less an admirer of the latter than André Malraux has said, '(She) is not an actress, like Sarah Bernhardt: she is a myth, like Phryne.' With all respect, it is a particularly inapposite comparison. Phryne was the great courtesan of the fourth century who tried to discompose her Athenian judges by throwing off her clothes. No Dietrich, she! Had von Sternberg been defending her, he would never have let her appear in court except fully clad from toes to neck, with perhaps a half-veil down to her nose-tip. And quite possibly he would have put her in breeches. For von Sternberg added mystery to Dietrich in the first place by the degree of concealment he devised for her. In matters of eroticism, he is the great coverer-up. One recalls why he favoured putting her in trousers at a time when the wearing of them by women was still a moral issue and when the Paris chief of police chose Dietrich's visit to the city as the occasion to allude meaningfully to an old ordinance against women dressing in men's apparel. Von Sternberg said he simply wished to prove that her sensual appeal did not depend on her bare legs, however shapely and celebrated. He would have turned his back in disdain on the Biblical Salome – *his* Salome would have donned her veils while she danced and, in doing so, raised her sexuality to the power of seven. In his memoirs von Sternberg says he did not bother to see Dietrich's film *The Song of Songs* (1933), which she made for Rouben Mamoulian – he adds, with something like a sneer, that there was in it a statue of her, nude.

In his films he wrapped Dietrich up in an erotic atmosphere which he composed with stupendous skill and detail – just how is something to be examined in the pathology lab., not the metaphysics class.

He created her mystery out of light and darkness and the way the camera lens registered them. The lens used to photograph Dietrich in *The Blue Angel* for example, was given to the cameraman Gunther Rittau by the American photographer of many of Mary Pickford's films, Charles Rosher. Called a 'Rosher bullseye', this custom-made lens duplicated the way a human eye sees in sharp detail only what it is looking at directly, while staying vaguely aware of related areas and objects. It clearly delineated Dietrich's main features, but let the rest of her face recede into ever-so-soft focus. The effect is that of a memory-image. A remoteness is created, a mysterious distance between ourselves and Lola Lola that no focus-puller could measure with his tape, for it exists only in the erotic imagination. Everywhere in von Sternberg's films, lenses, lighting, shadows and veiling create the same psychological comment on the actress: no secret ever came as well shrouded as Dietrich. The louvred shutters of the Foreign Legion town in *Morocco* (1930) stencil Dietrich the cafe singer, 'one of the legion of lost women', with a shadowy incognito. She stalks on to the platform in *Shanghai Express* (1932) with an eye veil that makes the lower half of her face look plastered with cold cream, it is so white by contrast, and establishes the chiaroscuro of Shanghai Lily's soiled soul. A bridal veil in *The Scarlet Empress* (1934) screens the wolfish concavities out of her cheeks and, aided by a glycerine tear, transforms her into an ikon madonna; while later the coarser net-curtaining round her bed, and the glint of a tear-drop diamond she is fondling against her cheek, restores her hardness and suggests the heartlessness of the future Catherine the Great. And when Shanghai Lily says of Clive Brook, 'Once upon a time we loved each other,' something more useful than this trite line comes out of her mouth – a cloud

Mary Pickford adopts an uncharacteristic pose as Kiki, the French chorus girl. Part of the plot required her to feign a cataleptic fit in order to foil her rival in love and remain in the flat of the hero, Reginald Denny. It was, perhaps, too abrupt a transition in Mary's roles for audiences to accept.

Above: Clara Bow, afloat in one of her early films, scarcely breaks the surface of the water. The flat-chested look, helped by the bandeau which compressed the breasts instead of emphasising them as the brassière did later, was the chief characteristic of the screen's flapper girls in the 1920s – Miss Bow came to the notice of critics when she was impersonating a boy. *Below:* The recumbent Mae West resembles the fascinating cross-section of a hilly terrain. In films, she emphasised her hips, and the padding in the Nineties period costumes she usually was found wearing amply enabled her to make more of what she had already got.

of cigarette smoke, wreathing round her face like the emanation of smouldering reminiscence. (Until one sees this effect, one does not appreciate how justly the Italians call their love-story magazines made up of photo-strips, *fumetti.*) Sometimes von Sternberg sectionalises Dietrich and lets a part of her imply the mood of the rest of her. Instead of showing Shanghai Lily at prayer, he photographs only her hands pressed together in the darkness like white shoots pushing their way up out of some buried spirituality. One of the half-dozen greatest lighting effects in films is Catherine the Great reviewing her officers and melting into the shadows, the spot-lighted white of one eye a diminishing point of roguishness.

When she eventually parted company with von Sternberg, Dietrich used to have a mirror mounted beside the camera so as to check the way she was lighted. Arthur Knight has said she could even judge it by the warmth of the lights on her skin. She had learnt her skill from a master, though one with an infinite capacity for giving pains. 'More often (than compliments) she listened to "Turn your shoulders away from me and straighten out . . . Drop your voice an octave and don't lisp . . . Count to six and look at that lamp as if you could no longer live without it . . . Stand where you are and don't move, the lights are being adjusted.'*

But much of Dietrich's mystery is also unquestionably due to her voice, with its veiled but faintly callous intonation, always perfectly in tune with the sexual taunts or the world-weary confidences she uttered or sang about. It is a voice that holds no major surprises, yet instantly demands attention. No one can anticipate how Garbo will phrase a line or sound a word: remember how 'bombs' somehow touchingly became 'bomps' in *Ninotchka*. But one can remember Dietrich deviating into this kind of thrilling unexpectedness only once, when she gave the word 'Shanghai' a strangely pendulous third syllable and an acoustically exotic first one, so that it came out like 'Chung-high-yee'. (Even this and much else in her vocal performance at that time, and in the curious slowed-up way everyone has of

* Josef von Sternberg, op. cit., p. 253.

speaking in *Shanghai Express* may be due to her early troubles with English *and* the slower tempo of some recorded dialogue to suit sound reproduction in cinemas in the early 1930s.) As a chanteuse on the stage today she is a mezzo-baritone with a range seldom more than an octave and a half. This strangely low register gives the effect of a lullaby, meant not to stimulate but to tranquillise. And the impression is corroborated by the fact that memories are the emotional material of many of her songs – while agelessness of the kind that many a young man might attribute to his mother is the physical illusion she strives to preserve. By contrast, the sentiments in the songs are frequently sensual ones: the sexual innuendoes of Jonny, the camp-follower attachments of Lili Marlene, and, of course, the greatest *femme fatale* song of all, *Falling in Love Again*. This paradox suggests why Dietrich is at her best in films, or in public, when surrounded by an audience in which men predominate, singing to them in tones that revive the muzzy security of sleepy childhood, while her words connect subtly with the male's sexual ego. She has said she picks her songs for the words, not the melody, in order to suit her small voice. How vital the words are to the spell she casts can be judged from the failure of the Hot Voodoo number in *Blonde Venus* (1932) which has visually everything working for it. The costume she wears, of blond fuzzy-wuzzy wig, long net stockings and feathers sprouting from her waist like *bandarillos*, is one of her most fantastic. But the words she sings are banal. They do nothing to project *her*; and consequently the suggestive voltage she packs is low.

* * *

If one dwells on how Dietrich was photographed, and how she sounds, it is because these erotic qualities are ones that predominate in the seven films which she made for von Sternberg. Save for *Blonde Venus* – a mother's sacrifice story he tried to leave Paramount before making – every one of the parts has been that of a *femme fatale*, a woman who attracts men at the cost of suffering to them and sometimes to herself. How well she knows her own strength is revealed by the story that she refused the leading role in Terence Rattigan's play *The Deep Blue Sea* on the ground that she could never be convincing as a woman who tries to gas herself because she cannot keep her lover or find other men. Vivien Leigh can convey the extremities of sexual despair, not Dietrich. Let her show herself for five minutes at a street window, one thinks, and Mr Rattigan would have been writing a different play. Though she has been married to one man since her German film days, her husband always keeps himself unfocused, in the background, seldom in her company: so that her public image reinforces the view of her as a rootless one, a *femme fatale* who travels alone. Of course it is not as simple as this. Dietrich has played many kinds of *femme fatale*; and the more one examines her career, the more clearly one fact emerges about the men she attracts and the code she lives by on the screen. Loyalty is as much part of it as love, and in some cases a great deal more.

She had been done a great disservice in this respect by her most famous film; for *The Blue Angel* is the least characteristic role she ever played. The really shocking thing about Lola Lola, the cabaret singer, is not that she deliberately destroys Jannings as the infatuated pedagogue – it is, rather, the impassive way she watches him destroy himself, throw up social position for sexual bondage, with padlocks for cufflinks on his clown's outfit and a slave's neckband in collar sizes, and wail out his grief over the footlights at the end in the famous rooster's crow of 'Cock-a-doodle-do!' that seems to echo back as 'Cuck-old-ed!' This humiliation was a typical invention of von Sternberg's: it does not occur in the original Heinrich Mann novel. Dietrich certainly tantalises her lover, puffing her face-powder into his beard and letting her lacy knickers float down from her upstairs dressing-room over his face. But most of the time she stands to one side of him on her 'provocative legs', as Siegfried Kracauer called them, and regards him coolly and egotistically. Instead of exploring their relationship, von Sternberg simply keeps on depicting Jannings's physical servility in front of her – for ever dropping on to his knees to pick up erotic postcards, or help roll on her stockings. Lolling back cross-legged in cutaway skirt, with black suspenders stretched tightly against her pale thighs, or dangling libidinously loose, Lola Lola is sex incarnate – but uninvolved. She is more of a narcissist than a *femme fatale*. What she keeps falling in love with again is her own image: no wonder that song has such a damnably introspective ring!

It is significant that Dietrich's image had to be changed before the American public were allowed to see her. For Paramount, the co-producers of *The Blue Angel* delayed its American première till January 3, 1931, to give von Sternberg time to rush out his protégée's first Hollywood film, *Morocco* premièred on December 6, 1930. Gary Cooper was the star of it, by virtue of prior American fame, and the story was made palatable to Main Street moviegoers by letting Legionnaire Tom Brown leave the foreign heartbreaker in the lurch at the end, staggering off into the desert with her own heart broken, to follow her man on those notorious high heels. By humiliating her, the film appreciably humanised her – made her capable of returning a man's love as well as accepting it. Not till *The Devil Is a Woman* (1935) – her last film with von Sternberg and their biggest box-office disaster – did she go back to playing a fatal woman, 'Concha the savage, the toast of Spain', who humiliates her lovers for no motive except the perverse pleasure it gives her. Outside of *The Blue Angel* no more heartless scene exists than the one in this film when she plucks the cigarette out of Lionel Atwill's lips and bestows it on the gigolo he has caught her with, pays the young man for his services with a bill from her protector's wallet, and sends him off with a flower tucked behind his ear broken off the bouquet Atwill has brought her. It is like a public degradation inflicted on a court-martialled officer whose buttons, ribbons and medals are stripped off on the parade ground.

In this sense, it is the reverse of Dietrich's characteristic passion. For her, love usually goes with loyalty. If not to the man, then at least to the code of life that he and she both observe. It is a military code: and it is the very heart and soul of Marlene Dietrich. With a father in the Uhlan Cavalry and a step-father in the Hussars, it would not be surprising if she grew up attached to the soldier's virtues of honour, loyalty and contempt for the pettiness of snug, bourgeois life. (Possibly her military background helped her accept von Sternberg's authoritarian command so completely.) What *is* surprising is the constancy with which such virtues appear on the screen, shaping her relations with men and giving her a comradeship with them that often precedes love and survives it. 'I am at heart a gentleman,' she was once reported as saying, a Garbo-esque communiqué the full text of which ought to have been, 'I am at heart an officer and gentleman.' Soldiers in Dietrich's films are always saluting her – not just out of courtesy, but in recognition that she wears the same uniform as they. And sometimes she does, literally. The male dress she often puts on in her films is not necessarily sexual in its undertones: generally it has a military association, too. Even the rakish clip she gives to her top hat whenever she appears in evening dress is in the nature of a masonic salute. *Shanghai Express* holds the beautiful surprise of seeing her, clad in an extravagantly feminine stole trimmed with fox fur and fully ten feet long, suddenly clap Clive Brook's army cap on her head just after kissing him – like a gage of loyalty. Even her growling boast that 'it took more than one man to change my name to Chung-high-yee Lily' makes one feel that the name is the posthumous battle honour of those who fought over her and fell, like Mons or The Marne.

Her opening remark in *Dishonoured* (1931), 'I'm not afraid of life, although I'm not afraid of death, either,' sounds like the translation of a regimental motto. This film, adapted from a von Sternberg story, uses a ludicrous plot about spying in World War One and the invention of an even more invisible kind of invisible ink, as a glorious excuse for stating Dietrich's sex appeal almost entirely in military terms. She plays an officer's widow who has turned prostitute and is picked for her work as a spy when cooing 'Hellooo?' with cool professionalism at the chief of the Austrian Secret Service. 'I need a woman who knows how to deal with men,' he informs her, and her eyes smile cynically at this recruiting euphemism. Her entrance into the Secret Service headquarters resembles that of a visiting general: a physical thrill stirs the roomful of uniformed men, as if they expect mobilisation of some kind to be declared. Later on, when she traps her first traitor, he acknowledges it by surrendering his sword to her.

'What a charming evening we might have had if you had not been a spy and I a traitor,' he murmurs before shooting himself. 'Then we might never have met,' she reminds him. Such is the ruthless logic of love and war.

Sometimes her sex appeal is exercised directly through the conditions of war. *The Scarlet Empress* shows the transformation of a frightened virgin princess into an iron-willed military autocrat galloping up the staircase of her palace in Hussar's uniform to confirm the power she has already learned to exercise over her Russia nguards in her royal bed-chamber. But although love for her is military in its appeal, and often in its trappings, it is by no means patriotic. She is a patriot for the heart, not for any king or country. (Dietrich sometimes makes a point in interviews for newspapers or radio of referring to herself as a wanderer in the world, giving the impression that she is almost a stateless person, with no home to go to.) 'Could you help me die in a uniform of my own choosing?' she asks the priest in *Dishonoured* when the Austrians who recruited her as a counter-spy are about to execute her for liberating the Tsarist spy with whom she fell in love. 'Any dress I was wearing when I served my countrymen, not my country,' she adds. Understanding man of God! – he brings her her old streetwalker's clothes. She makes up her face in the gleaming blade of an officer's sword, walks professionally out to the firing squad and gratefully utilises the brief reprieve when the officer in charge breaks down in tears to touch up her lipstick and straighten the seam of her stocking. The scene is absurd in recollection. On the screen it works like a *coup de théâtre*: she is so plainly meeting her execution as if it was an assignation. But the point is, it is a soldier's death she is privileged to die. And one's mind flashes forward precisely thirty years to Stanley Kramer's *Judgment at Nuremberg* (1961) in which she played the widow of a German general executed for war crimes. Dietrich's own sentiments about Germany are well known and it is usually assumed she took the role to help bring the war guilt home to the people who supported Hitler. No doubt this did play a part. But as Abby Mann wrote the character of Frau Bertholt in his screenplay, she corresponds more closely to a pre-Hitler Dietrich. She is a woman whose love for her husband excuses everything – she does not believe him guilty of war crimes – except the manner of his death, which outrages her own devotion to military ideals and dignity. 'He was entitled to a soldier's death,' she insists. 'He asked for that. I tried to get that for him ... Just that he be permitted the dignity of a firing squad. You know what happened. He was hanged with the others.'* No wonder von Sternberg was so angry when Ernst Lubitsch, as production chief at Paramount, insisted on changing the title of his film from *X-27* – Dietrich's code name – to *Dishonoured*. The lady, he protested, was not dishonoured by being shot: she was merely dead.

* * *

Dietrich spent six years under von Sternberg's direction. She has never ceased to give him full, and sometimes fulsome, credit for her performances, to which he has returned the laconic reply, 'With commendable instinct she turned herself into a martyr who praised the divine grace which favoured her with lacerations.'† Yet the relationship was one of steadily diminishing returns. Censorship, which began to really hurt Hollywood with the formation of the Legion of Decency in 1934, threatened the very type of character on which Dietrich's personality was moulded. She could not safely play a prostitute in terms of contemporary realism. The only time she came near it was in *Blonde Venus*; and censorship worries turned the character into a married woman who takes money from a rich lover to pay her sick husband's medical bills, and who does not go on the streets without her child. (An infant was a common sop to the censors then, and now, since it betokened a stricken conscience as well as being a physical handicap to any immoral proclivities.) The fact that Catherine the Great seduces only one of her guardsmen in von Sternberg's film is no attempt to whitewash history, but simply an acknowledgment that Joseph Breen, the chief censor, had his eye on the Empress of Russia. Von Sternberg suggests

* *Judgment at Nuremberg*, by Abby Mann (Cassell & Co.), p. 124.

† Josef von Sternberg, op. cit., p. 253.

her insatiableness, anyhow, in the hayloft scene where Dietrich mechanically feeds one ear of grain after another teasingly into her mouth as her lover removes the previous one – and a scene later she adds the last straw, provocatively plucked out of his paliasse in the barracks.

Censorship meant that Dietrich had to go on playing the *femme fatale* at prudently remote periods of history or else in vague and un-localised settings like an Orient express or a desert garrison. As her popularity declined, von Sternberg's mastery of pictorial effects increased. Today the psychological film, where the atmosphere is an extension of the characters and the mood suggests all the motivation needed, is better appreciated and has brought von Sternberg's work a growing acclaim. But in the 1930s the static, story-less quality of his films, coupled with the way he virtually dissolved Dietrich into the lighting and decor of his baroque imagination, cost them both their public. It would appear that von Sternberg had wanted to end their partnership after *Morocco*. 'I was finished,' he said at a much later date. 'But Miss Dietrich said to me, "You want to show the world you're a great director and that I am a bad actress. Isn't that what you want to do? You want me to go to another director?" '* Unwisely, they went on together. At heart, it seems, von Sternberg was a gentleman, too.

After the break with von Sternberg, several other directors made fumbled attempts to capitalise on his Dietrich – *The Garden of Allah* (1936), *Knight Without Armour* (1937) – or else tried to update her mystery and play it for light comedy, as Lubitsch did in *Angel* (1937) with great success, except at the box-office. In 1938 she and a number of other stars were publicly pilloried as box-office poison in a Hollywood trade paper. And there her career might have ended but for Joe Pasternak, the producer who persuaded her to star in the Western, *Destry Rides Again* (1939). Himself an old Berlin hand and a movie-maker wise to the ways of exhibitors, Pasternak changed her image by Americanising her. She shed her mystery, her European mannerisms and especially her dignity, and emerged as Frenchy, queen of the Long Chance

* Interview, *Films and Filming*, June, 1963.

Saloon in the town of Bottleneck. There is nothing perverse about her now. Instead of planting an ambiguous kiss on the lips of a very girlish girl, as she did in *Morocco*, she is the one who gets slapped by the customers – playfully, on the backside. Her singing voice startles one with its beery baritone. A lucky rabbit's foot in her garter brings those once-divine legs down to earth. She emphasises a very American part of her anatomy, which one hardly suspected existed, when she drops a few dollar pieces down her cleavage with the quip, 'I'd rather have money in the bank.' The only humiliation she inflicts now is to wager $30 against Mischa Auer's pants and win. And with total disregard for her dignity she grapples with Una Merkel in an Amazonian rough and tumble on the floor, at the climax of which she is doused with a tubful of water by Deputy Sheriff James Stewart, expels him from the saloon with a hail of bottles, then squelches up to the bar and musters the cheering men with the cry, 'Who'll buy me a drink?' It is the old touch of the man's woman that Ernest Hemingway loved in her. But now it comes with a Dietrich who can actually kid herself. The only other echo of the past is emitted, appropriately enough, by the wry, growling ballad, *See What the Boys in the Back Room Will Have*, written by *The Blue Angel*'s composer, Friedrich Hollander. Even it catches the new tone of ribaldry – Lola Lola might have thought its approach brash.

* * *

Destry Rides Again was a success and deserved to be. But in Hollywood such success is dangerous. Dietrich's post-Destry career landed her again in a rut. The studios now saw her as a sexy hoyden, with the glamour of brazenness replacing the glamour of mystery. French adventuress in *Flame of New Orleans* (1941), clip-joint hostess in *Manpower* (1941), saloon bar belle in *The Spoilers* (1942), harem queen with gilded limbs in *Kismet* (1944) – roles like these give a feeling of run-down momentum. Probably her best post-war film is Billy Wilder's cynical comedy, *A Foreign Affair* (1948). But even it depicted a Teutonic Frenchy – now called, with characteristic Wilder underlining, Von Schlutte –

who thrives on the Black Market and scores points off Jean Arthur's virginal Congresswoman. Dietrich hardly needed to act the role – but then how often has she needed to *act* any role? She is scarcely an actress in the sense of someone who sinks her personality untraceably into a character. It is hard to believe that the twist at the end of *Witness For the Prosecution* (1957), which requires one not to recognise that it is Dietrich got up like a skivvy with crooked teeth and Cockney accent, could really have fooled anyone unfamiliar with the play: admittedly this is a personal verdict. The same applies to her masquerade as an idiot maid in *Dishonoured*; while her Spanish cocotte in *The Devil Is A Woman* is an uncomfortable compendium of stamping heels, rolling eyes, heaving bosom, tossing head and boiling blood, with a mouth lipsticked into a Carmen Miranda fullness and costumes that run to fretwork haircombs a foot high. Where she does play against the grain of her personality more subtly and successfully is in the first half of *The Scarlet Empress* as the ingénue and timorous foreign bride of the future Tsar. Von Sternberg sends her scuttling round the court at the double, in ribbons, bibs and tuckers, looking in the words of Cecil Beaton – who did not intend a compliment – 'as if she had fallen into a baby's basinette'. Very tender lighting and very young hair-styles help her, but the nervous, jumpy rhythm is anti-Dietrich – and a revelation. The old rumour that she cannot play maternal parts will not lie down and die: but its falseness should be evident to anyone who sees *Blonde Venus* in which she makes a functional, practical, but devoted mother. Just as she gives a man her worldly *femme fatale* look and seems to search out the little boy in him, so in this film the small, unfussy, sensible gestures she makes as a mother, like tucking her child's handkerchief into his breast pocket, seem to flatter his latent manhood.

But it is true that her personality is very vulnerable to unsympathetic direction. It can disintegrate completely with bad direction, in a way the elemental Garbo's does not. Nothing of her survives the mystic hokum of Richard Boleslawsky's *The Garden of Allah* in which everyone talks as if aware an important plot is somewhere to hand, but just eluding them. Yet its scenes of

Dietrich and Charles Boyer setting out for a honeymoon in a sandstorm are no sillier than parts of *Morocco*, which remain mesmeric because her fascination is imposed so indelibly by her director on his own fantasy of love and fatalism in the Sahara. *Knight Without Armour*, the story of a Russian countess caught up in the Revolution, utterly quenched her mysterious glamour. What *could* be left of it when Jacques Feyder terminates a perfect von Sternberg set-up of Dietrich sitting down to dine with White Russian officers just as the table napkins are being shaken out?

'I – never – enjoyed – anything – in – a – film,' she said recently* with a heat that implied deeper resentment than justifiable discontent at being typecast, or understandable reluctance to face a film camera in her sixties. She went on: 'I had no desire to be a film actress, to always play somebody else, to be always beautiful with somebody constantly straightening out your every eyelash . . . I never see myself as an actress on the screen. When I sing my songs, then I am an actress. I act the lyrics.' Her film roles have got farther and farther apart as she has put her energies into being a *chanteuse*, a career she slipped into during the war, singing to men in uniform. From what one may deduce of her predilections, it is not surprising that this kind of role gives her more emotional gratification – nor that the song she has made most popular in post-war years should be *Where Have All the Flowers Gone?* in which she shares the sorrow of the fighting man at the waste of war. But this new career can also be seen as a reaction against her past, as one of the most slavishly 'directed' personalities in films. For now she is her own master, no longer subjected to 'a cold-eyed mechanic critical of every movement', but with only Burt Bacharach, or his successor, to give melodic unity to a stage act that she has supervised in minute detail – choosing her own costumes, doing her own make-up, arranging her own lighting, even on occasion seizing a broom and furiously brushing an unnoticed cigarette butt off the stage lest it subtract one fascinated eye from the impression she is creating. She is economical in all her gestures for the same reason: she does nothing unless it

* Interview with Derek Prouse, *Sunday Times*, November 22, 1964.

adds to her sensuous effect on the audience. It is a marvellously accomplished technique for projecting oneself and it recalls the one von Sternberg used, which he referred to as 'editing a human being' – with this vital difference. Now Dietrich does her own editing: now the goddess sets herself in motion.

CHAPTER FIVE

THE FUGITIVE KIND: GARBO

The only way of trying to penetrate the mystery that has gathered round Greta Garbo is to assume that it does not exist; to think oneself back to her screen beginnings; to refuse to be decoyed by the legends put out about her; to acknowledge the metaphysics of personality, but also to look for the less abstract ways in which she employed her talent to gain her effects; in short, to see Garbo plain. The approach may be anti-romantic and even disenchanting. But the Garbo myth has had such a long tenure that it is almost compellingly necessary to take a new perspective on its subject. For Garbo answers the need that people feel for something mysterious and inaccessible in life, though possibly *they* are the ones who have contributed more to her mystery than she has. To take one example. Nowhere in anything she said, either in the lengthy interviews she gave in her early Hollywood days when she was perfectly approachable, or in the statements snatched on-the-run from the publicity-shy fugitive she later became, has it been possible to find the famous phrase, 'I want to be alone.' What one can find, in abundance later on, is 'Why don't you let me alone?' and even 'I want to be left alone,' but neither is redolent of any more exotic order of being than a harassed celebrity. Yet the world prefers to believe the mythical and much more mysterious catch-phrase utterance. And though Garbo in this instance is not to blame, her films are – for she certainly has been heard speaking the words 'I want to be alone'. But it was in the character of Grusinskaya, the aging Russian prima ballerina who loses her nerve half-way through her gala performance, flees back to her suite in Metro-Goldwyn-Mayer's *Grand Hotel* (1932) and subsides on the floor in a flutter of tutu frills – looking, it must be admitted, more like the dying heron than the swan – and entones the legendary line associated with the real-life Garbo. It is an excellent example of art borrowing its effects from a myth that was reality for millions of people.

It is when a myth gets to be indistinguishable from reality in this way that a fusion takes place in the minds and emotions of filmgoers – and a star is made. Edgar Morin, in his work on the psychology of stardom, has put this more oracularly but none the less perceptively. "... The spectacle of the movies implies a process of psychic identification of the spectator with the action represented ... Man has always projected his desires and his fears in images. He has always projected in his own image – his double – his need to transcend himself in life and in death. The double is the repository of latent magical powers, every double is a virtual god.'* In short, filmgoers project their fantasy needs on to the star on the screen, as well as on to her in real life. 'It is when the mythic projection focuses on her double nature' – as actress and person – 'and unifies it, that the star-goddess is produced,' adds Morin.

But what happens when something frustrates the spectator's compulsive desire to project himself on to the real-life star? Then a Garbo is produced – a unique kind of star-goddess. From very early in her career she obsessively refused to let her admirers identify themselves with her. She shunned them. She soon gave up the ritual of attending the premières of her own films and waited instead until the film had been running a week or so before she sneaked in and viewed it, incognita in smoked glasses and a hideaway hat. Gradually she put an end to even proxy encounters with her public and withdrew from the other ritual of stardom, the Press conferences and individual interviews. Finally she retired herself into the most complete kind of inaccessibility that exists for a film star. She stopped making films. For millions of people today, the only possibility of identifying with Greta Garbo is on the screen, in one of the twenty-seven feature films that survive. And somewhere in her Swedish soul she probably regrets the necessity of having to admit us even to this sight of her. For Garbo, one suspects, the ideal film per-

* *The Stars*, by Edgar Morin (Transatlantic Book Service), p. 98.

formance would have taken place without a film camera being there to record it. She certainly on occasion seemed to be going as far as she could in this direction, barring visitors to the set, excluding even the technicians not directly involved in the shooting of the scene, having black screens erected round the set, and for one fraught spell making her director stand behind them and tender advice to her through a slit.

A queen of Egypt could hardly have ordered her own immortality better than Garbo has done, though almost certainly she never intended it to turn out this way. But this is what happened. By not leading the conventional life expected of a Hollywood film star, she unwittingly ensured that real life would never wear away the mystery that her public insisted existed. By severely limiting her public appearances to a hallucinatory screen image projected in semi-darkness before hundreds of people at a time, she unintentionally multiplied public curiosity about her and created the most potent kind of divinising distance between herself and her admirers. And by giving it all up at the age of thirty-six, at the height of her powers, she left behind a human enigma that keeps people guessing still, though it has obscured the real riddle that her personality poses. 'Why did she quit?' is what people first ask. What they should really seek the answer to is, 'Why did she become that kind of star?'

* * *

Greta Garbo was born Greta Gustafsson in 1905. Her parents were working-class Stockholm folk, her father had some lowly-paid kind of labour in the city corporation. But so far as early photographs offer any reliable guidance, it was from him that she inherited her feminine fineness of features, while paradoxically his farming ancestry came out in her long limbs, flat body, largish feet and broad yoke of collar bone that looks as if it was meant for harnessing to Mother Courage's wagon. So from birth Garbo's physique united the two sides of her nature, the feminine and the masculine, that she was able to deploy brilliantly for the emotional effects of her screen acting. Not that she was over-tall: she was a reasonable 5 feet 6½ inches. But the old lie about her excessive height persists because several of her best-known co-stars were comparatively small men, or wore costumes in their films with her that somewhat diminished them, and she had continually to condescend to them physically. Watch how often in *Marie Walewska* (titled as *Conquest* in the U.S.A.: 1937) she risks *lèse-majesté* by leaning against a table or chair, knees slightly bent, whenever Charles Boyer's Napoleon is seen beside her in long shot. In repose, Garbo was ungainly. In one of his very rare comments on her, William Daniels, her adored cameraman who photographed nineteen out of the twenty-four films she made for M-G-M, said, 'She was always taken in close-ups or long shots, hardly ever intermediate or full figure. The latter do not come out well.'

The irony is that the first impact Garbo made on Hollywood was a vividly physical one. When she was seen moving on the screen, her nature altered dramatically. Then her awkward proportions shifted into sensuous adjustment to each other, and gave the Americans a kind of animal movement that they had never before seen in their own pictures. This was especially remarked on then – and still would be now – in the love scenes she played, where the almost male intensity of her attack was played off strongly against the feminine spirituality of her looks. The Hollywood colony of Swedish stars and directors who had been imported in the 1920s, among them Nils Asther, Lars Hanson and Victor Seastrom, scoffed at the artistic banality of the first silent films Garbo made there, films like *The Torrent* (1926) and *The Temptress* (1926), laughable melodramas comparing badly with their own homeland's much more sophisticated productions, and they told her that her career was ruined. They were good critics, but poor prophets. They overlooked what captivated American audiences: the wholly new way in which Garbo, having at this date no voice on the screen, backed up her acting with her body. When other silent films, notably *Flesh and the Devil* (1927), featured her playing love scenes lying down, she aroused even more sexual expectancy among filmgoers, who would scarcely have cared to know that full-length shots of Garbo were best taken when she was supine. That way, too, there was less risk of her dwarfing John Gilbert.

Above: Jean Harlow is generally credited with shifting the emphasis of sexual interest in the 1930s from the legs of the previous decade to the breasts, though her conscious deployment of bare shoulders in some scenes in her films suggests she knew her appeal lay as much at the back as the front. (*Frame enlargement from 'Platinum Blonde'.*) *Below:* The lit-up face of Jean Harlow, suggesting that Life, intense and capitalised, is there for the living. Frank Capra dressed her in black almost to the neck for this first scene in *Platinum Blonde*, thus emphasising the eponymous feature that became her trade-mark. (*Frame enlargement.*)

Veiled Lady One: Marlene Dietrich as she first appears in *Shanghai Express*. Von Sternberg's favourite veiling effect gives her instant mystery, lends to her Shanghai Lily, the notorious China 'coaster,' the redeeming *chiaroscuro* of a woman whose goodness is only half-obscured by her worldliness. (*Frame enlargement.*)

Veiled Lady Two: 'Once upon a time w loved each other,' says Dietrich i *Shanghai Express*. An instant after she ha uttered the line, this veil of cigarett smoke conceals the banality of it b seeming to be the very emanation o nostalgic memory. (*Frame enlargement.*

A moment after kissing Clive Brook i *Shanghai Express*, Marlene Dietrich clap on his Army cap and gives it a rakish ti with a gesture that is also a kind of salu from a woman whose love is based on th same code of chivalry as the soldier' It is her most characteristic gesture an goes equally well with the top-hat sh wears with her tailsuit, except that suc 'mufti' makes it more masonic tha military. But the meaning is the sam (*Frame enlargement.*)

'They don't have a type like me out here,' she wrote home in 1926, and added a gloomy afterthought that echoed her fellow Swedes' prediction, 'so if I can't learn to act they'll soon tire of me, I expect.'* This was to be the tone all through her career. Success acted on Garbo like a depressant. By temperament she seems to have been pessimistic most of the time: which was a fruitful outlook when it could be incorporated into the tone of her films and make them very nearly plangent with fatalism. The screenplays turned out by Salka Viertel, Frances Marion, Clemence Dane, S. N. Behrman and others got to be very cunning about how they conscripted this and other characteristics of the star into their stories. The historical films lay down a red carpet of foreboding for Garbo to walk on to the exquisitely tragic point when one knows – and senses that somehow she knows, too – that she will stumble. 'I knew I was too happy,' cries Camille when required to give up her young lover for his own good, and to the banality of the line Garbo imparts a physical hopelessness, timed to a heartbeat, by suddenly sinking dead-straight-down till her chin is level with the bedspread – the camera duplicating her movement like a sympathetic confidante. Even when the note of doom is muted to a wistful envy, as in Queen Christina's remark to her favourite countess, 'How wonderful to be happy for no reason,' Garbo speaks it as if she is already rehearsing for her abdication. It was a characteristic pessimism that could also be played with tremendous effect against the grain of the film, so that in her last film, the comedy called *Two-Faced Woman* (1941), she answers the telephone with an utterly despondent 'Hel-lo' whose dying fall suggests that she expects to have the Last Trump announced to her this way.

But this was the plus side of a depressive personality that itself was the product of a badly scarred childhood. Garbo appears to have been a tense, withdrawn child who established a few jealously close friendships with girls her own age. According to one of her biographers, Friti of Billquist, she suffered at one time from anaemia, which persisted even after she became a Hollywood star and may be one of the reasons why she shunned social life. 'People take

* Quoted in *Garbo*, by Fritiof Billquist (Arthur Barker), p. 78.

energy from me, and I want it for pictures,' she explained in an early interview. How much, too, did this ailment shape the novel kind of bargaining tactics that helped her win her battles over fees and scripts with M-G-M? Instead of creating a scene, Garbo simply said 'No,' wasted no more energy in argument, but went home and stayed there, sitting it out till the studio gave in. Hers was the triumph of the apathetic will. She left school at thirteen and there is no doubt that her lack of education also made her shy and left her feeling socially at a loss for years until the small, protective circle of rich, influential and talented friends who were devoted to her enabled her to make up for her intellectual deficiencies by a process of osmosis. When she was fourteen, her father died. Garbo had had to take him regularly to a charity clinic for treatment; and witnessing the sick man being interrogated about his means, when he was desperate for treatment, must have been a shattering experience for the child. John Bainbridge in his biography of Garbo is probably right when he concludes that it taught her painfully early in life about the protective value of having enough money and made her excessively chary of how she spent what she earned.

But at a deeper level, one feels, it encouraged her cynical mistrust of the world: a melancholy expectation that the worst was always certain. And even more formative may have been the view of a man's world that she was plunged into on her father's death. To help support her family, Garbo, aged fifteen, took a lather-girl's job in a back-street barber's shop. There she soaped the faces of the customers, overheard some fairly uninhibited talk and ran the risks to which this kind of work, with its propinquity to men all day long, would be expected to expose her emotional development. One may, without wishing to do more than touch on a delicate aspect of her life, guess at some connection between the fairly basic and perhaps not reassuring insight into men that she got from this experience and her later cryptic attitude to men and marriage. Garbo certainly did not forgo male company in her private life, but neither did she dress or make up with the deliberate aim of attracting it. Whatever the degree of romance that the international Press was able to discern between her and some current escort, these associations were all inconclusive so far as marriage was concerned. John Gilbert fell passionately in love with her and, it was said, she with him; but she pulled back sharply in the middle of an elopement. Equally the courtship of Gayelord Hauser, the dietician, left Garbo fitter and for a time more sociable, but still single. What waiting reporters imagined to be a combustible romance with Leopold Stokowski was fanned into only a modest heat by their mutual passion for pre-breakfast calisthenics. Garbo's later preference was for men, among them the late George Schlee, who, like Mimi Pollak, Countess Wachtmeister and the other female travelling companions of her early years of stardom, had the financial power or knowledge of the world to ensure her privacy and throw a protective cordon around her whenever she moved from place to place.

Whatever determined her attitude, there is no doubt that Garbo's career profited from the curiosity and mystery that the independent woman always arouses. One thinks of lines like Queen Christina's 'I shall die a bachelor,' or 'I am Mata Hari: I am my own master,' which make the Garbo scripts sound like oblique commentaries on her life, or as if some coded message about her was trying to get through to us. The celibate roles strongly attracted her, so that at one time or another she considered playing Joan of Arc, Balzac's Duchesse de Langeais who jilts a lover to take the veil, and even St Francis of Assisi – 'What, complete with beard?' cried Aldous Huxley when summoned to write the screen play. Garbo with a husband is as hard to imagine as Elizabeth I of England with a consort. Oddly, she never hovered over that particular historical role – perhaps Queen Christina of Sweden had a prior call on her – though Garbo and that Tudor monarch were both women who managed to convert their enigmatic sexual status into very real power. For one of them 'bachelorhood' was a part of statecraft, for the other a part of screen myth. And any deviation into marriage would have made them vulnerable on these grounds alone.

* * *

In view of what has just been written, it may appear paradoxical that the Garbo myth has its origins in the character of a man: but this is almost certainly the case. She was not yet twenty when she met Mauritz Stiller, one of the leading film-makers in Sweden. Her screen career had already begun in a minor, amateurish way, with two advertising shorts for the department store she was then working in, and a 'quickie' comedy, *Peter the Tramp* (1922), in which she played a frisky, if lumpish bathing-belle. Thoroughly stage-struck, she then won a place in the Royal Dramatic Theatre's Training School, whose principal sent her along to Stiller when he was casting *The Saga of Gosta Berling* (1924). At that moment the screen acquired Garbo, the theatre lost her for good. What did Stiller see in the shy, awkward drama student? The scene has been described of him holding forth about her merits to his baffled film associates who could discern in her neither beauty nor talent. Precisely the same scene was to take place in Germany a few years later, when Josef von Sternberg nominated his 'discovery', Marlene Dietrich, to play in *The Blue Angel* against the vociferous opposition of *his* colleagues. In fact, the scene is commoner than might be supposed in the film industry with its unique scope for realising one's own fantasies while stimulating other people's. It occurs when a director-producer who is driven by an inner compulsion of which he may not even be completely aware comes across malleable feminine material and proceeds to make it into an image that feeds his emotional needs.

The Pygmalion drive was a very strongly entrenched part of Stiller's complex nature. A refugee from Russian rule, whose mother had committed suicide and whose father died soon afterwards, he had an innate ability to survive, great love of opulence, restless intelligence and a blend of artistic sensitivity and commercial hard-headedness. He was a dandy, a narcissist and an egotist: from contemporary accounts of him, he reminds one of Ibsen's Peer Gynt embroiled in moviemaking. There is a vital difference, though. Stiller was fond of women and liked to have them around him, but for vanity rather than sexual gratification: they completed the picture of himself he was always painting in his own mind. He was continually criticising other people and altering the way they looked, dressed, spoke or acted, so as to make them match up to the ideal he created for them. 'He compelled me to do what he wanted,' Garbo recalled later. 'I have him to thank for everything.' For a great deal, certainly. The name 'Garbo', for instance, the origin of which throws valuable light on their relationship.

Stiller had finished a very sophisticated and successful comedy called *Erotikon* in 1920, and he wanted to do another film of the same type since he had been intensely attracted to the film's leading female character – a professor's rebellious young wife who elopes with a sculptor, her own husband eloping with his niece. Stiller asked Arthur Norden, who had written the screenplay, to do another like it. 'But first of all,' he is reported to have said, 'we must get a name for the heroine, a name that is modern and elegant and international. A name that says just as clearly who she is in London and Paris as in Budapest and New York.' Norden, a history specialist, suggested the name 'Mona Gabor', inspired by the exotic patronym of Bethlen Gabor, a seventeenth-century Hungarian king. Stiller found the suggestion excellent, but kept trying out differently accented and spelled variations of it: Gábor, Gabór, Gabro, Garbo. Norden began writing the screenplay, but for some reason never finished it and the film was abandoned. At that precise moment Greta Gustafsson came to see Stiller. It is easy to believe that he gave her the name which had already excited his imagination.* Perhaps he settled for 'Garbo', instead of 'Gabor', because it is the Scandinavian word for a wood nymph and is often used as a term of endearment.

Whatever the precise explanation of the name that Stiller devised for her, a marriage of talents seems to have been solemnised between him and Garbo. Very flattered under her shy exterior by the attentions of so celebrated a director, she took on

* I owe the above information to Mr Christer Frunck, of the Swedish Film Institute, who obtained it for me from a memoir written by Norden in 1938. Mr Frunck also very kindly traced Garbo's application to change her name from Gustafsson, which was received at the Ministry of Justice on December 4, 1923. It has not been possible to learn when it was approved, but newspaper reviews of *The Saga of Gosta Berling*, in March, 1924, refer to her as Greta Garbo.

the name he wished her to bear, while he in his turn tutored her in social behaviour, taught her the techniques of film acting, and in the course of time influenced her outlook and personality so that many of his characteristics became her own. Stiller, for example, mistrusted newspaper reporters, and his dislike of being interviewed by them was communicated to Garbo at an impressionably early point in her career. Again, when bargaining with film people, Stiller habitually began with a show of disinterest or a blunt 'No'; and the effectiveness of this gambit must have been apparent to his protégée, while in any case it would be particularly agreeable to a person of her phlegmatic temperament. A perfectionist to a neurotic degree, Stiller made Garbo into one as well. Throughout her career she never arrived on the set anything but dialogue perfect; and it is probably to Stiller's early discipline that her refusal to welcome social callers – i.e., anyone not actually in the scene with her – on to the set while she was filming can be traced. To a person of Garbo's excessively shy disposition it would be far less torment to establish a relationship with one man, a film director, than to endure the nightly repetition of 'relating' on stage in front of an audience of strangers. (At a much later date, when a return to the stage was proposed to her, she is said to have agreed if the first half dozen or so rows of seats were removed.) Even so, the pains of film acting became apparent when G. W. Pabst directed her second major film, *Joyless Street* (1925). (She had gone into the film after the second film she was making for Stiller had collapsed for want of ready finance.) Pabst was dismayed to find her face developed a nervous tic when he tried to film it in close-up. Stiller acknowledged he had had the same trouble with her and advised Pabst to speed up the camera, so as technically to eliminate the twitch till Garbo gained confidence.

Her anxiety was intensified when Louis B. Mayer, head of M-G-M, imported her and Stiller to Hollywood in the middle of 1925. For Stiller's autocratic airs made him fall foul of the studio as soon as he arrived, with the savagely ironic result that after devoting so much energy and artistry to creating an ideal woman for his films to enshrine, he found himself being brutally excluded from directing any film starring Garbo.* Separated from her only intimate friend, at least during the working day, it is no wonder that Garbo, whose English was limited, retreated into herself. M-G-M's attitude to her giving interviews reinforced this. For her early interviews, which she did quite co-operatively, were full of banalities and naive remarks which embarrassed the studio: like her statement on arriving in Hollywood that she hoped 'to find a room with some nice private family' – hardly what was expected of an M-G-M contract artist. Garbo gratefully took the hint. Some of her fellow artists, like Lon Chaney, a man of mystery himself, advised her not to reveal too much about herself in public, M-G-M soon recognised the value of fostering the image of her as a remote, *mysterious* being, while her manager is generally given credit for having her billed solo as 'Garbo' – like Bernhardt or Duse. Thus outside pressures for once coincided with her own inclinations.

* * *

The ways of Garbo and Stiller now diverged professionally, though they remained the closest of intimates outside the studios. He went over to Paramount, she remained at M-G-M. Lonely, withdrawn, hating the hot dry climate, knowing next to no Americans and so shy at first that she took lessons in English from her Negro maid, Garbo sought out the most private place possible in which to hide herself: this time she found it in front of the camera, in the 'public solitude' of totally immersing herself in the character she was playing. Almost every eye-witness report of her at work stresses the same point: the amazing suddenness with which her nature changed the instant she started acting. Edmund Goulding, after directing her in the silent version of *Anna Karenina* (1927), observed: 'In the studios she is nervous. Rather like a racehorse at the post – actually trembling, hating onlookers. At the first click of the camera, she starts literally pouring forth Garbo into the lens.'† Later on her nervousness abated as she managed to channel her energy more fully into her remarkable

* He began directing *The Temptress*, but was replaced.

† Interview, *Picturegoer*, March, 1928.

power of concentration. Gene Markey, who adapted *As You Desire Me* (1932) for her from Pirandello's play, reported: 'She absorbs dialogue and situation instantly. She needs very little rehearsing and nearly always improves on the material she is given. This is not because she changes action or dialogue. It is because she adds to drama as much by virtue of her talents and herself.'*

It is sad there are no detailed accounts of the way Stiller – who had been an actor himself – coached and directed Garbo. But whatever the techniques he used to bring her to her pitch, they can only have refined the senses of a woman who was an instinctive Method actress long before that overworked and generally misapplied word became modish in New York and Hollywood. To read some of Stanislavsky's manuals on the actor's art after seeing a Garbo film is to find the nature of her performance virtually analysed and codified. This is not to say that Stiller knew of Stanislavsky's principles and goaded them into Garbo. They were as much hers by instinct or intuition as those of the great artists whom Stanislavsky studied for his theories. They are one of the reasons why her acting had such an exceptional impact on Hollywood. She was indeed a 'new type' in a way she did not appreciate.

One example of Garbo's art illustrates this with remarkable clarity. This is the famous furniture-touching sequence in *Queen Christina* (1933). One can think of no other actress in Hollywood who could have carried off a scene which is a classic Method exercise in the art of 'objectification', or relating oneself emotionally to the physical objects on a stage or film set. Garbo, playing the Swedish queen who is travelling incognita dressed as a man, has had her icy mistrust of marriage melted by having to share a bedroom in the village inn, and hence a bed, with the handsome new Spanish ambassador played by John Gilbert. The morning after, her sex revealed but not the fact that she is the queen, she moves around the room in an aura of softly filtered femininity, touching the objects in it as if each were some trysting place in Eden. While Gilbert watches, half-amused, half-mystified, she

* Interview, *The Daily Telegraph*, April 17, 1932.

uses her hands like a divining rod seeking the source of love, caressing the walls, stroking a spinning wheel, sliding across the bed and making a sensual pause on the pillow, finally flexing her breasts against the bed-post as if it were a man's chest. It is love transmuted into tactile joy. At length, with a half-catch in her throat, she murmurs an explanation to Gilbert. 'I have been memorising this room. In future, in my mind, I shall live a great deal in this world.' By any standard it is a marvel of a scene. But what makes Garbo's craft well-nigh incredible is how she contrives to play it simultaneously for sorrow as well as joy. Though Gilbert still does not know that she is the Queen of Sweden, she is wretchedly aware of the constitutional barrier to falling in love with the envoy of an unfriendly country. The words in which she speaks of preserving her rapture relay a boding undertone of someone preparing herself for loss and loneliness. And the inventory of love objects she has made on her tour of the room takes on the pathetic character of *memento mori*. Now one of Stanislavsky's techniques was to train the player's 'memory sense', to encourage him to summon up past moods and emotions and convert them to the needs of the character and scene he is playing. Can one locate the source of the extraordinary emotion Garbo must have drawn on for this sequence in *Queen Christina?* There is a reasonable likelihood that one can.

In November, 1928, Mauritz Stiller died in Sweden of an incurable disease. Garbo collapsed when she heard the news in Hollywood and warned M-G-M that her acting would suffer in her current film, *Wild Orchids* (1929): some critics did, in fact, detect an uncustomary constraint about her. Feeling bewildered, lost and even more lonely, she now refused absolutely to talk to reporters, dropped out of social life in which she had anyhow been only a peripheral participant, and built a wall of repression round her real self. Before the end of 1928, however, she returned briefly to Sweden and with Stiller's attorney she made a sad pilgrimage to the room where his effects were still in store. The lawyer has related what then took place. 'I remember vividly how she walked about the room, touching this item and that. "This was the suitcase he bought in America," she said, picking up the bag. "And those rugs – I remember when he bought them in Turkey." We stayed quite a time, while she walked round the furniture and paintings and all the other things and made sad little comments.'* Four years later she made *Queen Christina*. The case possibly will never be proved, but it is legitimate to speculate that the sensory immediacy of the love and grief of the bed-chamber scene is Garbo reliving emotionally her last sad contact with the man who had been her friend and mentor.

* * *

It will never be settled whether Louis B. Mayer actually wanted Stiller to work for him in America and got Garbo as a totally unlooked for bonus, or whether he set out to get Garbo and used Stiller as his stalking-horse. But he soon realised the rarity of the prize when he saw it on the screen. The movies in 1925 were just at the start of a reaction against the flapper girl's philosophy of free love and the Lillian Gish girl's continual battle for her honour. Garbo projected sexuality in a vivid way, of course, but with an underlying spirituality: the very combination that M-G-M, and the rest of Hollywood, had been seeking. For it permitted filmgoers to enjoy the spectacle of sinning womanhood without it entering their minds that the woman was enjoying it too. One well-placed Hollywood observer, the actress Louise Brooks, has commented on the pre-Garbo crisis: 'Mae Murray, fighting for her virtue against von Stroheim's direction in *The Merry Widow*, had proved the impossibility of transmuting established stars into the new gold. The worldly woman type, given a whirl with Edna Purviance, Florence Vidor and Aileen Pringle, was too remote and mature to intrigue the public. The passionate Negri, after being worked over by Paramount for three years, was dead at the box-office. And the producers were driving actresses out of their minds – dressing Barbara LaMarr in nun's veils to make her sympathetic and sticking a rose between the teeth of Hollywood's most celebrated screen virgin, Lois Wilson, to make her look sexy.'† Then came Garbo. And

* Quoted in *Garbo* by John Bainbridge (Frederick Muller), p. 129.

† Louise Brooks, *Sight and Sound*, Winter, 1958–59.

'the suffering of her soul was such that the American public would forgive all thirty-nine of her affairs in *The Torrent*.'

The way the spiritual and sexual natures are laminated together in Garbo's acting is what gives her scenes, especially her love scenes, their enigmatic character – this and her disturbing ability to change not only mood, but even gender, in the course of playing a part. *Camille* (1937) catches her at her most intensely feminine. Kissing Robert Taylor, she goes swiftly over cheeks, temples, nose, lips, in a series of little runs and swoops – brisk and sexy, yet very tender and pure. But where the character has a strong masculine side, Garbo can be literally grasping in her love, yanking her man down to her or up to her and, as Kenneth Tynan said, 'cupping (his) head in both hands and seeming very nearly to drink from it.' One feels Garbo really preferred screen lovers to be the passively romantic breed who rest *their* heads in *her* lap. The directness of her attack is sometimes dismaying, so that John Barrymore in *Grand Hotel* looks less like a Great Lover brought to bed than a drowning man beached by a female lifeguard. And yet it is as much a part of her rhythm as her signature is part of her writing. Garbo's kiss in her early vamp roles – 'Always the vomp, I am,' she lamented in one script wrangle with M-G-M, 'always the woman of no heart' – was open mouthed and direct on the lips. Suggesting a new technique in artificial respiration, it is marvellously at variance with her grip on a man which threatens to impede the flow of blood to his heart.

Garbo was seemingly one of those actresses whose sense of touch affords them emotional illumination, like Braille to the blind. Not that she needed to go into a clinch to project her sexuality. One recalls the moment in *Ninotchka* (1939) when Melvyn Douglas teases her with being jealous of the Grand Duchess. She appears to pull shyly back ten feet from him. Then her eyelashes flick down like a row of power switches and she utters a tiny, tremulous, girlish admission of – 'Uh-huh.' That is all – 'Uh-huh.' But it is like a pebble that has been dropped into a deep abyss – not the sound it sends back, but the depth it signifies is the impressive bit of evidence. Films showing intelligent women in love are less common than one supposes. It takes a very special class of actress to portray both states memorably and simultaneously. Greer Garson, Katharine Hepburn, Celia Johnson, to name a few of the very few, have managed it at times; but Garbo pulls it off nearly all the time. Her rich protector in *Camille* is particularly unperceptive when he says of her, 'So much heart and so little sense.' What intensifies her performance in that film is the balanced equation she makes of heart and sense. It is something for a woman so hotly in love as Camille, when told primly by her lover that her courtesan friends do not suit her, to retort, 'Nonsense. They are the only friends I have and I am no better than they are.' Likewise in *Queen Christina,* she halts a mob in mid-rush up the palace staircase to upbraid her for taking a Spaniard as a lover, lectures them on the duties and cares of being a monarch – then, as they shuffle out mumbling apologies, a sardonic eyebrow is arched at their child-like trust in life's text-book simplicities. Garbo sees the complexities of life so clearly that there are points in her performance of virtual premonition. Her refusal to use the knowledge to avert the tragedy is why one so often feels that she is a plaything in the catspaw of Fate.

But already one falls into error. Garbo exists so strikingly in her own right that she makes one forget that Fate itself exists by courtesy of M-G-M and the scriptwriters. For the same reason, one tends to forget that her scripts were vehicles just as man-made and earth-bound, until she got into them, as those of other M-G-M stars and fabricated quite as consciously to exhibit and enhance her personality. One aspect of this is worth dwelling on, since it is not widely known. It is the way Garbo's writers set out to link her personality quite deliberately with the elements of nature, a trick that one long-term M-G-M executive who was not at all dazzled by her screen divinity describes as 'the Nature Girl touch'.* Nature played a large role in silent films, of course, as a visual metaphor for human emotions too deep or too violent to be compressed on to the dialogue titles; and the Swedes like Seastrom had brought their native cinema's love of the elements with them to Hollywood. But the interesting thing is that, with the Talkies, dialogue was purposely written to endow Garbo

* Private information.

with a mysterious sense of having direct communion with the elements, even of being a part of them. 'Are you real, or born of a snowdrift?' is the unwontedly lyrical query addressed to her by Napoleon when they first meet in *Marie Walewska*. Queen Christina's pre-breakfast toilette is a brisk, orgasmic face-rub with a scooped-up handful of snow; and the first time in the same film that the hitherto hard, masculine lighting of Garbo's features is altered to an enraptured feminine glow by the use of a camera filter is just when she is murmuring longingly, 'The snow is like a wide sea – one can go out and get lost in it and forget the world and oneself.' (Of course when she does go out in it she meets her lover.) Winter, too, is given amorous preference over spring by Marie Walewska as being the 'truce' season when soldiers come home to their women – soldiers of the rank of Emperor, anyway. *Grand Hotel* ends on her plangent cry of 'The sun!' and Queen Christina on a keening note of 'The wind is with us' as she sets sail with her dead lover. Garbo's voice, that wonderful precision instrument for testing the tensile strength of every line, takes her scenarist's aims and transcends them: on her lips meteorology becomes a branch of metaphysics.

Her uncanny concentration likewise raised a line specially written for her into a higher class. When Garbo as the aging Grusinskaya croons out, 'My pearls are old,' she resembles one of those Japanese connoisseurs of *suiseki* ornamental rocks – she seems to be seeing right through to the centre of the mineral.

Garbo's directors, as befits 'women's directors' like George Cukor, Edmund Goulding and Clarence Brown, have been discreet about their contribution to her effects. What is open to the view in many of her finest films is the aid given by her favourite lighting photographer, William Daniels, in helping her key the mood of characters and scenes: he photographed all but two of her sound films. Every film star gets this kind of help, of course, with varying success depending on the cameraman's skill; but it should be recorded here because Garbo, being Garbo, has seemed to come self-created on to the screen. Yet lighting and make-up assisted her to the extent that a glance through a photo-album of her films suggests that she was at least twenty-four different women: a range no other screen actress can equal. The emotional moment is very carefully chosen in *Queen Christina* for the hard line of eye make-up that gives her a heavy-lidded, mannish look to be replaced by the soft mascara that brings out the woman in love. The very flattening of the hair by the weight of the crown as it is removed during her abdication sequence gives her features an immaculate, unreal symmetry embodying the transition stage from being a queen to being simply a woman. Daniels's lighting that robs her face of its feelings and her body of its life makes a powerful contribution to the famous last shots of Queen Christina standing at the ship's prow and of Camille lying dead in her lover's arms. And it is the hard angularity of the light falling on her face and gathering a shadow behind her head that adds callousness to Camille's rejection of the young man earlier in the film – he being held in a blameless white radiance.

To mention artifice like this is not to be anti-Garbo, simply anti-myth. It does not diminish her art, but it keeps one sanely aware that she was, after all, of this world. This is all the more necessary because the screenplays of her films, the very choice of stories, were designed to profit from the off-screen personality as it crystallised in the myth and the public's intense curiosity about her. The dour, melancholy, sexually enigmatic, neurotically shy Swede, who relaxed in men's clothes, viewed life fatalistically and talked like the archetypal Displaced Person of 'going home' – these much advertised traits were worked into films which developed historical, erotic or romantic reasons for them, or else played the story dramatically in opposition to them. Thus it was possible to publicise *Ninotchka* on the single slogan 'Garbo Laughs', since the story spoofed her style of humourless brush-off and converted it into an amorous crush. It is worth noting, though, that when M-G-M did not alert the public to the fact that Garbo laughs, when she starred as a gay, high-spirited *and laughing* girl in the opening reel of *The Painted Veil* (1934), five years before *Ninotchka*, many filmgoers conditioned by the myth of melancholy refused to believe the part was not being played by one of Garbo's studio doubles.

* * *

Why, then, *did* she quit? Surely not because, as Parker Tyler suggests, 'her destiny was to contribute an actress personality to films. That destiny had become monotonously fulfilled . . .'* It is true that *Two-Faced Woman*, her last film, was poorly received. But for this, Garbo is hardly to blame. It was made with the deliberate aim of compensating for the war-time loss of her always vital European box-office by popularising her with Americans as a fun-loving, energetic outdoor girl in a typical Hollywood comedy about an austere ski instructress who poses as a sexy twin sister in order to hold her husband. In retrospect, the film does not merit its cold-shouldering: 'Like seeing Sarah Bernhardt swatted with a bladder,' said *Time*. While *Ninotchka* is a hand-made job by comparison, though Lubitsch's hand got awfully heavy in the last reel or two which everyone forgets, *Two-Faced Woman* is a machine-made product. What preserves it, better than is generally admitted, is the American 'pace' which Cukor gives it, after an opening when the machine was running sluggishly. And Garbo not only takes to this new pace remarkably well, but in the scenes where she is inflaming Melvyn Douglas by playing hard to get puts a classic nip into her retorts. She is a wicked woman, he tells her, and she shrugs it off with, 'The good need us for contrast.' Have dinner with me tonight, he pleads – 'I've only just met you.' Then tomorrow night – 'I'll have forgotten you.' Is it because he is too old? – (A shy smile) 'I like older men, they're so grateful.' He promises her a star, a carpet to the moon, cream from the Milky Way, and she turns it down flat – 'What would I do with a star? A carpet to the moon, it's too bulky. Cream from the Milky Way, it's too fattening.'

Yet looking back one can see why the film flopped. The Legion of Decency, who effectively sabotaged the joke by demanding that the husband whom Garbo's *alter ego* is seducing be made aware of the deception, must bear some of the blame. But the chief trouble lay in the public's refusal to accept the Americanisation of Garbo, as they had accepted the Americanisation of Dietrich, in a style of comedy where they expected to find Katharine Hepburn or Rosalind Russell. Garbo was disconcerted.

* *The Films of Greta Garbo*, by Parker Tyler (Citadel Press), p. 19.

She felt her box-office power was waning. The war, too, had depressed her. And she was thirty-six, passing through the middle-age of her emotional life, though at the height of her artistic powers.

Yet it is hard to think that she deliberately resolved to quit. A simpler truth is maybe that she retired unintentionally – while waiting to see how things would turn out or what projects would turn up. Absence from the screen for any length of time, for any star, gradually builds up to the psychologically daunting point where it implies a 'comeback' with all the risks attendant on facing the public again. Garbo would have been forced to fight the Garbo myth: she would have been measured against a legend that was proportionately greater than any one mortal's talent. She was wise to decline battle. It is foolish to lament that her fabulous success did not give her greater confidence in herself. For Greta Garbo the screen star was a concept almost physically beyond Greta Gustafsson's sympathy and, perhaps, understanding. At some point – Mauritz Stiller's death? – the two fatally diverged. The greater Garbo became, the more strain was put on Gustafsson till in the end she resolved the dilemma by denying us Garbo. Our loss is to be deplored. Garbo was the greatest star the screen has produced. Among the many rare gifts that combined to make her, there was a unique one: it is the ability to suggest in one person the whole complexity of life. No wonder the source of her art finally evades us, for it is part of a much wider scheme of things. 'There is a mystery in you,' says John Gilbert to her in *Queen Christina*. And her answer must finally be our consolation – 'Is there not in every human being?'

A rare picture of Garbo actually being directed on the set. The studio caption reads, 'George Cukor directs Garbo . . . as she falls into a mood for a scene in her new dual-role Metro-Goldwyn-Mayer film, *Two-Faced Woman*.' It was to be her last picture.

Garbo as Queen Christina, the role she was said to have identified herself with most closely.

CHAPTER SIX

BODY AND SOUL: HARLOW AND MONROE

On none is the grandeur and servitude of stardom visited more brutally than on the sex symbols. Owing their fame to their bodies they seldom escape the indignity of being thought of as 'only a body', or 'the girl with the shape', or, simply, 'a piece of flesh'. Jean Harlow and Marilyn Monroe, the sex symbols of the 1930s and 1950s, certainly did not escape it. The trade show reviewer of *Daily Variety* passed a characteristic Hollywood judgment on both of them when he wrote about Harlow in her first starring part in *Hell's Angels* (1930): 'She'll probably always have to play these kind of roles, but nobody ever starved possessing what she's got.' Starvation in Hollywood terms means only starvation of the flesh. Constantly forgotten is the possibility that a sex symbol might have desires beyond the merely carnal or aspirations that are not reducible to vital statistics. The very way in which sex symbols are publicised brings out the latent sadism of a film studio more cruelly than the promotion of any other rank or quality of artist. Sex is what makes them valuable on the screen, but a studio exploits sex with a cynicism that is really a kind of self-loathing, or would be if the production machine ever paused for a moment's reflection.

For a sex symbol who has, say, ambitions to graduate to being an actress threatens the system that is geared to her glorification. She can be sure of bringing the studio's wrath down on her in the form of rebukes, humiliating publicity chores, or suspensions without pay – all devices aimed at cutting her down to size. Even if this is still several sizes above the norm, it is small on the scale of human dignity. A rebellious sex symbol may also incur the puritan backlash of the studio's preoccupation with the commodity she represents. Many film people with no financial stake in her continuing popularity nevertheless disparaged Marilyn Monroe when it was revealed early in her career that she had once posed, totally nude, for a commercial calendar. The same people would have readily condoned the same degree of nudity if it had been presented under Hollywood auspices. All actresses find it useful to cultivate ways of making themselves sexually attractive to their public, but sex symbols are forced to become sexual fetishes for the millions. And the emotional damage this can do to their psyche is severe. According to a recent biographer, Jean Harlow took a wilful revenge on the publicity department at her studio for the mechanistic way it had debased her sex appeal as she saw it: she hacked off the hair that had given her fame as the Platinum Blonde. She had to wear specially prepared wigs to the end of her short, frenzied life.*

Harlow and Monroe represent stars who revolted against the studio system that translates human beings into their *ad valorem* equivalent in 'flesh impact'. Monroe beat the system and, in doing so, turned herself into a screen phenomenon. Harlow was not so lucky: she became the system's victim, though she went under sensationally in her own way. What accounts for their respective victory and defeat is not simply the fact that they were different individuals – although their careers also reveal uncanny resemblances. There is also the matter of the different kind of sex that each of them symbolised for her era. When asked this very question, Monroe once made a touching admission. 'I never quite understood it, this "sex symbol" thing,' she said, then added with endearing innocence, 'but if I'm going to be a symbol of something, I'd rather have it sex than some of the other things they've got symbols for today.' Harlow, on the other hand, had no vagueness about where *her* sex appeal lay. Once when her agent telephoned with news of a new film for her, she simply demanded to know, 'What kind of whore am I now?' Would Monroe ever have referred to her role in a film so bluntly? She would not – but with tender concern for all suffering humanity, including whores, she might have enquired if the girl in the film finally 'gains respect'. Would Harlow ever have admitted that she was in the

* Quoted in *Harlow*, by Irving Shulman (Mayflower/Dell), p. 197.

dark, so to speak, about being a sex symbol? She would not – but with brash immodesty she might have said that if men liked you well enough you didn't need to be a symbol. Both stars were built to sell sex. But they went about it in ways that were as different as the hard sell from the soft – or the body from the soul.

* * *

Jean Harlow usually gets the credit for pioneering the shift of erotic interest from the star's legs to her breasts. It was the flat-chested flapper who symbolised sex on the screen at the end of the 1920s. The bandeau which flattened the bosom had not yet been ousted by the brassière which made things explicit. Breasts still had to be 'heaved' to convey deep passions, and it was far less wearing to kick up a shapely pair of legs to signify total abandon. The rolled stockings, tango dances, short skirts and open roadsters were more or less subtle ways of enhancing leg appeal. But legs looked sexiest when they were being displayed by Jazz Babies and by 1930 the mass public craved a maturer stimulation. Harlow supplied it. By today's tape measurements, her statistics of 34–24–35 are hardly freakish: Monroe's were 39–24–37. But at that era there were fewer competitors to breast the tape. Howard Hughes, who produced Harlow's first starring film, *Hell's Angels*, had no need to go back to the drawing board in his aircraft factory and design a bra to get 'more production' out of her bust, as he did twelve years later for another one of his discoveries, Jane Russell.

In any case, Harlow's eroticism did not depend exclusively on mammary impact. It was all over her body. Her skin had an unnatural but highly sensual whiteness. She looked aglow, on fire in the manner of phosphorus which has light but no heat: she radiated a luminosity that was the very blondness of blond, and it has been suggested that she had a trace of the albino in her. But whatever the reason, her orchidaceous appearance registered lividly on the less sensitive film stock then in use. She crowned the effect with a head of hair that lit up like neon. Her hair gave her, almost instantly, the first essential of any would-be film star: a unique screen identity. She became *the* Platinum Blonde. 'Female stars,' says Edgar Morin, 'are the object of a masculine attraction and of a feminine cult.'* Harlow fitted the description perfectly. Men were attracted by her beacon of hair with its promise of fun, women dyed their own hair in imitation and waited for the hoydenish allure to collect around them. By 1932 her studio had promoted over three hundred Platinum Blonde Clubs and the sales of cosmetic peroxide had gone up by thirty-five per cent. Harlow's face was not conventionally beautiful. Her eyebrows were shaven into antennae, perhaps to lighten a too-heavy forehead; the slightly cleft jaw was stubborn and had to be lighted extremely carefully; her mouth was painted slightly above the lip line and up at the corners in a smile of fixed expectation. It was a pepped-up face. It was also a tough face. It looked instinctively at a man to see if he was worth taking. It was a perfect face – too perfect – for the hookers, molls, B-girls and society parvenues she was to play.

Like Monroe, Harlow deployed her body very consciously on the screen, but not always the part of it that one might expect. 'Would you be shocked if I put on something more comfortable?' she asks Ben Lyon in a famous line in the World War One air drama, *Hell's Angels*. Then as she turns in through the bedroom door she lets her fur wrap slip off and expose her shoulders, bare and creamy white, with a thin chain that holds up her party dress cutting down low along the line of her spine. And she gives a sexy peek back over one shoulder. This is the erotic posture that later became almost a trade-mark of Harlow's. It has elements of strip-tease in it. It also serves to show that she is wearing no brassière: a bold omission in those days. The back view is so emphatically repeated in Harlow films that one wonders if it, and not the front elevation, constituted her erotic appeal for an audience. The bath scenes in her films, in rain barrels or conventional tubs, rely less on the nice adjustment of the water level round the star's Plimsoll line in front, than on titillating rear shots of her shoulder blades. Audiences are reported to have screamed when she commanded the man who was invariably present to 'Scrub my back.' If he were Clark Gable, he dunked her in the

* Edgar Morin, op. cit., p. 103.

water for her boldness. No matter. They screamed again when she surfaced, spiky wet and spitting like a platinum alley cat.

* * *

Nudity for sex symbols like Jean Harlow and Marilyn Monroe is a condition of existence – a way of life. Both made a practice of not wearing underclothes on the set, and off it, too, for that matter, though Harlow graciously made an exception for President Roosevelt's Birthday Ball to which she was invited in 1934. Both felt they needed to be as lightly clad as decency, or, rather, the Legion of Decency, permitted in order to project a feeling of nakedness on the screen. The urge to go nude was the strongest one they had in common. But very different motives circulated under the skin. Harlow behaved like a conscious sexual provocatrice who knew the effect her body made on men. Her nipples were said to expand as the room temperature went up and before Press conferences she would rub them with ice. She had a habit of fondling herself publicly, or being photographed caressing herself: the sure indication of a compulsive exhibitionist. For Monroe, on the other hand, nudity was akin to the proverbial state of innocence. When she took off her clothes she felt happy and secure – she felt people loved her. In a dream she had during a wretched childhood spent in an orphanage and then in half-a-dozen foster homes she had the impression that she was walking about a church with no clothes on and feeling no embarrassment but, instead, a strange sense of comfort and liberation. Years later she explained that being naked made her feel like other girls and not someone in orphans' clothing.

But although she never saw nudity as other than innocent, she was well aware of the exhilarating effect she had on males. In one of her early films a girl eyes Monroe enviously and says, 'To wear a dress like that you got to start laying plans when you're thirteen.' Monroe laid her plans even earlier. Before she was in her teens she was imitating older girls and had perfected the famous wiggle that turned a simple walk-off into an irresistible come-on. Later on she did setting-up exercises from a medical text-book on bone structure, so as to be able to assume at will the posture that suggested the required degree of sexiness – just that, and no more. The marvel was that she managed all this and still retained an appearance of innocence. Watch her swing round the firemen's poles in an early number in *Let's Make Love* (1960): it is more than just proof of how well she learned her anatomy lessons. From far off an Ape Man would throw out an uninhibited mating call, thinking she was his Jane; but swinging closer, something improbably virginal and pristine about his new playmate might make him stammer out, 'Me, Tarzan. You – Eve?'

Monroe was constructed on altogether softer lines than Harlow, though her early, small-part films reveal the Ur-Marilyn, a chorine cutie looking slightly overweight – the penalty for not wearing foundation garments – and obscured by make-up that might have been meant for a cigar-store Indian. But soon she was slimming here, developing there, and as her artistry increased her form got more insubstantial – till in the end her hair looked made of spun light and her face composed with an air brush. Her characteristic erotic attitude was the expression on her face. She would half-shut her eyes, and let her lower jaw slacken and her lips round into an 'O' shape. The look was variously interpreted as one of innocence, wonder, or orgasmic ecstasy. Actually behind it lay the rather unglamorous reality of poor lower teeth, which Monroe hid in this way in her early days till she could afford an orthodontist. The expression also affected her voice. For when one's mouth is agape, one's diction is pretty slack, too – like a little girl's. To come across such teasing vocal immaturity combined with very ripe physical charms is both appealing and disturbing. And much of Monroe's appeal lay in the way she maintained the purity of the child-woman she represented. No sooner did the 'woman' bring out the wolf in a man than the 'child' side of her turned him into a big-hearted guard dog. She managed this quite consciously with her voice. One early TV commercial for a make of automobile shows up her technique transparently. She accepts the keys of the convertible with a squeak of delight, as if the car were a pet poodle, turns to the filling station attendant, draws in a small breath, and then exhales it as she speaks her line so that the words come out in tiny puffs of girlish excitement: 'Garage man – please put some gas – in Miranda's tummy.' (Miranda, or some such name, was how she had then and there christened the car.) Later on, tutoring turned this penny-whistle effect into an instrument for uttering dialogue with the subtlety of a woodwind. Harlow by contrast, though six years Monroe's junior when she reached stardom, always seemed to act ten years older – for her voice was one of hard-bitten experience, spoilt, snarling at times, even grating on the ears of trade-paper reviewers, not usually men of delicate sensibility. Maurice Zolotow has suggested in his penetrating biography of Monroe – one of the best film-star biographies yet written – that her oddly melting diction may have been picked up from the English theatrical couple who provided one of her foster homes. It may indeed be the case. And it prompts the thought that Harlow's accent was one she might have acquired from being boarded out with gangsters.

* * *

The lives of the two sex symbols show remarkable similarities. Monroe was born as Norma Jean Mortenson in 1926. (Later Ben Lyon, then a casting executive at 20th Century-Fox, replaced her first names with 'Marilyn', derived from a vaudeville artist, Marilyn Miller, who had been Mary Pickford's sister-in-law: the 'Monroe' came from a family name.) She was illegitimate and fatherless, and soon became motherless as well when abandoned to the care of a Californian orphanage, a trail of foster homes and two zealous Christian Science aunts who did something worse than inflict the guilt of her illegitimacy on her. They inoculated her against reality by rearing her according to their own religious beliefs that the external world is what you make it in your own mind: a dangerously seductive philosophy for actors whose sense of reality is often already impaired by the illusions they live among and project in their performances. Perhaps this is what helps account for the beguilingly dreamy way in which Monroe moved through her films – and life – oblivious to any menacing element in her environment, apparently seeing no evil nor apprehending any. This was very funny in the fantasy life of the screen, when the threat came from Tom Ewell as the would-be wolf in *The Seven Year Itch* (1955). But the threat could also be embodied in a real and very angry film studio suing her for showing up only twelve times in thirty-two days during the shooting of her last film. And then to see Monroe remaining carefree, even euphoric amid the wreckage of this film and the hostility of Hollywood was a distinctly ominous symptom. Maurice Zolotow has convincingly traced her disregard for the realities of life to other incidents in her childhood. Time and time again work on a film could not begin, or would grind to a halt, because Monroe was taking a bath, powdering her body – 'I like to feel blonde all over,' she once said – or simply sitting bemused in front of her own image in the make-up mirror. At these times she was pampering herself to make up for the deprivations of her childhood when little Norma Jean had had to bath herself in water already used by half-a-dozen people in her foster home. Her chronic lateness, too, is traceable to a desire to inflict her importance on a world that at one time had ignored her existence, in which not even her mother had wanted her.

In the light of Jean Harlow's experience, however, the loss of one's mother – Mrs Baker had been admitted to a mental hospital – cannot be regarded as an unmitigated disaster. Harlow's mother was too much with her. She was a foolish, excitable woman, a rabid Christian Scientist like Monroe's aunts, who went through bookshops buying up and destroying volumes she considered inimical to her faith. Harlow was born in 1911, as Harlean Carpentier; but her middle-class parents soon split up and much of the emotional strain she later suffered seems to have been transferred to her by the guilt-ridden 'Mamma Jean' who tended to regard her daughter's screen fame as no better than a harlot's. She even contributed indirectly to her daughter's death, since she at first relied on the prayerful cure commended by Christian Science when Harlow was taken fatally ill with uremic poisoning.

'Being a sex symbol,' said Clara Bow at the end of her career, 'is a heavy load to carry, especially when one is very tired, hurt and bewildered.' Harlow and Monroe might have agreed, and added 'especially when one has grown up without normal affection, stable values, or any ability to face facts and foresee the consequences of one's acts'. The lives these two sex symbols led were filled with stresses, crises, scandals and tragedies both public and private. But an odd contradiction emerges. Though both were supposed to personify an all-American image of sex – liberated, healthy, un-neurotic and pleasurable – their own sexual drives were in startling contrast to the image. After both had got married when in their teens – Harlow eloped to get away from her mother, Monroe let herself be married off by her aunts to escape from going back to the orphanage – their subsequent husbands were practically their own antitheses in every way. Harlow's second husband, Paul Bern, was a quiet, balding M-G-M executive twenty-one years older than she was. To see their sex symbol marrying this fatherly homebody caused heartburn at a studio which, more than most, liked to believe its own legend that stars only marry other stars. In September, 1932, after less than three months of marriage, Bern was found shot dead, apparently by his own hand, with a note beside him which has been interpreted as an apology for his sexual impotence. If it was so, no wonder Louis B. Mayer tried to suppress it. Bern's suicide might add a lurid glamour to Harlow's image – and it did – but Bern's impotence could only make the Platinum Blonde Clubs wonder if the celebrated sex symbol really knew what it was all about. Harlow's third husband was Harold Rosson who had photographed four of her M-G-M films: another fatherly figure, sixteen years her senior, and closely resembling Bern in looks. That marriage lasted a year and her divorce suit charged that he read in bed. Again her studio gave a corporative wince. Where was the sex symbol's fabled power if it could not overcome a man's reading habits? So she added ambiguously that such an unwonted use of the bed-chamber left her next morning feeling unprepared for work. (In the film *Harlow* (1965), which purported to be a biography of her life, this third marriage is not even mentioned. The presumption must be that a sex symbol's husband who reads in bed forfeits his claim to have existed. Arthur Miller will hardly get left out of any film biography of Marilyn Monroe: but then Hollywood has always felt on surer ground with great writers than great readers.)

Harlow's off-screen life typifies the unsatisfied, uncertain sex symbol, unsure even of her own sex appeal: the star whose life is regulated by the same publicity that feeds her film image out to the public, so that the one infiltrates the other and destroys her chances of finding an identity for herself. Even her characteristic physiognomy – her bleached skin and platinum hair – had to be projected into the decor of her all-white Hollywood home with the limbo effect produced by its bedroom where she could contemplate a myriad nude reflections of herself in the wall mirrors. One of her films, *Bombshell* (1933), implies all that this meant. In it she playes a movie star, with a parasitic family much like her own, whose life is taken over by a stunt-minded press agent, played by Lee Tracy. The story plays the traumas she suffers for comic effect, but even the distortions are disturbingly credible as the Harlow personality is manipulated with heartless cynicism – till at last the only independent act of which she is capable is a shriek of frustration.

At first Marilyn Monroe sought the same safe domestic anchorage as Harlow by marrying Joe DiMaggio, a stay-at-home type openly contemptuous of the film colony's way of life. The marriage lasted nine months, its break-up coinciding with the Press acclaim for *The Seven Year Itch* which brought out into the open Monroe's dissatisfaction at being merely a sex symbol. Thereafter she embarked on an affair with the intelligentsia that began kittenishly with *faux-naive* confidences about her aspirations. 'Do you want to play *The Brothers Karamazov*?' a reporter asked her, and she made a memorable reply, 'I don't want to play the brothers. I want to play Grushenka. She's a girl.' There followed her coaching in Method acting which she absorbed with the sober deportment of a young bride taking instruction in the faith of her husband-to-be. Her marriage to Arthur Miller was a clinching earnest of her intentions. The scandals involving Harlow were the kind that added fuel to her sex-symbol image. But the way Marilyn Monroe made news was by conducting her education in public, defying her studio by holding out for better roles – i.e., roles that gave her the 'human rights' denied to a sex symbol –

marrying the intellectuals' playwright, and engaging a theatrical knight like Sir Laurence Olivier to co-star with her in her own company's production of a film that paralleled the aspirations of Marilyn Monroe to be taken as a serious actress in its story of Mary Morgan, chorus-girl, who is taken up by a Grand Duke. The film roles of Harlow and Monroe show the same pattern respectively of the sex symbol who could not change her image, and of the one who could and did.

* * *

Harlean Carpentier had taken her mother's maiden name of Jean Harlow and was earning housekeeping money as a Hollywood extra when Howard Hughes cast her as the female lead in *Hell's Angels*. She replaced the Norwegian star, Greta Nissen, whose voice had doomed her when the coming of the Talkies forced Hughes virtually to remake this costly aerial epic. Harlow played the English girl who flings aside respectability and seduces Ben Lyon of Oxford University and the Royal Flying Corps. Her Englishness is not at all apparent: her other qualities are – vividly. The flashpoint of her performance comes when, clad in that 'more comfortable' something – i.e., a black wrap of revealing looseness – she flings back her head at right-angles to her neck and flicking every feature into motion like the instrument panel of a high-powered roadster cries, 'I want to be free, be gay, have fun. Life's short, but I want to live when I'm alive.' It is laughably overdone. But her magnetism has already settled incandescently on her and her voice grates with the harsh conviction that Life, intense and capitalised, is hers for the taking. It is the debut of a new kind of star: a synthesis of vamp and sweetheart who was to be known as the good-bad girl for her possession of the former's erotic energy and the latter's good-sportsmanship. Edgar Morin dates her flowering from 1940, but Harlow is surely the type in the bud. She was more than an erotic symbol. She provided a focus for the social disarray of the Depression with its split between cynicism at the hollowness of accepted values and optimism that life was, after all, what you made it.

Five films with Harlow in the cast were released in 1931, the year after *Hell's Angels*. But no studio appeared to see her possibilities as a long-term star, rather than a one-hit phenomenon, till Frank Capra directed her in *Platinum Blonde*. This is the archetypal 1930s film: a story of an heiress who marries a newspaperman, tries to accustom him to her way of life, and loses him to his office Girl Friday. Harlow played the nympho-heiress whose family have to buy her out of marriage after marriage, Robert Williams was the foot-in-the-door reporter, Loretta Young the patient other woman. Capra handled the sexual antithesis in the manner of the class-clash attitudes in his later New Deal films. But he plainly made an acute analysis of where Harlow's sex appeal lay; for he sectionalises it, so to speak, and constructs his scenes and camera shots to present each part of it in turn to vivid advantage. In the early comedy between brash reporter and embarrassed socialites it is her hair that dominates the drawing-room like a bizarre burning bush, for she has her back to the camera and wears a black dress up to her neck. Her high-powered face radiating vampish energy only comes into close-up when she tries to seduce the newsman out of printing his story. Her body appeal gets projected with enormous impact in one unbroken tracking shot, lasting all of thirty-five seconds, of Harlow walking into the ever retreating camera, bosom cantilevered, hips swaying, arms swinging mannishly. Capra gained a curious hot-and-cold effect in a love scene that she plays opaquely behind a garden fountain whose veil of water suggests the refrigerated pane of a florist's show window. Her little-girl voice which she sometimes used on men like a spooky Shirley Temple is there, too, planted in a scene at her masseur's with an appropriate hint of puppy fat in her visible portions. (*Platinum Blonde* and his other bizarre film about a Chinese war lord's infatuation for an American girl, *The Bitter Tea of General Yen* (1932), show that the cinema lost a director of considerable erotic power when Frank Capra turned propagandist for the Roosevelt New Deal and took to showing that people are basically nice.) Harlow handled her dialogue so well under his direction that women were soon imitating her tough way of talking to, and about, men; though the same women appreciated the idea of this rich broad losing her man to nice homely Loretta

Young. Feminine psychology like this helped Harlow keep her female following – though it later cost her some heartburn when she grew discontented with her screen image and wanted to get the man herself.

Wide-ranging promotion tours for *Platinum Blonde* brought Harlow bodily to the American public, while the film's box-office receipts brought her on to the M-G-M star roster. Significantly, the nod to the Hollywood studio to sign her up came from the East Coast accounting end of the business. Monroe, too, was made by public demand, rather than studio policy. Exhibitors clamoured for films with her in them before the producers realised her potential – and it was really this and the demand for pin-ups of her created by the Korean War which electrified 20th Century-Fox. Such origins had the negative effect of making it even harder for the stars to live down their 'flesh impact' reputations.

The good-bad girl, as Harlow continued to play her, openly proclaimed that sex was fun. When she comes swinging off the Saigon river boat in *Red Dust* (1932), a triangle melodrama set in the rubber plantations, her undaunted reply to the news that the climate makes it hard to sleep is, 'Guess I'm not used to sleeping nights anyway.' One hardly needs to indicate which word the accent falls on. Harlow was a man's woman, but not to be confused with Mae West who is a more exotic flowering of the good-bad girl. Harlow's costumes were skimpy to reveal all she had got, Mae West's were padded to make more of what she had got. Harlow was all things to any one man – as ready to rub his cheek with sandpaper as hang a kiss on it. If Mae West was the saloon queen, Jean Harlow was its barmaid. Mae West stood no nonsense from her men, but part of Harlow's lot was to take plenty of knocks from her man before he finally fell for her. Clark Gable made great sexual capital out of this in *Red Dust* by resisting Harlow's provocation till *he* was ready. Not only does he dunk her underwater when she has the cheek to take a bath in the drinking supply. But in an even cockier moment, having let her remove his boots and taken off his shirt himself, he proceeds to strip off breeches and underpants (while off-screen) and chucks them insolently at her before climbing into bed, alone, and drawing the sheets coquettishly up to his chin. It is like seeing Madame Récamier suddenly upstaged by Monsieur Récamier.

However roughly she was treated, Harlow always had a residual loyalty to the man she genuinely liked. She was ever ready to clink whisky tumblers and sportingly offer to get a little drunk with him. When Gable stops a bullet, it is she who digs it out of him. (It might be surprising to see her operate with a bit of wire and apparently push the slug *through* him. Never mind – the thought was so right.) In *Hold Your Man* (1933) she even goes to prison for him – a prison where the inmates pay lip service to the Production Code by singing Onward, Christian Soldiers, though their expressions suggest parole is nearer their thoughts than redemption.

Yet the effect of all these roles on Harlow was depressing. Their similarity wore her down. She craved a breakaway part where her body would matter less than the acting talent she believed she had. A bizarre manifestation of this was her attempt to play lady-like roles like the American girl back from England in *Saratoga* (1937), her last film, where she puts on a hoity-toity accent, experiments with 'Charmed, I'm sure . . . It would be a great kindness,' and burbles about stately homes, old traditions and punting with Clark Gable on the Thames. The comic intention is not so clear that one can laugh comfortably. She fancied herself as a stylish comedienne in the manner of Myrna Loy, whose cool ease with smart quips she particularly envied since it complemented the urbanity of William Powell. And she was romantically drawn to Powell, a paternal kind of screen playboy who bore a marked resemblance to her two previous husbands. But though she softened her diction and dressed to conceal rather than provoke, Harlow's appeal was that of a sexy hoyden and *it* could not be concealed – though it might be effectively burlesqued. In *Dinner At Eight* (1934) she plays a spoilt wife eating chocolates in a huge white-satin bed, buffing her nails, dabbing her body with a powder-puff – voluptuous and nit-witted. Basically she is still a broad, but snobbery and not sex now motivates her. Her aim is to gatecrash high society. Her bouncy vulgarity suited the role and she played it amusingly. Even so, the part reveals a mortal truth about her which the last wisecrack in the film dispatches like a poisoned arrow to the heart. Trying to scintillate intellectually as the guests go in to dinner, Harlow remarks to Marie Dressler, who is cast as a Grand Old Dame of Broadway, 'Do you know, machinery is going to take the place of every profession.' 'Oh my dear,' retorts Miss Dressler acidly, 'that is something *you* need never worry about.' One laughs. At the same time, one is painfully aware that seldom have one star's artistic limitations been so bitchily but precisely intimated by another.

* * *

Marilyn Monroe gained stardom right at the post-war peak of America's material prosperity. Yet her unique achievement was to render her appeal virtually immaterial, in the sense of impalpable and intangible. On the screen she little by little liberated herself from the flesh and stood out against the trend of the times. All round her, society was obsessed with sex and making it appear extremely complicated. Monroe's charm was to make it all seem blessedly simple again. Simple *and innocent*. She developed a way of taking the sexual appeal she at first crudely projected and turning it into something nearly transcendental.

It did not happen quickly. The Marilyn who scored two rapid-fire hits in *The Asphalt Jungle* (1950), as Louis Calhern's 'niece' stretching fetchingly for bed but remembering to lock her door, and in *All About Eve* (1950), as George Sanders's protégée calling the butler 'waiter' because there might be a Mr Butler present, is an entertaining dumb blonde – but not yet the girl whose trustfulness keeps the male at bay better than a door lock and whose dumbness is beamed to us on a positively spiritual wavelength. Where she begins to appear is in *How to Marry a Millionaire* (1953). It was long odds against it happening in a film like this. A nominal society comedy about three women out to sink their hooks into rich husbands, it shows no awareness that its characters have the commercial morality of whores, without the latter's honesty in business dealings. One simple, absurd fact saves Monroe from this reproach: she plays a girl who wears glasses. Whereas Lauren Bacall and Betty Grable are beady-eyed for loot, Monroe goes through the callous husband-hunting with a weak-sighted air of vagueness about what they are all up to. Her gold-digging is put into forgiving soft-focus – since half the time she shyly refuses to wear her spectacles and cannot see the man she is meant to exploit. Her dumbness, too, is the result of an optical effect that invites our amused pity. A man tells her, 'You're reading your book upside down,' and she stammers, 'I'm no such thing,' after checking her sitting position. We are right back in the surreal world of 'Do you want to play *The Brothers Karamazov*?' – 'I don't want to play the brothers. I want to play Grushenka. She's a girl.' The film revealed another endearing characteristic: the almost maidenly delicacy of her approach to sex, so that a word of such suggestive possibilities as 'passes' is shyly eliminated as she explains her fear that 'men aren't attentive to girls who wear glasses'.

By the time of *The Seven Year Itch*, in which she played the girl upstairs who makes the romantic imagination of the summer widower downstairs crash its gears, every bit of the Monroe image is present: the dazzling smile, the vague but excited voice, the kookiness that makes her keep her undies in the ice box in a heat wave, the child-like rapture of standing over a subway air vent and letting her skirt billow up round her . . . And there is a vital new quality. Her love is now linked with pity. In this film and in *Bus Stop* (1956) she is a girl cursed by possessing an irresistible body, but quite ready to take pity on any man who finds it too much to bear. 'This has never happened to me before,' gulps Tom Ewell, after an abortive pass at her. 'Oh it happens to me all the time,' she tells him solicitously. And the same forgiveness flies out to Don Murray, the virile cowpuncher in *Bus Stop* whose rodeo tactics in love make her run till she realises that the poor, deprived boy's life up to then has been all cattle. Monroe developed this marvellous talent for playing against the sex appeal of her body – which thereby acquitted her of any offence and left the sin firmly lodged in the eye of the beholder. Not by one dubious inflection does she hint at an innuendo in *The Seven Year Itch* when crying, 'My fan's caught in the door' as the camera goggles at her behind like a Via Veneto voyeur. Had she realised how some lewd

'I want to be alone.' This is the moment she actually did speak the words that are, almost invariably inaccurately attributed to her; but she did so in the person of the aging Russian ballet dancer in *Grand Hotel* who has just run away from her gala performance. Not for the first time, Garbo's screen character profited from the star's public myth.

Elizabeth Taylor as the free-living artist in *The Sandpiper:* her face holds tensions the way a sponge holds water, her dark hair hanging down in unruly undress adds to the wildness of her looks, the scrupulously made-up eyes are the central features and the mark of a temperament which an Elizabethan poet would have called 'gypsy.'

people might confuse 'fan' with 'fanny', one feels sure she would have changed the line to, 'My electrical equipment . . .'

By the time of *Some Like It Hot* (1959) her pity for the love-lorn male is so transparently beyond reproach that she can volunteer her body in a big-hearted effort to raise a spark of passion in Tony Curtis who is playing a Casanova pretending to be impotent. Monroe's death showed how essential she was to such *risqué* sex comedies: when other sex symbols were cast in roles written originally for her, the films turned out disconcertingly salacious. But even more astonishing was how she extended her sympathy beyond the immediate male to take in all created things, animate and inanimate. *The Seven Year Itch* had hinted at this. When Monroe expressed pity for the monster of a horror film, she made The Creature from the Black Lagoon seem like a homeless kitten. But not till *The Misfits* (1961), her last film, did one realise how far she had pushed her soft-hearted altruism into a radiant pantheism.

The Misfits is the story of a girl with the gift of life who changes the ways of three cowboy misfits in mid-twentieth-century America when they are reduced to rounding up wild ponies for dog meat. Please Don't Kill Anything is the message of the film: it is also the title of a story Arthur Miller once wrote about his wife. Monroe's whole appearance is altered in the film. The old undulations are still there, but now not quite corporeal. The sex symbol has become a nature symbol. Her Roslyn is a luminously white, whispering, wistful lost child who loves everything, suffers with the leaves of grass if they are trodden on, mourns for the rabbits that Clark Gable wants to take pot-shots at, and sways all alone in a formless dance in the moonlight to the sound of music that only she can hear. The actress who made seriousness her aim has ended by making soulfulness her achievement.

Yet the price was high. A man may be intrigued by the Monroe in *The Misfits*, flattered, moved or amused by her; but it is far from easy for him to feel fulfilled by her. Her love for humanity is now too big for any other person to reciprocate. Arthur Miller's screenplay was taken at the time to be a celebration of his wife's qualities. But in the hindsight of their separation and divorce, it is *The Misfits* rather than the play he subsequently wrote, *After the*

Fall, which seems like his attempt to exorcise her spirit. For if Clark Gable in *The Misfits* represents the average sensual man, then the film's lesson is a disconcerting one. Whereas Jean Harlow's callow platinum blonde boosted Gable's ego as he manhandled her in *Red Dust* nearly thirty years earlier, now Marilyn Monroe as the life force incarnate actually breaks his spirit in the way he once broke the wild horses'. The moral appears to be that in the films it is far less harassing to live with a 'body' than to settle for marriage to a 'soul'. In life, too, the same perhaps applies.

In reacting against being known as just 'the girl with the shape', Marilyn Monroe raised herself to the Nth degree of spirituality. This is not contradicted by the fact that one of the last things she did, before she was found dead from an overdose of barbiturates in 1962, was to negotiate the magazine rights of photographic studies of herself in the nude. For when she said in explanation, 'I want the world to see my body,' it was in the mood of a woman who wanted the world to have her body. There seems to be an almost metaphysical link between the degree of unreality that entered into her relationship with picture-making, in the number of delays, accidents, hold-ups and final suspension of work which her last film suffered, and the ethereal impression she made in the few moments of her that appear on the screen in this abandoned version of *Something's Got to Give*. There is a tragic appropriateness in the thought that at the very moment of gaining her soul, she lost possession of the world.

CHAPTER SEVEN

STAR SYNDROME: ELIZABETH TAYLOR

When the auditors finally got down to the task of tracing where the estimated forty million dollars spent on *Cleopatra* (1963) had gone to, there was at least one sum they could do in their heads, although perhaps with mixed feelings. Grateful for the neatness of it, astonished at the enormousness of it. 'To Elizabeth Taylor, star: one million dollars.' No other woman in films could then command so much money for playing one part – and go on commanding it. The fee she was paid for *Cleopatra* is the sum Elizabeth Taylor has obtained by down payment, or by guaranteed percentage of the profits, for every film she has made since. Her agent later justified it by saying: 'Elizabeth had never lost money with any film . . . So when they planned a big film like *Cleopatra*, they had to have (her) as security. So I said, "Elizabeth has to be a major partner with a guarantee of a million dollars." I knew they had to pay it, otherwise they wouldn't have a picture.' Yet to ask if she is worth it is to miss the point completely. One might as well ask why Raphael's angels do not wear shoes to stop their feet getting cut when they land on the rocks. A million-dollar fee is real enough in hard cash, but it has an importance over and above the feeling of neediness it relieves – as the appropriate market price of a myth in the creation of which Elizabeth Taylor's talent for acting has not played the major part.

It is not through her performances that she keeps her hold so securely on the public's imagination. These are always professional. But unless she has a temperamental affinity with the role, or is working with a director of inspiring talent – nothing more than professional. One would have said that until her marriage to Richard Burton she had no wish to be known as a great actress – no desire at all to play Grushenka. If she now acquires the desire, it will be like a late pregnancy. She is certainly not affected by the commonest neurosis of stars whose screen life is so much bigger and more dramatic than the life they lead off screen, so that they feel devitalised by their double up there in Technicolor or black and white, using their name and enjoying bizarre sensations they are denied. Such stars usually fall victim to acting out their movie roles in public.

The exact opposite is true of Elizabeth Taylor. In her case life does not ape art, but transfuses it. She magnifies any film she makes simply by being in it. She guarantees intense and profitable public interest in it, however bad it may be, by endowing it with the attributes of stardom she has acquired off screen. Such attributes include her huge fees, her very special quality of looks, her appetite for new and usually disordered emotional experience, her complete disregard of public opinion, even her apparently extreme vulnerability to misfortune, accidents and near-fatal illnesses. Wealth, beauty, sex, taboos and the imminence of tragedy and death: all are potent factors in making an individual into a popular myth. With more remote stars, like Garbo or Mary Pickford, it is necessary to dispel the mythology that has been gathering round them over the years in order to see them as they really were or might have been. In the case of a contemporary star like Elizabeth Taylor, what is vital is to be aware of the myth-making taking place.

Elizabeth Taylor was a film star from childhood and consequently, as she later put it, 'My toughest role was learning to grow up.' This already sounds perilously like a cliché. But then her early life reveals a pattern that many a film scenarist would consider too cliché-ridden – or too classic – to make into convincing fiction for the screen. She was born in London, of American parents, in 1932. Her mother's acting career stopped when she met her husband, a successful art dealer, and the birth of Elizabeth and her brother gave her a chance to continue her stage ambitions through her good-looking children once they were old enough to act. Today daughter and parents are on the warmest of terms, but there were signs of friction when they moved to Hollywood during the war – where Mr Taylor's art interests gave him an entrée to the film colony – and the mother's ambitions for her children were not whole-heartedly backed by the family. Her brother obstinately declined a screen test. But gaining a contract with Metro-Goldwyn-Mayer, Elizabeth took well enough to animal films, like *Lassie Come Home* (1943), to force herself to grow several inches in as many months and capture the starring role in *National Velvet* (1944), for which she had been thought too small. Her parents' Christian Science was a strong influence on her at this age: for a faith which believes that reality can be modified by will power is always a spur to ambition. (It can also be a comfort in an often hostile environment like a film studio, as Marilyn Monroe found.)

As a child star she had her life arranged for her by her mother and the film company. Mrs Taylor supervised her acting on the set, fought for better parts for her, and even handpicked her boy friends not only out of any ordinary mother's prudence, but to flatter her daughter's professional image. The studio also seems to have played the role of a deputy father. For she was their investment and had to be protected against emotional upsets or unsuitable matches in much the same way that a wealthy parent would act out of self interest while keeping a benign eye on his marriageable daughter. In her early M-G-M films she played children of her own age and was co-starred with race horses and collie dogs. But her physical development quickly outstripped her emotional growth and the roles she began to play carried a risk of making this disparity more permanent than it would be in any ordinary childhood. At the age of sixteen she was playing a woman of twenty-four and co-starring with Robert Taylor. During the filming of *The Conspirator* (1949), she would be taken out of her classroom in the school at the studio, directed in a love scene with her co-star, then returned to her arithmetic. It is not surprising to find this kind of emotional jump disconcerted her. As she later acknowledged, 'I have the face and body of a woman and the mind of a child.' And some of her best acting vividly conveys the presence of this kind of dislocation: it runs through her performance like a water-mark, giving it an authenticity conspicuously lacking when she plays other roles. An edgy intenseness is the form it takes on the screen: the wilfulness of a woman who has set herself a lot of emotional living to do. In all likelihood, it is a reaction against the oppressively close supervision of her personal life in childhood and the all-invasive rights which a film studio at that date could claim over its contract artists.

* * *

Elizabeth Taylor was bound to revolt sooner or later against being treated – in her words – 'like a freak'. The impetus of the revolt is what still carries her along. It helps to explain both her disregard of convention and her disinterest in setting the public record right when columnists and other commentators may have got it wrong. In this she is like the star she most resembles in other respects, too: Gloria Swanson, who gave the public what they expected of a screen goddess, but had a very just appreciation of what they did not expect. 'The public didn't want the truth and I shouldn't have bothered giving it to them,' Gloria Swanson declared. 'In those days they wanted us to live like kings. So we did – and why not? We were in love with life. We were making more money than we ever dreamed existed, and there was no reason to believe that it would ever stop.'* One can detect in those words the tone of Elizabeth Taylor, except that she takes such grand indifference one step further: she gives no appearance of caring deeply *or even knowing* what the public think of her. After wearing leading reins for so long, it must be a tremendously liberating feeling to be able to behave in this imperious way and still not fall flat on one's face. For this she has to thank the myth that began taking shape from the moment she took charge of her life.

Marriage is the matrix of the myth. Elizabeth Taylor has, like Gloria Swanson, been married five times and thus, whether it pleases her or not, she has generously fulfilled one condition of stardom: the mass public's craving to participate vicariously in a star's love life, which seems to them to be an extension of her screen life. In the old days before mass media enabled the news to be 'managed' in a much more sophisticated fashion, the commonest technique of a film studio's publicity department was the 'arranged' affair. Stars were publicised as being in love with other

* Gloria Swanson, quoted by De Witt Bodeen, *Films in Review*, April, 1965.

stars, and romancing couples were co-starred in their films. The premise underlying this was that fans would assume that the stars had the same irresistible sexuality as the creatures they played in their films. The ferment of curiosity would then boost the box-office receipts. (It sometimes also hoisted the fees of stars with agents who were unromantic enough to put a price on their clients' affairs.) The same ferment has been produced periodically in Elizabeth Taylor's case through her successive marriages, with the advantage that this time it is for real. Even the myth propagated by the silent cinema and early talkies, that the kiss which lovers exchange on the screen leads to real-life romance, was sensationally realised during the filming of *Cleopatra*.

Elizabeth Taylor's first marriage at the age of eighteen, to the heir of Conrad Hilton, the hotel owner, was a way of cutting loose from home ties; but it lasted only three months and foundered on the couple's mutual immaturity. Her next marriage, to the actor Michael Wilding who was considerably older than herself, was also unsuccessful; and she has since recognised that it represented a search for security. Mike Todd, her third husband, was a big-business dynamo. And although somewhat immature himself in his conspicuous extravagance and compulsive desire to impress people, he gave her for the first time the sense of a world beyond herself. Her fourth marriage to the singer Eddie Fisher, was very much the instinctive rebound from early widowhood following Todd's death in an air crash; but it was associated with the break-up of Fisher's marriage to Debbie Reynolds and led to much unwelcome publicity. (In one of those periodic fits of morality, to which Hollywood is prone, the Theatre Owners of America re-routed their annual award to Deborah Kerr, with the pious observation that 'to award Miss Taylor at a time like this is out of the question'.) Even greater was the now celebrated commotion surrounding the double divorce which preceded her marriage to Richard Burton.

But instead of damaging her box-office appeal, this kind of serial polygamy only enhanced it. The reason lies in the fact that a lasting marriage is not what fans expect, or even want, from most Hollywood stars. A syndrome has formed over the years whereby a star marries in the morning and by nightfall her fans are confidently expecting the news of her up-coming divorce. Traditionally each marriage is entered into with every indication that it is nothing if not permanent; and the bride's statements are infused with an earnest spirituality to this effect. Elizabeth Taylor's reported assurances run true to form in both respects:

'I am now Mrs Hilton. You can take it from me that my romantic life is settled for ever. There is no other future for me than as Nicky's wife.'

'It is wonderful marrying a man like Michael (Wilding) who is twice my age. He is so mature and that is what I need.'

'I have given Mike (Todd) my love. My eternal love.'

'I love Eddie (Fisher) dearly.'

'Richard (Burton), unless he wants to divorce me, will never be divorced by me . . . I love him enough to stand by him, no matter what he might do, and I would wait.'

A star's divorce may bring her indiscretions to lurid light. But in general, as Hortense Powdermaker remarked in *Hollywood, The Dream Factory*, 'the studios' worry about (such scandals) is not because of their effect on fans, but because of fear of organised pressure groups who are self-constituted censors of morals.'* But the curiosity of the moviegoing public was stronger in Elizabeth Taylor's case than any feeling of righteous indignation which might have been aroused by groups or individuals, like the Congressman who proposed barring her and Richard Burton on moral grounds from re-entering the United States. In contrast, moral outrage of the same smugly offensive kind undoubtedly helped to turn Ingrid Bergman's fans against her when the nature of her relationship with the Italian director, Roberto Rossellini, became widely publicised. She, too, was attacked in Congress, stigmatised by one Senator as a 'free-love cultist.' But the wider public's disapproval of her was partly their reaction to the feeling that they had been deceived by the image which had been built up of Bergman as a healthy, wholesome, happily married woman living a blissful home life between pictures. A whole new image of her had to be created by 20th Century-Fox when the studio gambled

* *Hollywood, The Dream Factory*, by Hortense Powdermaker (Little, Brown & Co.), p. 250.

successfully on restoring her career and popularity by starring her in *Anastasia* (1956). One Fox executive said, 'I felt if we could convince the public she was a courageous, long-suffering woman who had sacrificed all for love, the American people would accept her again.'*

Elizabeth Taylor's image was never vulnerable to the same kind of scandal. Conditioned by the marriage-divorce syndrome of stardom, the public saw her as a woman of instinct, without any driving passion to put her life in order: the messes must just be cleared up as she goes along. Even when so-called 'illicit love' becomes 'married love' in the course of time and the decree nisi, there has remained what she herself recognises as an intriguing suggestion of 'rampant sex' in the rumbustious life she is pictured leading with her latest husband.

This kind of star thrives on 'scandal'. However unjustified it may be, or however painful it really is when old friends shun her and complete strangers hiss or spit at her, it is nearly always financially advantageous. Elizabeth Taylor's fee at the height of the Fisher scandal is said to have gone up to $500,000 per picture, and Debbie Reynolds's to $100,000. The real loser, as Ruth Waterbury pointed out in her biography of Elizabeth Taylor, was the man, Eddie Fisher, who temporarily forfeited a lot of his popularity. The moralists punished him, just as they did Ingrid Bergman, for misleading them into believing he was a settled homebody. Very different was the fate of Richard Burton. He was already accepted as a rebel against convention and the circumstances of his marriage to Elizabeth Taylor fortified his image and defined his rebellion as one against marital convention. His hitherto sluggish film career picked up spectacularly. So did his box-office value. Soon he was receiving a consort fee of $500,000 a picture when co-starring with his wife.

* * *

Next to marriage, wealth and beauty do most to promote the myth of a star. The tag 'Million Dollar Woman', with its hypnotic row of zeroes when printed in figures, is a power symbol which a

* Quoted in *The Real and the Unreal*, by Bill Davidson (Harper), p. 172.

star like Elizabeth Taylor can turn into real power by deciding which film she will appear in, how she will play the role, where the film will be made, frequently who will make it. It is curious to note that in the history of the cinema, figures of this astronomical amount have nearly always had a feminine association. Mary Pickford became known as 'the first woman to make a million', Gloria Swanson as 'the first woman to spend a million'. In the case of female stars, it would seem, the size of a fee is directly linked to the fluctuation of their sex appeal. This is less often the case with male stars, where a high fee usually represents the uniqueness of a personality and thus, being less visibly related to a perishable commodity like sex appeal, may even mature with them like a good endowment policy.

But it is hard to see Elizabeth Taylor as a sex symbol, like Loren, Bardot or Lollobrigida. Not for her the sexy hip-flip or the roll-and-pitch of the bust. Her physical beauty is the kind that an Elizabethan poet would have called 'gipsy'. And it is not generalised, but local – centred on her large eyes, delicate nose and dark hair that always looks more effective when let down. Her looks hold the appeal of sexual tension. They generate expectancy among filmgoers that her actions will be impulsive, high-tempered, possibly destructive. (No doubt such filmgoers are reading her own turbulent, off-screen life into her looks: but stardom depends on precisely this kind of identification.)

A vital, though tragic aspect of the intense interest Elizabeth Taylor arouses has been her perilous health and the way misfortune seems to follow her around. What might have been minor illnesses in others have often had a way of engulfing her dramatically. Her worst crisis occurred in February, 1961, when she fell ill while filming *Cleopatra*; and to the other alarms of that accident-prone picture was added the scarcely credible news that its star was dying. Complications developing during pneumonia had put her in a coma, her temperature was 105, and several times she came as near death as she ever would. In a speech made later at the Los Angeles Medical Fund dinner, she clearly detailed her conviction that she had actually 'died'. 'And then I coughed. I moved. I breathed. And I looked. That hanging lamp – that most beautiful light my world has ever known – began faintly to glow again, to shine again.' Modern life lacks clear-cut tragedies. But the dying star is one that still focuses people's collective imagination like an old-time morality play. The situation is a morbid form of intimacy for some: it is as if by reading the newspaper reports, or telephoning the studios for the latest bulletin, they can boast of knowing the stricken celebrity. But for many more, perhaps the majority, it intimates that film stars are human, mortal, and essentially folk like themselves. And so a wave of sympathetic identification is built up that may turn into an orgy of grief if the star dies. But once let a 'miraculous' recovery take place, and the star is restored to her fantasy dimension – only now that little bit more 'immortal'. Elizabeth Taylor's crisis touched off this kind of reaction. If she deserved an Oscar for her acting, there were worthier occasions than the one offered by the film *Butterfield 8* (1960). But the Academy Award ceremony came immediately after the high drama of her illness and gave Hollywood an opportunity it could not resist – to bracket her recovery with its own gold-plated token of movie immortality. Thus the fact of death contributed to making her larger than life.

The way a star lives – as well as 'dies' – enhances her importance. A serious study should be made of all the conglomerate courtesies and rites that a star like Elizabeth Taylor is able to use to confirm her rank. One small, but not unimpressive, example is the panoply of semi-royal privileges publicly extended to her and her entourage on arrival at a major airport. It is extraordinary how air travel, the most 'modern' form of transport, is the means of perpetuating an almost feudal list of distinctions based on inherited or acquired importance. No doubt there are sound commercial or safety reasons behind it, but the VIP concept confers or confirms off-screen stardom in a way that adds to the mythical personality of the star on the cinema screen. 'AM ARRIVING WITH THE MARQUIS TOMORROW. PLEASE ARRANGE OVATION', Gloria Swanson cabled ahead to Hollywood on returning there with her new French husband. The way that international airports operate today makes it unnecessary for super-stars of the screen to spend money on cables. (It is entirely apt that one of Elizabeth Taylor's recent films should have been called *The VIPs* (1963): Terence Rattigan's screenplay flyly recognised thrt, with the downgrading of the Grand Hotel, the VIP lounge at an airport was the last ambiance from which a dramatist could borrow a ready-made importance for his characters.)

For a star who has minimal physical contact with her fans, such rites are additionally important. So is the scale on which she lives – and the zest she puts into living. 'I have decided that when I am a star I will be every inch and every moment the star.' Again the words are Gloria Swanson's: and again they apply to Elizabeth Taylor who reaches her mass public vicariously through the reports spread of her fabulous extravagance, or her expensive whims, or her bulk purchases of couture gowns, or her block booking of whole hotel floors to accommodate her retinue of bodyguards, secretaries, cooks and governesses. True or false, it creates an aura of fascination round her most mediocre film. And even when she makes a point of seeing how simple folk live – sinking a pint of beer in a pub, cheering on the Welsh at international Rugby football – both interests taken over from her husband Richard Burton – the effect is not dissipated. It is the 'common touch' of a queen.

* * *

Such a life, of course, is no guarantee of emotional adjustment: rather the reverse. The effect of it on a highly-strung temperament like Elizabeth Taylor's must be unusually severe. Where does she go to look for stability, for relief from being 'every inch and every moment the star'? Two answers suggest themselves, both of them in the nature of paradoxes. One is that she seeks stability in marriage: the other is that she seeks relief in film acting. Five marriages, three of them dissolved, and one of them terminated by death, may indicate a run of incompatibility and misfortune, but is not conclusive proof that she is anything but serious. Indeed, implicit in each of her marriages is a strong desire for security and emotional stability. 'I need strength in a man more than any other quality,' she has said; and marriage seems to be a time for testing the man's strength to sustain her – sometimes even endure her. Her marriage to Mike Todd was happy and successful precisely because Todd's own masterful nature was reassuring to her, so that even the occasional public difference of opinion between husband and wife became a trial of strength which she did not mind losing. Being between marriages, separated from Eddie Fisher but not yet free to marry Richard Burton, was emotionally a very damaging state. She has referred to the 'panic' induced in her at such moments. Quite obviously she was not thinking of the merely legal complications – disagreeable though these must have been – but of the frustration of her own search for a meaningful relationship.

Her marriages suggest she has repeatedly tried to assuage the 'panic' by attaching herself to some stable or dominant characteristic of her current husband's. It has sometimes been his religious faith. For a bride to take instruction in her future husband's religion is commonplace in mixed marriages; but Elizabeth Taylor set herself to embrace Nicky Hilton's Roman Catholicism with a quite remarkable intenseness of purpose. When she married Eddie Fisher she became a Jewish convert, and still drops the occasional Yiddish word into her small-talk. Mike Todd provided her with the lay faith of wheeling and dealing, and, incidentally, showed her how to gain people's attention in public and hold it. With Richard Burton as her husband, she has worked hard at his Welshness – and succeeded in mastering demotic tongue-twisters like *cwtched*, or 'hugged'. She has given public poetry recitals with him, which must have been a nerve-ridden break-away from the security of the closed film set. Having taught him some of her own tricks of personality projection on the screen, she now seems intent on penetrating his repertory of stage experience and Classical acting, with the non-speaking part of Helen of Troy in the Oxford University production of *Dr Faustus* as her matriculation test, and the film version of *The Taming of the Shrew* (1966) as her graduation piece.

For the man, of course, this constitutes a risk – of having his personality completely absorbed by his partner. Burton's well-known curt and candid remarks about his wife's looks and shortcomings appear calculated to repel any such threat. He has the actor's need to be the centre of attention: what emerges from some of his published short stories and interviews he has given is a strong longing not to be left out of things. One feels he was only half jesting when he began his marriage with a husbandly warning that he meant to hold the stage – 'Elizabeth will be in the wings – knitting.' To which she replied, 'A man has really to love a woman to go to such lengths to dominate her.' It is in this kind of tension that Elizabeth Taylor's life off-screen achieves its intermittent stability.

On the screen her emotional 'panic' can be artistically electrifying provided the right part is there to act as a lightning conductor. Ruth Waterbury in her biography of Elizabeth Taylor suggests how the 'panic' can be self-induced; and though the incident is sentimentally recounted, it is illuminating too in relation to her later roles. While honeymooning in Rome with her first husband, she thought it would be fun to appear as a Christian martyr – an extra's role, done strictly for a joke – in the M-G-M epic *Quo Vadis* (1951) then being shot there. 'Elizabeth had been laughing over it . . . until the lights went up for action. But then, suddenly, the solemn meaning of the scene swept over her, and she began to cry. The thought of her own death, the remembrance of idealism struck her, and while she surged ahead on command with the other extras, she could not conceal her sobs.'* Her early adult roles seldom asked her to do more than look beautiful and sometimes supplement her features with an expression, or practise her diction on a line like the one in *The Last Time I Saw Paris* (1954) – 'Is the war really over? Because I want to give you silk shirts, silk socks and silk shorts.' But a significant exception was *A Place in the Sun* (1951), where George Stevens seems to have detected the highly-strung girl under her professional self-possession and drawn it out in a well-written role.

Her most noteworthy performances since then have been in *Cat on a Hot Tin Roof* (1958) and *Suddenly Last Summer* (1959). It is significant that both films came from Tennessee Williams's plays about women under obsessive and uncontrollable stress, who are pushed beyond the limits of endurance. Some of the incantatory power of her long, harrowing monologue at the end of *Suddenly*

* *Elizabeth Taylor*, by Ruth Waterbury (Robert Hale), p. 101.

Last Summer comes from the way the director, Joseph L. Mankiewicz, fills part of the screen with her anguished face, while letting her reviving memory of the poet Sebastian's death fill the other half with fluttery, incandescent fantasies of perversion and cannibalism. But much of the power also comes from her own sustained hysteria that is a vocal *tour de force* which reportedly left her in a state of collapse.

Her gift is for playing women out of control. But more and more in recent films she has taken to playing women in command – not always happily. *Cleopatra* best displays her strength and limitations in this respect. What drew little critical comment at the time was how Joseph L. Mankiewicz, who as well as directing the film was writing its script almost nightly, took the opportunity of refreshing ancient history with modern psychology. Mankiewicz, with *A Letter to Three Wives* (1949) and *All About Eve* to his credit, is one of the most penetrating character-analysts of the modern American woman; and in *Cleopatra* he took the opportunity to build up a full-length portrait of her. The film is Plutarch infiltrated by Kinsey. In the first half of it, Elizabeth Taylor has to play Cleopatra as a sexually precocious kind of co-ed who knows more about such matters than the dean of women, as one might designate the palace eunuch. Her acting of this role is excellent. Her infatuation of Rex Harrison, as the ageing Caesar, is managed with kittenish ease. But in the second half of the film, she has to switch to playing a matron whose ambitions for her mate are too much for him to fulfil. It is not the love which Antony betrays so much as the ambitions which he cannot consummate that dominate this part of the film. It hardly begins to be a love story. Elizabeth Taylor, so compelling when playing Tennessee Williams heroines in the grip of hysteria, was unequal to the part of a woman born to command – her every imperative tended to turn into a snarl. The way she makes love is like a war of emotional attrition, finally humiliating Antony after he loses the Battle of Actium by taking away his sword.

Her part in *The VIPs* is also motivated by the inadequacy of her screen husband, a millionaire played by Richard Burton again, who can only give her the 'cheque-book affection' that drives her to run away with a gigolo. Like Shaw's *Candida*, she goes back to him only when she realises how weak and helpless he really is. (Perhaps *Candida* has already been earmarked as a property for future film-making by these two stars.) *The Sandpiper* (1965) continued to make her the present of the upper hand. She plays a Bohemian artist, living in highly picturesque and hygienic simplicity on the coast of Big Sur, who seduces her son's headmaster – an ordained minister played once more by Burton. Her own brand of pagan pantheism is promoted far more exuberantly in the film than Burton's muddled Christianity which makes him try to lead her to God through art by designing stained-glass windows for the school chapel. She does not lose a chance of tempting him or humiliating him by showing him the weakness of his flesh, the worldliness of his Church and the ineffectiveness of his God, till at last he is praying unavailingly over the bonnet of his Ford station wagon: 'Oh God, allow me a little remembrance of honour.' At the end of the film he wanders dazedly off, without his job, without a reputation, with his marriage in ruins, to reflect on fate, cheered on his way by the school choir which has spontaneously burst into the anthem, 'There is mercy for the sinner.' Meanwhile Elizabeth Taylor, with her vigour unimpaired, is dashing off a fresh seascape. This foolish film – scripted, let it be recorded, by such otherwise respected talents as Dalton Trumbo and Michael Wilson – did record business at the box-office. The analogy with the break-up of Burton's own marriage did not escape filmgoers – nor, it is reported, Burton himself when he first read the script.

Since *The Sandpiper*, the films that these stars are shooting or have in prospect consistently follow a pattern of stronger and weaker mates in romance or marriage. In *Who's Afraid of Virginia Woolf?* (1966) she played Edward Albee's neurotic and ultimately pathetic shrike-wife to Burton's masochistic campus-husband. It is her most dramatic and subtle performance to date: it might be called the triumph of the shrew. Gone is every defence that a beautiful actress might have relied on to give her an easy ride over Albee's heaving sea of marital nausea. She enters with a fatted face, slip strap showing, a braying voice, a greying wig that lashes around at moments of temper like a bundle of snakes, and a body that looks hard enough to take knocks and rubbery

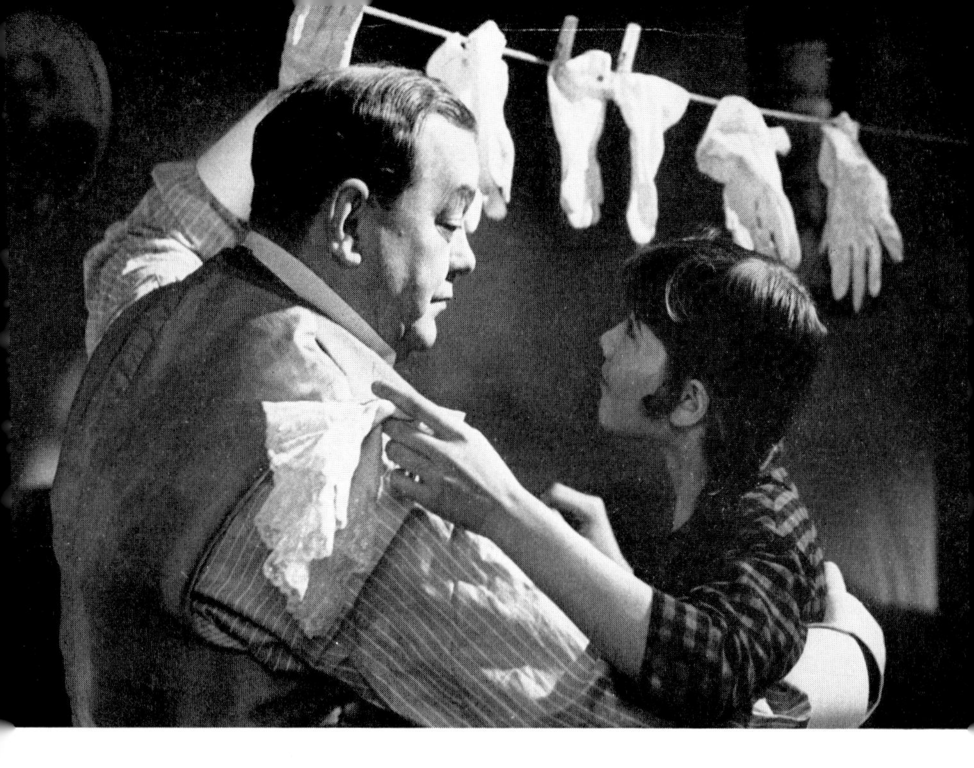

Above: Seduction of the Innocent: Ake Grönberg, as the middle-aged stranger, dances with the little girl in Mai Zetterling's film *Loving Couples*. It was a few seconds after this shot that the scene was cut. *Below:* Seduction of the Mature: James Mason, as Humbert Humbert, paints the toe-nails of the Coke-sucking nymphet played by Sue Lyon in Stanley Kubrick's *Lolita*.

Threat to the Young: Lori Mortin, playing Gregory Peck's daughter in J. Lee Thompson's suspense-thriller *Cape Fear*, suddenly comes face to face with Robert Mitchum. It was the menace directed towards the child by this vengeful ex-convict that the British censor sought to tone down.

enough to bounce back again. In unerring intuitive strokes, she builds up Martha's sluttishness with physical details like the casual drag at a cigarette filched from her husband's lips. She is the blazing equal of the big scenes of humiliation when she taunts Burton with his ineffectualness, his dead-end job, even his physical impotence, till, unlike Antony, he turns on her and literally chokes her off. Yet she is infinitely touching at the end of Mike Nichols's film, when her termagant trumpeting is muted into a lament for the child she never had and one detects the sad inter-dependence of the couple whose marriage is a public sparring match. How appropriate that after Albee's envenomed version of the games people play they should immediately film *The Taming of the Shrew* as a rumbustious knockabout comedy which will for once give Burton the dominant role – though this novelty should be balanced against his announced desire at some future date to play opposite his wife's Lady Macbeth.

There is an odd paradox here. The proven box-office appeal that this partnership possesses makes them freer agents in picking themes, stories and roles for themselves than many other film stars who have status without any corresponding power. Yet the films they have made are, for the most part, the very opposite of those which one might have expected them to make, judging from their off-screen remarks about the qualities they believe are necessary for a compatible marriage relationship. Elizabeth Taylor who has spoken of her need to be dominated, has nevertheless been presented on the screen as the dominating woman. Richard Burton who has announced his intention to keep the upper hand off screen, has nevertheless excelled at playing the flawed and vulnerable man on it. At this point, their film careers begin to look less like ways of satisfying their artistic drives, and more like part of an adroitly established *modus vivendi* in which a destructive relationship on the screen, with the dominant and submissive roles reversed, enables them to preserve an orthodox relationship in real life. Stars, after all, may be no different from the audiences they exist to entertain. They, too, need to seek their fantasies in the movies.

Part Two
THE GUARDIANS

'To state the matter shortly,
the sovereign has, under a
constitutional monarchy such
as ours, three rights – the
right to be consulted, the
right to encourage, the right
to warn. And a king of great
sense and sagacity should
want no others.'

– Sir Walter Bagehot in
The English Constitution.

CHAPTER EIGHT

ONE MAN'S MEAT: BRITISH CENSORSHIP

A large and pleasantly sited room overlooking the leafy centre of Soho Square, London, has probably heard more obscene words and pornographic allusion traded to and fro in the course of serious business than any lodgings ever tenanted by Henry Miller or William Burroughs. It is the office of the secretary of the British Board of Film Censors. The present censor – as the secretary is usually if loosely described – is John Trevelyan* who came to the job in 1958 after a career in education and a spell as one of the board's small staff of examiners. Lean, leathery and tirelessly articulate about his work, Trevelyan might have been created by C. P. Snow for one of his 'Corridors of Power' novels about the dying art of secret negotiation and the cagy confrontations of the devious and the devout. The room's old-gold wallpaper radiates a mandarin light: an appropriate ambiance for some of the decisions he has had to make during his tenure.

Risking a generalisation, one can say that censorship in Britain is singular, in America plural. The Hollywood Production Code Administration is only one among many proliferating groups, State or local, official or unofficial, lay or clerical, which have a say in what the moviegoer sees. In Britain this is largely one man's meat. Unlike his American counterpart, Trevelyan has no written Production Code which the film industry has approved and which he is empowered to administer. His office *was* set up by the film industry, in 1912, mainly to avoid the multiplicity of censors who have hounded Hollywood producers; and it is financed by companies who handle films and who pay to have their product vetted

* At the time of writing, 1966.

and given an 'A', 'U' or 'X' Certificate.* (If the product is refused a Certificate altogether, they still pay.) But Trevelyan's decisions are uniquely his own and his board's, the product of their collective outlook, or more often, his personal judgment. So are their acts of courage or enlightenment: so are their misjudgments. Like the British Constitution, film censorship is an imprecise, changing thing which reflects what goes, and what does not (yet) go, in the view the public has about contemporary morals. Generally this means sexual morals; and generally it is what Trevelyan thinks the public is thinking about them that goes. His power is not absolute, however. His own panel of examiners have a strong say-so which he is bound to listen to, though he may overrule them. So has the president of the British Board of Film Censors. But it is not a widely known fact that, while the president can guide long-term policy and is always available in a consultative capacity, the power to make day-to-day decisions on specific matters is reserved to his secretary.

The more insidious checks on Trevelyan's powers come from local authorities who have the right to overrule, or alter, his Certificates. Very occasionally they have banned outright a film he has passed, as Warwickshire County Council did in the case of *Saturday Night and Sunday Morning* (1960) which was held by some to be a slur on the morals of factory floor workers in the Midlands. Sometimes the local authorities have been more lenient than the censor: it was they who let the goose-pimply rash of nudist-camp films spread on to the screen in the late 1950s, though the censor had denied them even an 'X' Certificate fig leaf. Reacting quickly to 'this useful test of public opinion', the board reconsidered the films, in most of which people threw off their inhibitions along with their clothes and romped through some sempiternal sunshine and carefully angled photography. Most of them were given 'A' Certificates and now usually get a 'U', though few such films now come up for censoring, the makers having acknowledged that sex

* A classification based on the British view that children are the ones who need protection in film-going. Any child may see a 'U' Certificate unaccompanied, an 'A' Certificate if accompanied by a parent or *bona fide* adult. No child under 16 may see an 'X' Certificate film at all.

does not thrive where nudity is the norm. It would appear that a few local authorities do not bother to see the films they ban or pass, but rely on publicity hand-outs and synopses; while others who are unaccustomed to censoring films often fail to spot why the London censor has found them objectionable. There was the case of the Albert Zugsmith production of *Fanny Hill* (1964) which Trevelyan declined to pass. One of his objections was to a scene in a haystack where Fanny and a young rake are sheltering from the rain. To protect her dress, she asks him to help her off with it and while fumbling behind her she suddenly exclaims that she can feel a mouse in the hay. A few seconds later she cries out that she can feel the mouse again, only now it is bigger. Some local authorities who had begun giving the film an 'A' and even a 'U' Certificate entirely missed the implications of this erection joke. To them, a mouse was a mouse. They took Fanny's word for it.

Though sometimes irritating to the censor, and always a potential danger to his authority, local censorship of this kind has little effect on morals in the wider sense. Much more influential in fixing the shifting frontier of sexual morality is the dialogue always going on between the censor and those who produce, direct, write, distribute, exhibit and even review the films. The involvement of the censor in almost every phase of film-making is the biggest change in the last few years. More than any of his predecessors, who have tended to be either exceptionally prudent or else inconveniently stubborn men, Trevelyan is 'in' on many a film from the time it is just a gleam in the eye of the producer and his banker. If invited to do so, he will pass an opinion on a subject, vet a script for trouble spots, visit the set for the shooting of a tricky scene, even sit in at the screening of the partially finished film before he 'officially' receives it. All this is done to forewarn the producer and does not commit the Board either way before their final verdict. But inevitably it affects his attitude to some degree. And film-makers realise this. Like the monarchy, the censor has always had certain rights, two of them being the right to encourage and the right to warn. To them, Trevelyan has virtually added the third royal prerogative: the right to be consulted.

* * *

It is still up to film-makers whether they choose to consult him or not, or whether they heed the advice he gives. But some who do not later regret it. Jayne Mansfield was revealed to be so lightly clad in one British thriller called *Too Hot to Handle* (1960) that the censor ruled the film too hot to show. As no alternative material had been shot in or around Miss Mansfield, artists had to be employed with air-brushes to spray a decent density of paint on to her on the film print: it was a tedious retouching job. When Trevelyan saw *The Chapman Report*, a story of sexologists inadvertently stimulating the American community they simply go to survey, he refused to pass scenes of sexual violence. No script of the film had been sent him in advance of shooting, though his views on the value of this had been made known to the Hollywood studios, at least one of which had orders from its president to do so. Moreover since George Cukor, who directed *The Chapman Report*, specialised in long, uninterrupted takes, there was no substitute material available. The result was censorship cuts which made the film jump as if the cameraman had been kicked. Couples were repelled as if their lips generated electric charges, rapist and intended victim were thrown to opposite sides of the room, and Claire Bloom in the role of a nympho-dipsomaniac was bounced from rape on the bar-room floor back to her ranch-house bungalow in one traumatic cut. It added an unexpected dimension of hilarity to an already absurd film.

These are all extreme cases of the censor *not* being consulted at any stage prior to censorship, or his advice not being taken. But as soon as he is consulted, he ceases to be merely a censor making moral judgments. Whether he likes it or not, he becomes a person involved in the production of a film. And he would be less than human if his moral outlook was not coloured by his artistic sensibility. This is made easier for him than for his Hollywood counterpart, since he is not bound to abide by any Production Code view of morality. Thus as well as being the guardian of public morals, Trevelyan has progressively become involved in the work of evaluating the artistic merit of films that may impinge on those morals. The skill with which a film is made, the integrity of its aims, even the reputation of its makers may come into the reckoning of how far it should be permitted more sexual licence than usual. Among other things that count are some that few people realise even concern the censor: the way the film will be received by critics, or publicised by distributors, or advertised by cinema owners.

What helped widen the scope of censorship in this way was one outstanding film in the late 1950s: *Room At the Top* (1959). Yet exactly how Trevelyan viewed the film when he came to censor it has often been misunderstood. It was a breakthrough British production in several ways. It made an international star of Laurence Harvey, gave director Jack Clayton a brilliant debut in feature films, won a Cannes Film Festival award for Simone Signoret – but, most of all, it injected a new sexual candour into British films. It took an unhypocritical view of the advantage that sex could be to a young man ruthless enough to exploit it for material gain: a form of realism more often Gallic than Anglo-Saxon. Its most startling innovation was the sequence where Harvey seduces the industrialist's virginal young daughter on the river bank. There were two extraordinary aspects to it. For the first time in a British film, the sex act was talked about and, even more daring, it was pronounced to be pleasurable. 'Oh Joe, wasn't it super?' the girl cries breathily, while Harvey, as Joe Lampton, takes the post-coital male's silent, ruminative view of what is past. The girl's enthusiastic chatter continues as they stroll away, giving the scene an ironic sense of anticlimax.

Though it may seem anticlimactic in another sense, it must be recorded that the scene did not perturb the censor at all. What did puzzle him were the compliments that film critics paid him for being bold, wise and progressive enough to let such a scene be screened. In fact, the changes he did suggest were all to do with the film's taste, not sex. One of them referred to Harvey overhearing a girl at an office party going into lurid detail about Simone Signoret's messy death in a car crash. The censor felt that the shock point had already been strongly enough made by the very news of such a death – no need to lay on the details. This was agreed. *Room At the Top* was regarded by the censor as a film that treated illicit sex with artistic integrity, and he gave it an 'X' Certificate which had been specially designed to permit the adult treatment of themes that were too controversial to be covered by an 'A' Certificate. Although some film-makers had deliberately sensationalised their films so as to give them the forbidden allure of an 'X', it is true to say that at this time the film industry had a certain bias against the 'X' Certificate since it reduced the potential audience for a film to people over sixteen years of age. Despite this, the distributors of *Room At the Top* released it with the censor's 'X' and had the satisfaction of seeing it become one of the biggest post-war hits at the British box-office.*

Such success had several results. It softened the film industry's resistance to the 'X' Certificate, which helped the censor award it more easily to films he would have had to cut if the makers had insisted on an 'A'. It encouraged film-makers to reconnoitre subjects that were even more socially and sexually daring. And it hastened the day when the censor would have to let a film's artistic worth figure prominently in his reckoning of its possible impact on morals. This was the real work accomplished by *Room At the Top*.

* * *

Often overlooked is the help that television has been to the British film censor. Ironically the medium that reaches right into the heart of the family has been freer for the probing of once-taboo subjects – partly because it is regarded as a news medium as well – than the cinema which is traditionally regarded by the film industry in Anglo-Saxon countries as a medium of family entertainment. This freedom is truer of Britain, however, than the United States. When Hollywood set out to lure back its vanishing audience in the early 1950s, it looked for themes and stories that were *not* available on the sponsor-wary television networks and the result was a spate of films that treated sex more explicitly, though hardly with more truth. But British television viewers were accustomed to having 'controversial' sexual themes discussed or dramatised and film-makers profited from the atmosphere of frankness this helped create. It also provided the censor with an argument that he could hardly exclude subjects from the large screen which had

* It was denied a seal of approval by the Motion Picture Association of America. Even so, it did good business there too.

already been seen on the small one. One of these was homosexuality, which the Wolfenden Report of 1957 brought out into frank public debate. As early as 1958 Trevelyan announced that his board would not ban homosexual scenes in a film, provided they were done responsibly. 'Responsibly' usually included close consultation with him, which he got from the makers of the two films about Oscar Wilde that quickly followed: *Oscar Wilde* (1960) with Robert Morley and the superior production *The Trials of Oscar Wilde* (1960) with Peter Finch. In doing so, he showed how quickly British censorship could respond to a change in the public's attitude in contrast to the position in Hollywood where a cumbersome amendment to the Production Code had to be engineered before such themes could be permitted on the screen.

But one report current in film industry circles at this time neatly illustrates the opportunism that a censor of liberal outlook has to be on his guard against. A certain screenplay submitted to his board opened with a love scene which filmgoers would think unmistakably homosexual. Later they would have had to reclassify it as heterosexual in intent, since one of the youths underwent surgery for a change of sex. Trevelyan may have doubted if filmgoers were capable of this degree of retrospective subtlety. His doubts must have been settled on learning that the film proposed showing the sex operation in some detail. It has not been made, yet.

A quite different matter was Joseph Losey's film *The Servant* (1963). This contained all the things that weigh in the censor's equation of artistry and morality. Its plot seems quite irredeemably immoral. A rich, idle, upper-class young Englishman, a little stupid under his charm and *eau de Cologne* engages a manservant and lets himself be imperceptibly and then inescapably corrupted by him. The last shot of the film shows Master Tony, his free will sapped by drugs and his self-respect poisoned by his servant's sexual pandering for him, looking on helplessly while Barrett and his girl-friend move into the master bedroom. Homosexual undertones abound in the antagonistic, yet intimate relationship of the two men: there is also a heterosexual seduction scene of erotic intensity. In allowing the film to reach the screen without a single cut, Trevelyan reasoned as follows. Harold Pinter, the distinguished stage playwright, had written the screenplay with a brilliance that earned respect. Moreover Losey's previous films showed a skill and sincerity of purpose that had gained him the censor's trust. To this extent, then, *The Servant*'s references were impeccable. Now the American censor in vetting the screenplay would have had to apply the test of 'moral compensation' – the principle that underpins the Hollywood Production Code. It means that every sin the characters commit must be compensated for by their punishment or repentance, or both. The British censor could ignore this pathetically crude slide-rule, and instead vet the story for moral and artistic integrity.

As Trevelyan saw it, watching one ruthless man deliberately debauch a weaker one is never edifying. Yet *The Servant* made one accept the essential rightness of it. For while Barrett is a predator on his young master, Tony is equally a parasite upon society – an obsolete ornament, in other words, who comes apart in the hands of a callous class-enemy. Viewed this way, the story was a soundly based if disturbing study of social retribution – and as such, acceptable. As for the sexual elements, two things eased the censor's mind. One was that Harold Pinter's screenplay is 'suggestive' in the best sense. Brilliantly oblique, it uses words like sequins to glitter darkly on the surface and suggest depths of corruption underneath. In plotting Tony's descent into degeneracy, Barrett and his girl-friend scorn even to whisper – they operate by a kind of lower-class telepathy conveyed most effectively by Dirk Bogarde and Sarah Miles. The homosexual episodes are equally indirect – tellingly present for sophisticated filmgoers, likely to be overlooked by others. (The natural inequalities in the distribution of intelligence is a great asset to censors in cases like this.) Trevelyan told Losey that his Board's main worry might in fact be the seduction scene where the girl and Tony, played by James Fox, are absorbed into the great dark leather lap of a Swedish-type swing chair. Though most of their bodies are never seen, the girls' legs and thighs dangling over the side of the chair suggest that she is naked. Suspending judgment till he saw the edited film, Trevelyan suggested that Losey shoot the scene in such a way that if cuts had to be made they would not disrupt the action like those in *The*

Chapman Report. Losey agreed. As it turned out, the eroticism of the scene was held in place so securely by the rest of a serious, intelligent film that no cuts were judged necessary. *The Servant* was released with an 'X' Certificate and did extremely well.

The Servant is by no means an uncommon example of the usefulness of good relations between the censor and the film-makers. Much depends on each recognising they possess a sympathy, if not an identity of interest. This in turn comes from personal trust. Like most creative people, Losey is rightly suspicious of the institution of censorship: on this occasion he found the censor an agreeable and useful person to work with.

* * *

The risk inherent in this kind of understanding is that it may draw an accusation that some film-makers are being given favoured treatment. But a censor who takes a film's artistic merits into account must accept such a risk. Placed as he is at the very centre of the industry, on intimate terms with people in all branches of it, he soon learns to distinguish the genuine pioneers. Three case histories show how a similar theme, treated by different directors, can pose vastly different problems for the censor. The theme is sexual assault. It is one the British censor regards very gravely, especially when the violence is aimed at children. The fear is that it may stimulate maladjusted filmgoers to go out and do likewise. Himself the father of a young family, Trevelyan is quick to call in a consulting psychiatrist if he senses any risk of this. But often the film does not offer anything as crude, and easily censorable, as actual violence. The threat of it can be more effective in film-making terms, more insidious in terms of censorship. Here, if anywhere, the reputation, intention and craftsmanship of the film-maker weigh with the censor – and also the former's willingness to consult with him.

J. Lee Thompson, an effective director of action and suspense films, chose to oppose the censor over *Cape Fear* (1962), an American thriller which starred Gregory Peck as a small-town lawyer and Robert Mitchum as the ex-convict he sent to prison. The story's aim was to show how thin civilisation is, and it did so disquietingly well. For when the released convict comes back to town and hangs around Peck's home and family, a peripatetic menace, the lawyer gradually finds there is nothing he can legally do to protect himself unless, and until, he is attacked. Or, rather, until his little girl is attacked. For the film implied a continuous threat to the child. The nature of this threat is never stated in so many words, but since it was known that the intruder had been jailed for a sex crime, it was natural for audiences to imagine the worst. Trevelyan saw the film as a skilfully made exercise in shock. But the very skill used to set an audience's alarm bells jangling only made *Cape Fear* a worse risk, he felt, from the point of view of potential child assailants. He requested some fifteen cuts, totalling about five minutes' screen time, and added the charges of 'brutality' and 'sadism' to his main concern over the film. By some confusion, possibly a semantic one over what constituted a 'cut', the director alleged that the censor had insisted on over 150 cuts and he refused to make them. The affair boiled over in more charges and counter-charges, then simmered down – as such affairs have a way of doing when distributors realise that the disputed film may be a long time in their vaults, gathering dust and bank charges, unless a settlement is more discreetly reached. *Cape Fear* was eventually shown with the censor's cuts. They were detectable, if one was looking for them. But it was still a compelling thriller in the convention now, not of child assault, but of the good citizen who suddenly finds out how much alone he can be left. Having reduced the part that the child played in the emotional tension, the censor felt he had achieved his main aim and could let the director tighten the screw on Gregory Peck and his family. The menace in the plot had been generalised: it was now far less inflammatory.

The film version of *Lolita* (1962) seemed fraught with censorship problems when Stanley Kubrick announced his decision to make it. Its theme of a middle-aged man's obsession for a twelve-year-old nymphet had already alarmed several reputable publishers. Kubrick chose to make the film in Britain, possibly because there was less risk of harassment from pressure groups there than in America. The censor saw Vladimir Nabokov's screenplay ahead of shooting; and it was immediately clear to Trevelyan that the scenarist and the director had resolved many of his own apprehensions, often brilliantly. There was only one major compromise. Lolita in the novel is twelve, in the film she is said to be fourteen, and in some scenes she looks sixteen. That this sop to censorship did not ruin the film was due to the seductive infantilism and 'eerie vulgarity' that Kubrick's direction teased out of Sue Lyon. The eroticism of the book also underwent a transposition. Kubrick created a striking visual metaphor for Humbert Humbert's perversion: as the credits appear at the start Lolita's bare leg is thrust out imperiously into the screen and a man's hand advances and cushions the soft little sole of her foot while his other hand proceeds to paint her toe nails with infinite tenderness. It portended the pathetic fixation of the grown-up man who is enslaved by the child he loves. Once the film proper got under way, Kubrick and Nabokov turned the eroticism into visual comedy that never for an instant lost its undertones of irony or pity.

Like Lubitsch, a director who was a censor's delight, Kubrick got the maximum effect out of what taste or discretion decided him *not* to show happening on the screen. We do not actually hear the details of the 'game' that Lolita is proposing she and Humbert Humbert play when they wake up in the morning – his attempt to seduce her during the night having been frustrated by the slapstick mechanics of a folding cot – but his dawning astonishment at what the child is whispering in his ear telegraphs the news that Lolita is already a very cankerous bud of American adolescence. But it was the way the film opened which was particularly helpful to the censor. It begins with retribution being meted out before sin has been committed. Amid the dust-sheeted furniture, marble statuary and Citizen Kane bric-à-brac of Clare Quilty's mansion, James Mason as Humbert takes revenge on the man who seduced Lolita away from him; and Peter Sellers as a superb Quilty leaps up and down like a ticklish kangaroo as the bullets hit home in a way that makes the sequence both goonish and grisly. A more realistic opening not rooted in the realm of surreal fantasy might have made the story, in the censor's view, that degree more probable and thus more likely to stimulate imitation.

According to one film industry source the screenplay caused him only one major anxiety. It concerned Humbert Humbert's theory of nymphets, which in a passage in Nabokov's novel begins: 'Now I wish to introduce the following idea. Between the age limits of nine and fourteen there occur maidens who, to certain bewitched travellers, twice or many times older than they, reveal their true nature which is not human, but nymphic (that is, demoniac); and these chosen creatures I propose to designate as "nymphets".'* In Nabokov's original screenplay James Mason's voice is heard saying, 'Now I wish to propose the following idea . . .' and then as his narration continues on the sound track the camera swiftly illustrates it by quick-cutting through a series of nymphet-type adolescents – schoolgirls, store girls, cinema usherettes, etc. What disconcerted the censor was the explicitness of this 'proposal'. The oblique and sophisticated depiction of the idea he was prepared to permit, but he did not relish the risk of putting Nabokov's possibly stimulating theory of nymphets so directly into people's minds. Moreover, it offered a dangerous generalisation from a case history that censors would prefer audiences to believe was rare and specific to Humbert Humbert. The sequence did not appear in the finished film.

Much of the censor's work in the case of *Lolita* was done for him in the sense that his objections were anticipated by Kubrick and Nabokov – both, incidentally, brilliant chess players skilled at seeing moves well ahead – who then absorbed them artistically into the construction of their film. The outcome was not nearly so happy in the case of Mai Zetterling's *Loving Couples* (1965), a Swedish film based on a once-daring novel about sexual emancipation and upper-class immorality in the 1920s. The sequence that particularly worried the censor was a flashback showing one of the three heroines as a child being picked up outside a confectioner's by a portly, middle-aged man who indulges her sweet tooth, then takes her back home with him, serves her wine and with elaborate courtliness waltzes slowly round the room with her. In the uncut version of the film he then becomes more physically affectionate, at which the child whimpers and pushes him away. The scene ends with the man deeply ashamed of what he has tried to do. It was

* *Lolita*, by Vladimir Nabokov (Weidenfeld & Nicolson), p. 18.

extraordinarily pathetic. The cut requested by the censor came at the moment in the scene when the pair are dancing, so that it ended as they both waltzed past the camera. While this excluded the man's grosser display of affection, it also excluded any evidence that the child resisted it. As a result, the cut sequence became disquietingly ambiguous and at least one influential critic on a London paper, who had not seen the uncut film, referred to the scene as if the child had acquiesced in her own seduction.

The censor obviously erred on the side of caution. He preferred to have the scene misinterpreted rather than risk it stimulating a sexual psychopath who might have seen it uncut. But his artistic caution may also have been induced by the fact that Mai Zetterling, an accomplished actress, had still to make her reputation as a director. If the sequence had come in, say, an Ingmar Bergman film, it is quite possible that Bergman's proven artistry and world-wide renown would have got it more tolerant treatment.

Loving Couples is not the only case where censoring of a scene has inadvertently made its implications appear worse. A sequence in John Schlesinger's *Darling* (1965) showed the career girl of the title, played by Julie Christie, being taken along to a smart Paris brothel by Laurence Harvey to witness a sexual exhibition. In the uncut version these two characters are sitting round the room along with with other clients while a lady in a plastic raincoat sits alone on the bed. Everyone is obviously waiting for something to happen. What happens is that footsteps are heard running down the corridor, in bursts a young man already stripping off his clothes and apologising profusely in French for keeping the company waiting. '*Le parking est affreux*,' he gasps out, or words to that effect. The scene then fades out, having made its ironic point that even those who indulge rich voyeurs have to take account of mundane matters like parking restrictions. In the cut version the effect was quite different. There the scene was faded out well before Plastic Raincoat's partner made his belated entry. The impression given to some filmgoers was that the people in the room were there to witness not a sexual display by two performers, but a solo performance by the woman. Again it seems an ill-judged cut.

But it is instructive to ask what exactly the censor was censoring when he made it. It reminds one of an earlier film, Delbert Mann's *Bachelor Party* (1957), in which a bunch of office friends, having a stag night out, are glimpsed viewing a 'blue' home movie. Nothing at all of the movie is seen: only the expressions of the men's faces, some bored, some fascinated, some embarrassed ... But the sequence was deleted when the film was screened in Britain, at the request of Trevelyan's predecessor who was a much more rigidly orthodox man. Presumably he was censoring the thoughts passing through the men's minds – or the thoughts that such a sequence might suggest to filmgoers wondering what the men might be thinking! Now a censor cannot be expected to approve of orgy-watchers, even ones as old-fashioned as the people in *Darling* who go over to Paris for their spectator sport. But in cutting the sequence short, it is likely that the censor was not indicting their moral turpitude as much as the artistic taste of a film that often left one in doubt about where its own sense of values lay. *Darling* was meant to expose the English *dolce vita* set through the corrupt rise of a cover girl who uses sex to procure herself wealth and status till she finally gets her come-uppance in the shape of that modish twentieth-century malaise – boredom with it all. The censor saw the screenplay in advance and viewed a rough cut of the finished film. The story's episodes were linked by a commentary representing Julie Christie talking about herself to a glossy-magazine interviewer. It was the contrast between her story as she was sweetening it for publication and as one actually saw it happening which the censor expected would give the film a moral framework. It did not work out like that. The Christie narration in the completed film was so vague and intermittent that it hardly impinged on the main story at all. *Darling* did not try to excuse how the people in it behaved, but its view of them was frequently out of focus. Penelope Houston summed up this criticism which was much more general in Britain than in the United States, when she wrote: 'Its disillusionment looks like that of a gossip columnist who has left the party with a monumental hangover, but will be back next day to see how all the awful people are contriving to amuse themselves.'* The brothel scene in the censor's view told one nothing new about the

* *Sight and Sound*, Autumn, 1965.

characters, emphasised nothing that had not already been clear; and to a censor already perturbed by *Darling*'s blurred morality it seemed artistic self-indulgence to stage a sequence like it simply for the sake of an ironic pay-off. It was not foreseen how perversely suggestive some people would find the cut scene.

* * *

Darling ran into censorship trouble in the United States because of Julie Christie's fleeting nude scene near the end of the film.* Nudity, partial or complete, tends to be treated more tolerantly in Britain, though again it must be justified by the context, the skill or reputation of the film and its maker. The American censor is said to have requested some fifty cuts in *The Amorous Adventures of Moll Flanders* (1965) to satisfy the Legion of Decency's objections about the amount of bosom displayed in it by Kim Novak as Defoe's picaresque trollop. Trevelyan was faced with similar though far, far fewer objections from some of his examiners. Nevertheless, he passed the film uncut on the grounds that its bawdy literary origins and the farcial tone of its story rendered Kim Novak's obtrusive charms rather innocuous. The scene he *did* hestiate over passing was a long shot of Moll emerging from a lake, apparently nude, when surprised by highwaymen. This finally got by on the producer's assurance that all the decencies were observed during the shooting. A film that arrives with prestige behind it can be fairly sure of the censor's artistic sympathy with its use of nudity. *Une Femme Mariée* (1964), Jean-Luc Godard's dissection of Parisian adultery, was passed quite uncut despite its nude love scenes – likewise *Woman of the Dunes* (1964), an erotic fable directed by Hiroshi Teshigahara about a man and woman who are forced by circumstances into living together in a deep sand pit in wild Japan. The censor decided it would utterly destroy the point of such films to cut them. Yet it is worth noting the type of nudity they involved. It was not at all easily censorable. In *Une Femme Mariée*, the lovers' naked bodies were posed together, bit by bit, an arm on a shoulder, hands round a thigh, fingers across a breast, like still pictures of an anatomy lesson, chopped up further by surgical editing, clinically

* See next chapter for fuller account.

lighted. As far as sex went, it was a vivisectionist's view: *morceaux choisis* scarcely stimulating, and even curiously dissatisfying to anyone not in a suitable mood of empathy.

Woman of the Dunes with its sand-brushed bare bodies was more tangibly erotic. But again the camera went in for isolating parts of the anatomy, this time magnifying them to a degree that made it hard to be sure of exactly which part of the human figure one was looking at. Sex was reduced to practically abstract art: a form more resistant to censorship than any representational style. A man is going to feel very foolish if what he takes to be a groin turns out as just a magnified thumb joint.

While the censor can have the last word in deciding cuts, bans and classifications, it should be remembered that the British Board of Film Censors does not differ markedly from any human group where opinions are not to be synchronised like watches. Disagreements do occur, for not all the panel of examiners travel at the same speed of enlightenment. It is not often, of course, that disagreements persist; but when they do, some diplomatic compromises have had to be evolved. There was the case of *The Balcony* (1963). Director Joseph Strick filmed this version of Jean Genet's play as a Hollywood fringe production on the low budget of $200,000, with Shelley Winters playing the omnipotent madam of a brothel – now adapted to look like the set on the sound stage of a film studio – whose clients purchase new identities and work off old obsessions. A clerk buys the fantasy of being a judge and extorts a confession from a prostitute; a milkman buys the fantasy that he is a general and tries to saddle a whore; and a meter-reader buys the fantasy that he is a prelate and prepares to absolve another prostitute. Trevelyan felt that the film's origins and Strick's direction made a most interesting and responsibly handled film, one which would have a limited appeal that ought not to be exploited in order to draw in the mere sensation-seekers. But there were doubts among his examiners; and he himself had to consider the possibility that some of the Press reaction to the film might overemphasise its sexual aspects to its detriment and the board's embarrassment. So while witholding a Certificate for the time being, he looked around for a way of testing public opinion and newspaper reaction and hoped to find it when the film was entered in the 1963 Edinburgh Festival where it did not need to have a censorship Certificate. Instead, most of the critics, very inconveniently for Trevelyan, merely noted the film's existence and said they would review it at its London première.

It is quite legal for club cinemas in London to show films which have no censor's Certificate; but at that date some of the highly reputable club cinemas which have sprung up since did not exist. Trevelyan was unwilling to see *The Balcony* included in the usual programmes of 'nudies' which the others screened. It was therefore suggested to the distributors of *The Balcony* that they apply to the then London County Council (now Greater London Council) for a special licence enabling the film to be shown publicly in the L.C.C. area. This was done and the licence granted. On went the film. Out came the reviews. The majority were favourable. And with this test of public opinion to support them, the censorship board were able to give the film an 'X' Certificate when the distributors wanted to show it outside London. It was a typical British compromise, all parties feeling they had won. Trevelyan still wonders, however, what the consequences would have been if the reviews had gone against the film.

British film critics do more than they are sometimes aware of to encourage the censor's liberalism. Press clippings from a wide range of national and provincial papers are received by the censor in the course of his work and often quoted at recalcitrant film-makers whose opportunism outruns their artistry, or at local councils who censure the censor for being 'the tool of the cinema trade'. But this is not usually a two-way process. No distributor has yet felt like appealing to critics in order to help him obtain a Certificate for a film he anticipates will be banned. Sometimes one senses a reluctance to embarrass the censor by letting him in for this type of controversy. One such film from Sweden dealt with a rehabilitation centre for delinquent boys, but managed in the course of its story to include a homosexual government official who seduced the boys, an orgy aboard a merchant ship, a student counsellor who turns pimp, a beatnik girl who shares the boys' dormitory and a scene in which the girl is held down while an

Alsatian dog – to judge from the off-screen panting it makes – is forced into intercourse with her. The chance of this film getting a Certificate was bleak. It eventually opened at a club cinema, where it did not need one, but the critics were not invited to review it although other films at the same club cinema had been Press shown. Presumably the distributors had decided that Press comment would be unlikely to create a public opinion in favour of giving the film a wider showing – and a Certificate. No doubt this suited the censor's view of it too.

What the censor may decide to do with a film often depends on what the distributors intend to do with it. Obviously it is not in his interest to have a film he has passed exploited for the 'wrong' reasons. He has no control over the way films are advertised: that is left to self-regulation by the film publicity groups and local authorities. Sometimes the way a film is advertised is so sex-obsessed and sensational that the censor catches the blame for passing a film that may have been wildly misrepresented on the posters or in the newspaper advertisements. Certain cinemas even make a practice of plastering their marquees with graffiti of pejorative Press quotes – 'Disgusting', 'Sickening', 'Perverted', etc., to lure in audiences who wish to partake of the promised feast. Joseph Losey's distinguished film *Eve* (1962), which featured Stanley Baker and Jeanne Moreau, was advertised outside one cinema as 'A Dirty Sexy Film Brilliantly Acted and Directed', no doubt in the hope of appealing to both the purists and the prurient.

However the title of a film can be – and is – regulated by the film censor. The board permitted a film called *Girls' Dormitory* (1953), but turned down the title that had previously been submitted – *French Girls' Dormitory*. It has also insisted that a Brigitte Bardot film be called *Warrior's Rest* (1962), a literal translation of the French title, *Le Repos du Guerrier*, instead of the distributor's first choice – *Love on a Pillow*. It is easy to quote these examples and imply that they show how small-minded and intolerant the censor is. It is often ignored that it is in such ways as these that the censor signifies his displeasure at commercial opportunism taking advantage of his liberalising policy. Small harrying tactics can be more persuasive than major show-downs.

Sometimes a censor will pass a film uncut, but make a gentleman's agreement with the distributor concerning its screening and advertising. If it is destined for exhibition in cinemas catering for sophisticated audiences, and if the advertising is 'responsible', well and good. But if it eventually gets wider distribution through the circuits, or chains of cinemas, the distributor agrees to re-submit it to the censor for a second look at it in this new context. Occasionally the distributor will request the censor to take a second look at a film with an 'X' Certificate and make cuts to change it into an 'A' Certificate and give it a wider audience. This can have some ironical results. One Continental film made by a distinguished director received an 'X' Certificate from the censor who felt that while it contained a violent scene of sexual assault, its overall integrity and artistry were plain to see. The film did extremely well in London and came to the attention of one of the big cinema circuits who booked it for country-wide distribution largely on the strength of the uncut sequence in the original version. However, the distributor, honouring his gentleman's agreement, referred the film back to the censor and by the time the film went on release the sequence had been somewhat trimmed. Much later the censor accidentally discovered that the eminent director of the film had been under pressure from his producers to make the sexual assault in the film look as sensational as possible. One would like to think that the moral of all this is that integrity is not so easily mocked. It may seem to some that the censor was being over-prudent in cutting the film for a wider audience. But the kind of sensationalising treatment that a film is given in the publicising of it rubs off on his censorship board and it pays him to be wary. After making one agreement with distributors about how they should advertise a certain film, he was disconcerted to see it publicised as 'The Hottest Picture Since *Room At the Top*.' The distributors lamely replied that as it was a 'weak' 'X' Certificate film, it had had to be 'beefed up.'

* * *

At the end of 1965 new censorship regulations for London were announced by the Greater London Council. The general aim of them was to restrict the scope of the Council's film censorship 'to preventing those kinds of harm which the Law seeks to prevent in relation to the printed and spoken word.' The arts, it was observed, 'are sometimes intended to be disturbing'. Moreover, in determining whether the effect of a film is such as to tend to deprave and corrupt persons who are likely to see it, the film should be viewed 'as a whole'. Some critics of the British Board of Film Censors have interpreted these new regulations – which only operate if a distributor appeals to the G.L.C. against the film censor's decision – as being much more liberal than the censorship board's. But in effect they are the endorsement of policies that the censor has been evolving in a characteristically pragmatic way and are likely to make him feel surer of his ground in deciding to give Certificates to films that hitherto would have had to be screened in club cinemas. But the new situation does have one unrevealed irony.

In 1960, Lord Morrison of Lambeth – formerly Herbert Morrison, the Labour Party stalwart and Government Minister – was appointed President of the British Board of Film Censors. His experience as a skilful tactician at all levels of politics, national but especially local, was regarded at the time as a great asset to the board in its dealings with local authorities. The board was then discreetly sounding out opinion for an 'AA' Certificate – which would simplify the censor's task when he had to decide between a straight 'A' or 'X' for a film. It would be a double warning to parents that the film was unsuitable for children, but would not prevent the former from bringing their children if they so wished. (It would also please film distributors who disliked losing the 'family audience' and who took a fairly cynical and probably correct view of the average parent's preoccupation with the films his children saw.) Lord Morrison, however, despite being an ex-chairman of London County Council, failed to stir up any clinching enthusiasm for the scheme among the county and municipal associations. The plan for an 'AA' Certificate was quietly shelved. This was disappointing. But much more disturbing in the opinion of many film makers, was the way Lord Morrison, once installed, gradually began to make his own moral judgments on some of the films the board was asked to certificate. He was ill-equipped for this highly sophisticated task. A man of the widest humanity so far as his

The scene that successfully challenged the Hollywood Code: an actress in Sidney Lumet's film, *The Pawnbroker*, revealed herself partially nude and, for the first time, bare breasts were adjudged no disqualification for the Motion Picture Association of America's Seal of Approval, though the Legion of Decency still protested that they were 'never necessary.' (*Frame enlargement.*)

Stages of Seduction: a series of shots from the sequence in Joseph Losey's film *The Servant*, in which Sarah Miles

seduces the spoilt young master played by James Fox. The British censor passed it uncut.

Love Vivisected: *Above:* Macha Meril, and lover, in Jean-Luc Godard's *Une Femme Mariée. Below: Une Femme Mariée*, was made with enough visible integrity to be passed uncut by the British censor, despite its nude scenes. At the same time, its characteristic way of showing only parts of the lovers' intertwined bodies—and seldom the more traditionally erotic parts – made censorship unusually difficult.

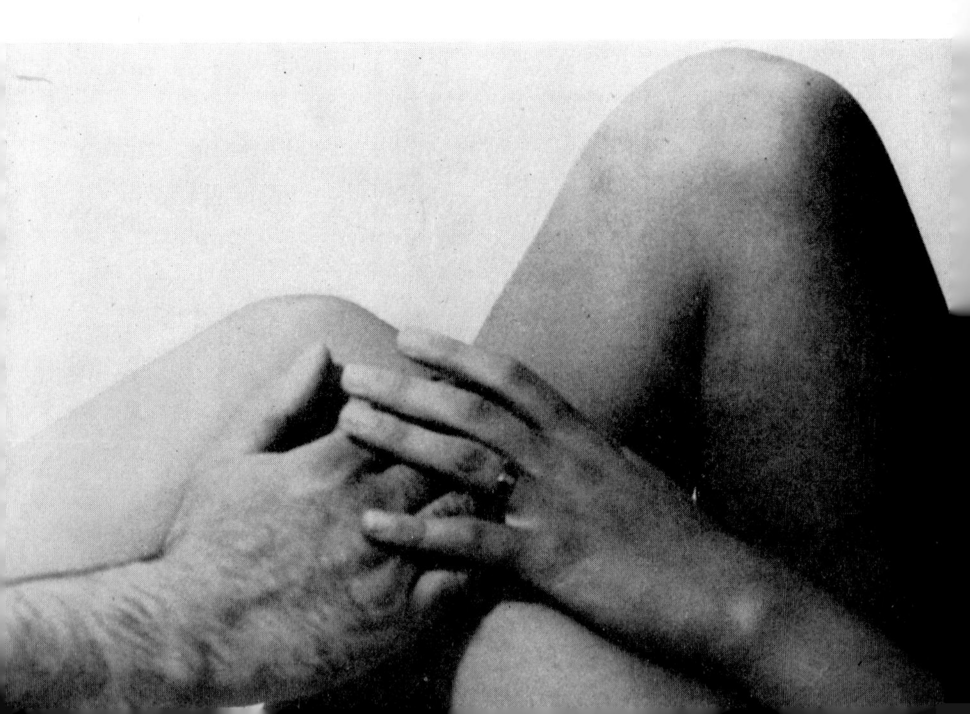

fellow men were concerned, he proved to have a much narrower outlook in specific respects. He made no secret of the fact that he disapproved forcefully of homosexuality, of loose living among teenage youth, and of whores and tarts, and his disapproval was vented on films which featured these things. A political radical in his youth, he turned into something of a moral reactionary in his semi-retirement. He knew nothing about aesthetics. If he had had his way, some films would have found it extremely hard to get a public showing. While executive authority in this respect had been lodged with the board's secretary, Lord Morrison was responsible for more general censorship policy and he would have made it much more difficult for the board to pursue an enlightened policy on moral and artistic values. His appointment as president was for a period of five years and he died shortly before its expiry. It is unlikely that he would have been re-appointed. He did not live to see London County Council, his old feuding ground and the scene of the party political victories of his youth, endorse a policy on film censorship which he would have viewed with grave misgivings.

The new attitude to morality played a significant part in the choice of Morrison's successor, Lord Harlech, formerly Sir David Ormsby-Gore who was British Ambassador to Washington under the Kennedy Administration. Lord Harlech is a relatively young man with a teenage family – assets in a job which calls on him both to protect the young and also keep up with the changes in sexual morality, which is largely a young person's morality today. His first-hand experience of America is of value to the censorship board in its negotiations with Hollywood companies, while his cultural background is of advantage in the increasingly frequent adjudication on a film-maker's artistry.

A pragmatic system of censorship like Britain's is bound to have inconsistencies, hypocrisies and easily mockable compromises. But would abolishing it really increase the bounds of sexual and artistic freedom in any beneficial way? It would almost certainly increase the pressures on many film-makers of repute to ignore standards and values. 'Money is Hollywood's guiding light in living with censorship,' says the American critic Murray Schumach.* He was referring to the American film industry's massive opposition to any plan for classifying films on the lines of Britain's 'A', 'U' and 'X' Certificates. Hollywood has always been afraid of such a system. The fear is that it would cut back box-office profits by limiting the audiences for certain kinds of movies. Yet it is in precisely this system that the source of the British censor's power is lodged. It has enabled him to impose standards on film-makers motivated solely by commercial profit, yet at the same time relax restraints to assist what he judges to be the truly creative talents. If this benevolent autocracy went, it would assuredly be replaced by the rule of money. It is an attractive argument to say, keep the system but change the censors. Many sincere opponents of British film censorship believe that an autocrat, however benevolent, is not the best guarantor of an artist's constitutional rights. But it is not at all certain that, say, an elected board of review would do better, or even as well. Inevitably its members would lack the power of discrimination which comes from cultivating personal contacts with film people, gaining inside knowledge, keeping an eye on all the stages of production, giving off-the-cuff advice when it is requested and generally evolving a sense of strategy for the day-to-day dealings with the industry. Moreover, such an anti-censorship view ignores the fact that the film-maker does not work in a constitutional democracy. The industry of which he is a part is made up of dozens of autocrats, many of them by no means benevolently disposed towards his artistic integrity. At the very least, the censor acts as an official conscience. But he can also, if so minded, if he has the will and ability, play an unofficial part in the creative side of film-making. The aim of this chapter has been to present him not necessarily in the best light – simply in this unaccustomed light.

* Murray Schumach, op. cit., p. 255.

CHAPTER NINE

MANY MEN'S POISON: AMERICAN CENSORSHIP

On March 29, 1965, a woman in an American-made film opened up her frock, exposed both of her breasts to the full, unobscured eye of the camera, thereby broke Section Seven, Sub-section Two of the Motion Picture Production Code – 'Indecent or undue exposure is forbidden' – and nevertheless succeeded in gaining the Hollywood censor's seal of approval. Quite a number of countries with film industries and censors had already met the challenge of similar scenes in their films without any perceptible quickening of breath. But this was the first time that nudity had been officially sanctioned in Hollywood; and one hardly knows whether to laugh or cry – probably both – at the sensation caused by such an example of late-in-the-day liberalism. It was hailed in film circles as a 'breakthrough' and a 'precedent-shattering step'. One commentator wrote: 'For the first time in the history of the Hollywood Production Code, official recognition has been given to the good taste and artistic merit with which a subject is treated, not only to whether it hews to the current standards by which the Code is interpreted.'* And the headline writers of *Variety*, those sardonic encapsulators of film industry mores, spelled out the same consequences with succinct pep: 'FILM ART REQUIRES NO BRA.'

Making allowances for the feverish mood in which they were uttered, all these pronouncements were soundly based. For over thirty years one of the most restrictive, unrealistic and hypocritically observed codes of conduct ever clamped on creative people had compelled Hollywood, in the name of morality, to conform to a series of anachronistic thou-shalt-nots. Now in the name of art the entire Code was threatened with revision, if not extinction. Never had Hollywood felt so emancipated – or so apprehensive.

* Ronald Gold, *Variety*, April 4, 1965.

The film that had successfully challenged the Code was called *The Pawnbroker* (1964). It hardly appeared iconoclastic. Directed by Sidney Lumet and starring Rod Steiger, it was the story of an East Harlem Jew going about his daily pawnbroking business, but being reminded by many a humdrum incident of his war-time ordeal in a German concentration camp. But there were enough unorthodox aspects to certain scenes for its backers to withdraw it from the major Hollywood studio for which they had intended to make it, and assign it instead to an independent producer, Ely A. Landau. After completion, *The Pawnbroker* was the official United States entry in the 1964 Berlin Film Festival. Landau then submitted it in the routine way to the industry's own self-regulating body, the Motion Picture Association of America, for a seal of approval. A seal is not required by law. Some films, notably Otto Preminger's comedy about virginity, *The Moon is Blue* (1953), have been refused seals but nevertheless been released and sometimes gone on to make enormous profits. But this is uncommon. Lack of a seal generally cuts down drastically the business a film can do. Many cinema chains are pledged not to play it, military establishments cannot screen it, TV networks shy away from buying it and local pressure groups turn their fire on it. The M.P.A.A.'s censorship arm, the Production Code Administration, ordered a cut to be made in *The Pawnbroker* – or no seal. The scene objected to showed a Negro harlot stripping to the waist to try and entice the old pawnbroker to pay her more for a trinket she was pawning. The sight of the half-naked woman made the pawnbroker remember his own naked wife being forced to submit to Nazi guards. Far from being put there for titillation, the producer insisted, the scene made a dramatic point and made it vividly.

In vain. The Production Code Administrator, Geoffrey Shurlock, replied in effect that he was bound to observe the letter of the Code, not the artistry of the film. Refusing to make the cut, Landau carried the case to the M.P.A.A. Appeals Board. A rare procedure: there were only six appeals between 1954 and 1964. On the board sit representatives of the major film distributors, independent producers and cinema owners; and plainly they knew the effect it would have on the industry when they upheld Landau's appeal and ordered his film to be given a seal, uncut.* They did not spell out their arguments publicly, so one can only guess at them. Perhaps they were satisfied with the scene's dramatic validity. Perhaps the fact that the woman was coloured counted as well: for films have always regarded the exposure of dark skins more indulgently than white. Then again the pawnbroker was an immigrant Jew who had suffered under Nazi tyranny; and many people in the American film industry are warmly responsive to the immigrant's experience and the Jewish tragedy in World War Two. At an informed guess, one would say this particular scene had quite a lot of emotional weight on its side. But the Appeals Board recognised the unique nature of their verdict by passing the word back to the chief censor that one pair of naked breasts did not licence a Saturnalia: and he was to continue, as before, turning down scenes of undue exposure.

This was an unrealistic piety. To some people it spelled the worst. Monsignor Thomas F. Little, the redoubtable executive secretary of the Legion of Decency, predicted that *The Pawnbroker* decision would 'open the flood gates to a host of unscrupulous operators out to make a quick buck'.† Bare breasts, he contended, were never 'necessary'. Presumably he meant 'necessary' to make a dramatic point; though the history of the Legion of Decency since 1934 might make one doubt that his words were to be interpreted in this narrower sense. (They irresistibly recall Marilyn Monroe's famous comment, 'The trouble with the censor is that he worries if a girl has cleavage. He should worry if she hasn't any.') Mgr Little refused to acknowledge the existence of any impasse in *The Pawnbroker* case. There was a blindingly simple solution. 'They could have had the same scene,' he was quoted as saying, 'and shot it from the back.'

* * *

Whether the American censors wished it or not, *The Pawnbroker* decision was to have all the consequences of an unexpected pregnancy. Just as one could not be simply 'a little pregnant,' so

* The British Board of Film Censors found no difficulty in passing the film uncut, with an 'X' Certificate, when it was submitted to them in 1966.

† *Variety*, April 4, 1965.

one could not hope to confine the effect of the Appeals Board ruling to one picture. Producers who thought their films had similar borderline scenes would now have a strong case for demanding similar licence. And why should it not be retroactive? What would happen if Elia Kazan, say, put back the nude scene deleted from *Splendour in the Grass* (1961) and asked for a seal of approval? As described by Murray Schumach, one of the few critics who saw this untrimmed scene, it showed Natalie Wood, driven hysterical by a sin-fixated mother, fleeing totally nude from her bath down a short hallway into her bedroom – she was seen only from the rear and in long shot. Speaking of the film some time later, Kazan said: 'I did the nude scene . . . because I thought it was the honest way. I still think so. It was not done for sensational reasons or as a promotion stunt . . . I was trying to stress the hysteria. A girl in her state would not stop to dry herself and put on clothes.'* The Hollywood censor ordered the scene to be cut, since 'complete nudity, in fact, or in silhouette, is never permitted'. And Kazan abandoned a lingering hope of convincing them of his artistic sincerity when he learned the Legion was against him too, with the effects that would have on the film's commercial fate.

More recent possibilities come to mind. *Darling*, the British-made film about an English playgirl's apotheosis into an Italian *principessa*, was released in America with a Code Seal, but without a brief nude scene. In this Julie Christie, as the heroine left all alone in her *palazzo*, wanders dispiritedly from room to room, finishing up in her bedroom with the unattractive prospect of, for once, going to bed alone. Wearily she draws her petticoat over her head – she has been undressing as she walks through her private apartments – and reveals herself fleetingly nude before falling face down across the bed in a spasm of wretchedness. The nudity was filmed from the back, but presumably the indulgence that the Legion of Decency grants this angle extends only down to the waist – for that shot had to go. Then some exceptionally sharp-eyed person, a true vigilante, detected that in falling on to the bed, still clutching her petticoat to her, Miss Christie had momentarily exposed her bosom. What a fractional infringement of the Production Code this must

* Murray Schumach, op. cit., p. 8.

have been is evident from the steps taken to rectify it. The frames of the film in which the alleged exposure occurred were enlarged in a laboratory, the excess of breast was shaved off, and then the whole was reduced again to almost standard size. A strip-tease girl reflected in a distorting mirror in one sequence of *The Spy Who Came in from the Cold* (1965) also had to have her image adjusted in the same way.

With the precedent of *The Pawnbroker* to back them, film-makers like Joseph Janni, producer of *Darling*, or Martin Ritt, producer-director of *The Spy Who Came in from the Cold*, could have appealed for a seal of approval if they so wished. The lesson for the M.P.A.A. was disconcertingly clear. To extricate itself from an untenable position, it needed a new set of standards by which to judge films. It needed, in short, to revise the Production Code. Those who had set themselves up to say what was moral were now being forced into a position where they had to say what was art. Some people felt an ironic satisfaction in the reflection that it had all been precipitated by the promiscousness of a screen harlot.

* * *

The *Pawnbroker* affair was one of several far-ranging dilemmas that were changing the nature of American film censorship in 1964–65. A cauldron of incompatibles that had simmered fretfully for three decades suddenly boiled over into a morality crisis. Basic to the crisis was the fact that Hollywood's hankering for greater latitude in the choice and treatment of sexual themes could no longer be held in check. The relaxation of the ban on nudity coincided with a series of blows that shook the whole system of censorship. There occurred a wave of aggressively candid sex films. The Roman Catholic Church accused the film industry of practising the sin of 'moral brinkmanship'. The Legion of Decency clashed head-on with the Production Code Administration. And the progressives were greatly emboldened by the verdicts of several Courts affecting the power of State boards to censor films in advance of their public screening: one such judgment was summed up in *Variety* as, 'NEW YORK MUST POWDER BLUE NOSE'. Blue noses everywhere were put very much out of joint by these events.

The one thing which created the atmosphere conducive to all the other things happening was the growing unreality of the Production Code. This amazing document, written by a Jesuit priest in collaboration with a Roman Catholic publisher, was adopted in 1930 by film chiefs in order to ward off State or Federal censorship. To bring home how its obscurantist absurdities have persisted, it is only necessary to mention that *in the year 1965* it still officially ordained that adultery must not be explicitly treated, brothels might not be clearly identified as such, open-mouthed kissing and lustful embraces were not to be shown, seduction should never be more than suggested, and while abortion might be referred to, it must never be referred to by the word 'abortion'. Instead of having one individual who was empowered to use his discretion over a wide area of movie morality, as was the case in Britain, the American film industry abdicated power to a document that specified in black and white which of the facts of life could be filmed and which could not. Even so, Hollywood might have slipped its head out of the noose little by little, and left its critics feeling that at least it had shown itself willing to acquiesce in its own artistic strangulation, but for the formation of the Legion of Decency in 1934. The Legion gave the Code militant backing. It turned it from a declaration of piety into a dictatorship of virtue. The Legion itself decided what was 'virtuous' by grading films all the way from the 'morally unobjectionable for general patronage' up to the stark dismissal – 'Condemned'. It backed up its classifications with pledges committing Legion members to 'condemn indecent and immoral pictures' and to 'stay away from places of entertainment which show them as a matter of policy'. In short, it buttressed movie morality by the fear of boycott.

In assessing the ratings it gave to films, the Legion paid no attention to artistic, technical or dramatic values – only moral content. This content is judged from the viewpoint of the Roman Catholic Church, even though the Legion's attitude when translated into censorship cuts affects the freedom of non-Catholics to see what the film producer might wish to show them. The concept of 'freedom' in this case means the freedom to act as one ought. The Legion has stated many times that it has never initiated the censor-

Mastroianni rampant: the public image of a masterful lover or incorrigible ladies man was subtly assisted by cinema posters, such as the one for 8½ – which actually depicted the phlegmatic hero's amorous fantasy.

Mastroianni couchant: the 'schoolboyish eagerness' of the historical Casanova is replaced by the anxiety of a modern lover in *Casanova 70* who finds himself unequal to the opportunity.

ship of a film – that the film-makers always approach it for an opinion. This is probably quite true. But it is hardly significant. It merely indicates the prudence of the producers, not the liberalism of the Legion. Major film-makers have been chary of attacking the Legion publicly, though some have talked in private of testing the legality of action that they allege to be in restraint of trade. None of them has yet done so. The official censors at the Production Code Administration have to keep watch on both flanks. If they are too rigorous, they risk angering the Hollywood film industry. If they are too broadminded in granting seals of approval, they risk the wrath of the Legion of Decency. There is a third risk, too. If they refuse to approve a film, it is still open to the producer to submit it to the Legion of Decency for a rating. It is long odds against his getting anything less than a 'Condemned' classification; but the barest possibility of it must be an unspoken consideration in the adjudication of border-line films.

The censors are often accused of obeying the letter of the Production Code, not the spirit of it. This is too simple a view. The truth is, if they only obeyed the letter of it, the Code would be unworkable. From its adoption in 1930, the Code has preserved a view of morality that is both utopian and sectarian. Critics of it sometimes make the mistake of concluding that because the main body of supporters for the Code were Roman Catholic clerics and laymen, its principles must enshrine Roman Catholic doctrines. They do not. Though penned by a Jesuit priest, Father Lord, they are quite non-denominational in their *wording*. It is the principle underlying their *working* that reflects their Roman Catholic inspiration. For it is based on the belief that the sinful can be redeemed through the technique of penance. In the censorship manual, this goes under the name of 'moral compensation'. It means that whoever commits a sin or a crime in a film must be made to suffer remorse, or repentance, or retribution – the degree of each to be apportioned to the gravity of the offence. The man credited with the development of this technique was the late Joseph Ignatius Breen, a former Roman Catholic newspaperman who was appointed chief censor in 1934. (He retired in 1954 and died in 1965.) Ruth A. Inglis, in *Freedom of the Movies*, describes how Breen used to figure out compensating moral values for the screenplays submitted to him for approval before shooting. A good Roman Catholic, he would appear to have secularised his Church's technique of expiating sin in order to make the utopian morality of the Production Code workable in terms of film making. His technique has outlived him. 'Details of sin,' the present chief censor has said, 'have to be balanced against details of compensation. There would be no sense in too much retribution for too little sin. This, of course, is not our problem. Ours is the other extreme of too much sin and too little compensation.'* This principle which makes the Code workable is responsible, more than any other, for making it also practically worthless. It has fostered a view of morality that is frequently false and hypocritical – in which sin and punishment are nicely adjusted to each other, yet the link between cause and effect is seldom made convincing. The Code's moral imperative of a virtuous ending is no more conducive to a realistic view of life than Hollywood's old commercial imperative of a happy ending. Moral compensation opens the screen to subjects specifically forbidden by the Code, on condition that film-makers do not treat them honestly. Moreover the sophistry of the film censors in this branch of their work has been matched by the increasing sophistication of the film-makers, so that no longer need sensational themes be treated crudely. The 'quality' movie that dangles the salacious promise of sex can accommodate its bland dishonesty to the requirements of the Code more easily than one that deals honestly with the sex act itself. Nowhere is this trend more in evidence than in the treatment of the Hollywood Prostitute and in the use made of what one can call Auditory Sex.

* * *

The Hollywood Prostitute is the favourite playgirl of film censors. She bears little resemblance to the prostitute found in other cities of the world. She is the creation of movie morality. Traditionally, she is depicted with a heart of gold. And this is not her only organ or faculty which has been adapted for the screen's peculiar morality. She has a roving eye, but it is a curiously

* Quoted by Murray Schumach, op. cit., p. 45.

unbusiness-like one. She is sexy, but in a way that suggests sex is not the first thing in her thoughts. She must never be shown as actually willing and able to sell her body for money: the transaction should be sentimental rather than commercial and yet must not be made enjoyable. *Never on Sunday* (1959) was released in America without a seal of approval from the censors because the eupeptic Greek whore played by Melina Mercouri actually relished being the life, body and soul of the Piraeus waterfront.

Vice can be depicted going on all round the Hollywood Prostitute: but frequently her role is so passive, or half-hearted at best, that the story seems to have planted her in the brothel simply to explore the much more titillating environment around her. She should never appear to have chosen her profession, but rather been pushed into it. Consequently she is usually found to have been given an upsetting start in life – e.g. rape by a relative or stranger at an impressionable age. Getting out of her profession, dead or alive, with Production Code seal or without it, depends on the degree of contriteness she shows, though the rules can be bent if she shows a sufficient degree of maladjustment to her work. Promiscuity seems to be pardonable by the censors: nymphomania has led to some messy car crashes in the last reels.

John O'Hara's story in *Butterfield* 8 illustrates a basic type of Hollywood Prostitute. As its wanton heroine, Gloria Wandrous, Elizabeth Taylor started one up in the censor's favour, having the mitigating circumstance of a disagreeable childhood experience to explain what has made her take it out on men ever since. The opening scene finds her on Sunday morning, the Scotch on her breath, in the bed of a married man – Laurence Harvey. But since he is out when she wakes up there is no censorship problem. Eddie Fisher is then introduced as moral collateral for giving Gloria the benefit of the doubt: he plays her steady boy-friend, a teenage father-figure, who has loved her platonically since they were so high. By now the Moral Compensator is working full blast. Gloria continues her bed-hopping, but entirely without desire for gain: she gets angry with men who offer her money and scrawls 'NOT FOR SALE' in lipstick on their wall mirrors. What she wants is pure love. The censors might understandably have been anxious at her persistence in seeking this quality in motel bedrooms, instead of in marriage, were it not for the fact that her constant quarrels with Harvey show her having a miserable time. When things do take a dangerous turn towards a happy *and* immoral ending – he has left his wife, she has left her analyst, so both are free to settle down in sin and live comfortably ever after – a mink coat separates them. (The Production Code gives plenty of employment to such Anti-Cupids.) By stealing the mink out of Harvey's wife's closet, Gloria somehow forfeits her status as an amateur whore. This damns her. A car crash kills her. Her lover is left choking over a surprising epitaph – surprising, that is, to all but the official assessors of moral compensation. 'Everything in her,' says Harvey, 'was struggling to be respectable.'

The truth is that everything in *Butterfield* 8 was struggling to be sensational, with a free abuse of such words as 'lush', 'slut', 'lechery', and 'brothel', but masking its intentions with a cloud of moral compensation. Given a redeeming touch of honesty, the theme might have been tragic instead of merely sordid.

The Hollywood Prostitute probably achieves her most soulful incarnation in Capucine and Carroll Baker. To find a realistic equivalent for the contemporary brothels they inhabited in *Walk on the Wild Side* (1962) and *Sylvia* (1965) respectively, one would need to go back to the age when the first brothel was a temple and the resident goddess was worshipped in the person of the sacred prostitute. But however smoothly this worked in Antiquity, it seems out of place amid the folk ways of twentieth-century America. Nevertheless Capucine as the prize boarder of a New Orleans brothel is the Production Code equivalent of the sacred prostitute, incredibly pure, untouchable, preoccupied with things of the spirit. Except for suggesting that she is rather indolent by nature, the film offers no explanation for her choice of profession. She adds nothing to the profit of the brothel, though plenty to its tone, for she is a sculptress in her off-hours. If she condescends to importune a client it is with a request to buy her a Brancusi. If she quotes anything at him, it is not her price but a line from T. S. Eliot. Artistic talent is, in fact, a common way of working moral compensation into a sex picture. A touch of Bohemian temperament, it is felt, helps excuse a character's excesses. Sculpture is popular for the obvious reason that it permits partial nudity, or the suggestion of total nudity, with at least a plausible defence of necessity. Thus Elizabeth Taylor, a sculptress in *The Sandpiper*, poses nude to the waist for a fellow artist, chastely covering her bosom when disturbed by the minister she seduces. And Susan Hayward in *Where Love Has Gone* (1964) is a society sculptress, 'one of the truly greats', whose nymphomania is handily implied by the statues of male nudes which she sculpts from models picked up on the San Francisco waterfront. The only model one actually glimpses, bolting from her bedroom, is wearing sweater and slacks: it may not be the Greek ideal of male beauty, but it at least allows Hollywood to combine artistic integrity, the sex drive and censor-proof suggestiveness, all in one shot.

Capucine's brothel in *Walk on the Wild Side* has an antiseptic atmosphere in line with the Production Code's ruling that 'brothels in any clear identification as such may not be shown'. Identification in this film is so tentative that Laurence Harvey, as Capucine's ex-beau, imagines she is housed in some kind of Y.W.C.A. hostel, in spite of the girls who drift around in lacy nighties in mid-afternoon.

Yet there is one significant shred of realism in this picture: the madam is a Lesbian and is played as such by Barbara Stanwyck. *Walk on the Wild Side* was one of the first films to take advantage of the Production Code's special revision of October, 1961, to permit 'sex aberrations' to be shown if treated with 'care, discretion and restraint'. This was a belated effort to update the Code in one respect at least, but its effect on the Hollywood Prostitute was baneful. She became less real than ever, certainly less real than the scene around her which now filled up with enough sexual activity, normal and abnormal, to furnish the curriculum at an institute of sexology. As the whore got purer, the environment got kinkier until at last the Code was virtually stood on its head. Previously it had banned prostitution from the screen 'unless shown in contrast to right standards of behaviour'. Now it looked as if the prostitute existed primarily to provide a moral contrast to the wrong standards of behaviour she had to tolerate around her.

This trend reached a climax in the movie *Sylvia*. What such a film would suggest to a cynic is that the benefits of a good brothel far outweigh the combined advantages of a finishing school and a convent education. Sylvia, played by Carroll Baker, gets the standard start in her kind of life by being raped by her drunken step-father. But once again culture is the salvation of her. A lady librarian has already introduced her to the works of Jane Austen, so that Sylvia is able to enjoy the whore's traditional prerogative in an altogether superior way: she gives her body, but keeps her mind for literature. She only quits her trade when one caller shocks her with a book that is less than wholesome; and she goes off to acquire 'Europe, travel, culture,' before settling down in Beverly Hills on some wisely invested immoral earnings. There she writes poetry, cultivates prize roses and receives a proposal of marriage from a millionaire.

The whole tale of vice triumphant was made acceptable to the censors by several strategems. Although there is little evidence that Sylvia was ever corrupted, it cannot be denied that an ex-prostitute who advances from whoring to horticulture has been thoroughly rehabilitated in the eyes of the censors. Then again the film is riddled with moral compensations. When she hires herself out as a hooker in a night-club, it is simply to pay another whore's hospital bills. Thirdly, Carroll Baker plays her as if the character had gone through life in a sanitised wrapping. Not as much as a sneeze does she catch from a cast of sleazy types around her, all of them waving a Production Code dispensation on the grounds that they are necessary to contrast with 'right standards of behaviour.' As well as the rapist step-father and the librarian who seems to be Lesbian at the edges, they include a con-man preacher, an adulterous salesman, an alcoholic saleslady, a well-connected pervert and a transvestite club-owner. These characters were acted and directed more sharply than the null and void Sylvia: they made the film more entertaining than it deserved to be. One is not objecting to their presence on the screen on moral grounds, but simply to the mechanistic division of virtue and vice that *Sylvia*'s makers had to resort to in order to get the characters on the screen at all.

It is worth noting that while *Sylvia* got a Production Code seal, it was attacked by the Legion of Decency which gave it a 'B' rating – 'morally objectionable in part for all' – and caused a cut of forty-five seconds to be made in the rape scene which, in the producer's view, left it 'more lurid than it was before' since it no longer showed the girl's distaste for her experience. 'Now I can't tell whether the rape was enjoyed or not,' he complained. The Legion apparently had no such doubts. And indeed why should it? Where bare breasts are deemed to be never 'necessary', is it to be conceived that rape is ever 'enjoyable'?

* * *

In 1960 the rotund and restless showman-producer, Joseph E. Levine, was named Motion Picture Pioneer of the Year. Mr Levine was later to produce *The Carpetbaggers* (1964) and *Harlow* (1965), two of his best-known films; but what he had pioneered in 1960 was the sales technique of buying up a third-rate, Italian-made, sex-and-action 'epic' like *Hercules Unchained* (1958) for a modest $120,000, spending at least $600,000 on ballyhooing it, and grossing some $5,000,000 on it. In envious Hollywood such success tended to obscure another pioneering feat of Levine's, namely the technique of Auditory Sex. Auditory Sex consists of putting into the dialogue the sexual implications that the censors would not allow to be put explicitly into the visuals. The sex in a Levine film is strictly for the ear, not the eye, though publicity must suggest that the eye is catered for, too. In *The Carpetbaggers* and *Where Love Has Gone* lust, lechery and perversion are continually being implied by the characters – but by word rather than deed:

'What do you want to see on your honeymoon, darling?' – 'Lots and lots of lovely ceilings.'

'For once the hero is going to let the heroine show herself properly grateful.' – 'Properly?'

'My films add dignity and culture to the movie industry.' – 'And three starlets a week to your bed.'

'What's the wildest thing you've ever done?' – 'I was hoping I hadn't done it yet.'

'The fans write in for her autograph. If only they knew that just by pushing her doorbell they could get everything.'

'You have only one concept of love, a vile and sinful one.' – 'If you're dying of thirst you drink from a mud hole.'

'I was shocked to find you could write such letters.' – 'Are you jealous, mother?'

'You say your daughter was a very ordinary girl. At her age, most ordinary girls are (pause) virgins.'

'He was no good at double-entry book-keeping, but he was a real pro at double-entry house-keeping.'

The dialogue is the most sexually pithy part of such films – otherwise they give the impression that sex is something regulated by clockwork mechanism, that the characters are coupling every hour on the hour. Next to its Auditory Sex, what provides *The Carpetbaggers* with its liveliest moments is not love-making: it is money-making. One suspects that it is with this drive that the producer really identifies. His films seem to one to be perfect examples of the work of a film-maker for whom story options, production budgets, collateral financing, box-office grosses, percentage contracts, net returns and, above all, high-pressure salesmanship have more fascination than sex, which is merely the commodity being merchandised. The Production Code stands four-square against the honest depiction of many kinds of sexual relationships, yet permits the cliché treatment of the same relationships simply for commercial entertainment. For example, though incest is not named specifically by the Code, it probably falls into the penalty clause referring to 'illicit sex' – not to be explicitly treated, nor justified, nor made to seem right and permissible. Perhaps it would be just possible to make a serious, searching film about incest that observes all these restrictions, but significantly no one has yet tried to make it. Yet an obtrusive aspect of the more commercially blatant sex films is the prospect of illicit sex between two closely related characters. In *The Carpetbaggers* it is the young tycoon who has just stepped into his dead father's shoes and is almost immediately incited by his over-sexed step-mother to jump into her bed. And for a considerable stretch of the screen biography of *Harlow* one is led to suspect the Platinum Blonde's Italian step-father of an attraction towards her which she does not reciprocate. Then, suddenly, without any logical motivation – unless the trouble in

Sylvia over the step-father's rape counselled prudence – Harlow's step-father is assuring her with pained innocence that it is against his nature, nay, against his Church, to feel that way towards her. Meantime the audience have had their titillation.

It is arguable that the enormous commercial success which Joseph E. Levine made of promoting his films helped precipitate the morality crisis that Hollywood found itself in at the end of 1964. High-pressure salesmanship of the Levine brand, and its envious imitators, put the emphasis on the sexy tone of the films. Inflammatory titles, advertising copy with a built-in leer, and magazine photo-spreads of nude, or near-nude, scenes said to have been shot for the films but somehow not included in the released version: these were the commonest ways of making the mass of moviegoers imagine that a film's sex content was higher than it in fact was. Unfortunately such techniques could not help impinging on individuals or pressure groups who never went to see a movie, or, at least, that *kind* of movie, but were stirred up by the publicity to rail against Hollywood's moral brinkmanship. At the start of 1965 a *Variety* correspondent wrote: 'A mood, rather than a movement, in favour of film censorship begins to assume unmistakable shape around the United States. It is marked by the readiness of many citizens to sound off against films in general, and titles in particular, without bothering to view the films . . . Indeed the outcries against the film business are probably three parts against the "sell" and one part against the "content".'*

Paradoxically the swelling civic agitation to 'do something about censorship' came at a time when the Courts *were* doing something about it – curbing it. When the Production Code was written, in 1930, there were some ninety city censorship boards and twelve State boards, all with a say-so in what local cinemas could screen. They held on to the powers despite the Code, but time and changing tolerance whittled them down to thirty city boards and four at State level – New York, Maryland, Kansas and Virginia. In 1963 the New York State Censorship Board denied a licence to the Danish film, *A Stranger Knocks* (1959), alleging that a seduction scene in it was obscene. The decision was overruled two years later

* Robert J. Landry, *Variety*, February 10, 1965.

by the United States Supreme Court, a member of which, Justice William O. Douglas, had said in a similar case in Maryland: 'I would put an end to all forms and types of censorship and give full literal meaning to the command of the First Amendment' – guaranteeing freedom of speech and the Press.

Thus at the beginning of 1965 the burden of proving that a film was unfit for public screening had been put on the censors; and instead of withholding a licence, while litigation dragged on for years, they should in future let the film be shown publicly or take legal action against it themselves. On the face of it, Hollywood would benefit from this liberalising policy. For the news that the Supreme Court frowned on arbitrary censorship by small-town worthies should diminish the zeal of police officials or power-drunk J.P.s whose function was usually interpreted by Hollywood, on the screen at any rate, as simply that of making sleeping couples respectable. But in hard box-office terms, those to benefit by the new tolerance would be the companies which imported well-made but uninhibited – by Hollywood standards – European films, or else the product which the trade calls 'sexploitation' pictures, mostly second-rate home-made or foreign films with a lurid sexual appeal. The quaintly named Audubon Films is one of the largest specialists in the latter line of product, with titles like *Warm Night and Soft Pleasures*, *Soft Skin on Black Silk* and *The Weird Lovemakers*; and one of its executives reported at the beginning of 1965, 'Despite the talk of censorship and so-called public outrage, more and more theatres are playing this product all the time.'* This was the very same public that the major Hollywood producers were trying to reach by insinuating more and more aggressive sex into their films and backing it up with inflammatory publicity. Consequently when legal rulings on censorship began to fall like fig leaves round the country, the temptation to take advantage of the new freedom was intensified irresistibly.

But it was hard to make the running if one was still hobbled by the Production Code and the Legion of Decency. And as well as gaining freedom and leeway, one also needed to have talent and taste. Hollywood films throughout 1964 and 1965 reflected this

* Quoted by Vincent Canby, *Variety*, February 10, 1965.

conflict of forces inside and outside the studios. Films that sought to be outspoken rarely chose their words with skill. Often they failed to rise above the bad best-sellers on which they were based. Attempting to be frank about sex, they ended up by being simply vulgar. Something much more positive than throwing away one's inhibitions was required to break the habit of decades spent in falsifying life out of deference to the Code and the Legion. It was startling, for example, to find a scene centred on the erogenous areas of the body inserted with lubricious relish in an otherwise ingenuous comedy like *Sex and the Single Girl* (1964): one got a creepy feeling of Junior cracking off-colour jokes about the adults. Even a film as sensitively made as *Love With the Proper Stranger* (1964) began as compassionate realism about a young, unmarried couple grappling with an abortion, then swerved violently into domestic comedy, betraying its makers' uncertainty about how far they could go with the life-like treatment of a ticklish theme.

By the end of 1964 the Legion of Decency was implying that Hollywood had already gone too far. In its annual report for the year ending 12th August, 1964, it stated that it had reviewed and classified 270 films, of which 208 were American. Only forty-two of the latter were judged fit for the entire family, the smallest number in the Legion's thirty-year history. Fifty-three of the Hollywood-made films were rated for adults only, compared with thirty-five in 1963; and there were fifteen foreign and domestic productions, most of them important pictures, which were approved for adults 'with reservations'. This was a small increase over 1963 and showed the steady trend in such films. Forty-three Hollywood-made films were rated as 'morally objectionable in part for all', a leap of seventeen over 1963. At least half of them were made by major studios. But the severest rap was reserved for the sixteen films that were 'Condemned' outright: the highest muster in the Legion's history. Among these were Roman Polanski's *Knife in the Water* (1961), condemned 'because of nudity in the treatment', and Ingmar Bergman's *The Silence* (1963). The Legion took objection to the latter because: 'His selection of images is sometimes vulgar, insulting to a mature audience, and dangerously close to pornography. In spite of the author's good intentions, therefore, he has seriously violated artistic taste and sensitivity and leaves the film's presentation open to sensational exploitation by the irresponsible.' The single gratifying note, said the Legion's report, was that the Production Code Administration had not approved any of its 'Condemned' films.

* * *

But if ever there was a case of biting off one's tongue as soon as the words are out of one's mouth, this was surely it. For at the very moment its annual report was published, the Legion was to be found thundering the charge of being 'patently indecent and immoral' at a major Hollywood film, branding this maverick's flank with a sizzling 'C' for Condemned, and furthermore castigating the Production Code Administration which had actually given the film its seal of approval. 'It is difficult to understand how such approval is not the final betrayal of the trust which has been placed by so many in the organised industry's self-regulation.'

The film that brought the morality crisis to a head was Billy Wilder's sex comedy, *Kiss Me Stupid* (1964). It is the story of an amateur song-writer in the dead-end town of Climax, Nevada, who tries to sell his compositions to a big-time singer in exchange for the adulterous services of his wife, though he borrows a stripper from the local honky-tonk to impersonate the latter. But getting sexually jealous of the singer, he takes the tart to his own bed. The singer accidentally ends up with the wife, anyway. It was a traditional comedy of substitution: the French boulevard theatres have dozens like it. Most lay critics scarcely found it indecent or immoral – merely plodding and unsavoury. The chief sin was in the casting. It needed Marilyn Monroe, not Kim Novak, to bring an antiseptic innocence to the stripper. A heart attack had made Peter Sellers drop out of the song-writer's role, and he had been replaced by Ray Walston who was seemingly required to act with the finesse of a burlesque house comic whose motto is 'Leave 'em leering'. This coarsened the film's stag humour. Yet it got a Code seal without any requests for changes. No doubt if one cared to computerise the plot's switches, they would be found to contain an equal balance of moral compensations.

But the Legion blasted the film as 'a bald condonation of immorality' and fulminated not only against its release at any time, 'but especially during the holiday season of Chanukah and Christmas'. (Note the call for allies implicit in the reference to the Jewish festival.) Such timing was alleged to be 'a commercial decision bereft of respect for the Judaeo-Christian sensibilities of the majority of the American people.' Voltaire once remarked to a friend, 'It is said that God is always for the big battalions.' A latter-day cynic who observed the Legion's strategy might reflect on the corollary – that the big battalions are always for God. 'FILM CODE'S CREPE-HUNG XMAS' was how *Variety*'s headline writers chronicled the morality crisis. (How long did they agonise, one wonders, before rejecting 'CREPE-HUNG CHANUKAH'?) It was true that Hollywood's maladroit timing had resulted in a heavy sexual fall-out over the nation's Christmas box-office. In addition to *Kiss Me Stupid*, the unseasonable releases included *Sex and the Single Girl*, *The Americanisation of Emily* (1964) featuring a heroine who offered her bed to soldiers on the eve of battle and a U.S. officer who turned unrepentant coward on the eve of D-day, and *John Goldfarb, Please Come Home* (1964) in which Shirley MacLaine put on scanty disguise as a houri in an Arab harem and fell into bed with a footloose Jewish U-2 pilot. (Though sometimes a more vulgar film than *Kiss Me Stupid* this one astonishingly drew no charge from the Legion that it offended Judaeo-Christian-Islamic sensibilities.)

By early 1965 large sections of the American Press were reflecting the morality crisis by taking an increasingly restrictive attitude towards film advertising, which is one of the most lucrative sources of newspaper revenue. The new advertising code that many papers adopted made the Production Code look mild. Among forbidden subjects were: 'Bust measurements, intimate positions, couples in bed, double meanings, excessive bosom, cleavage, horizontal embraces, nude figures, silhouettes, nymphomania, perversion, promotional use of the word 'sin', short bikinis [sic], suggestive dress or undress, vulgar display of anatomy and' – a catch-all classification – 'violation of normal moral standards.' Lists of taboo words that would not be accepted in film advertisements included, 'Cuties, girlie, homosexual, immorality, Lesbian, lust, naked, nothing on, nudies, nudist camp, professional girls, prostitute, rape, seduce, sexpot, sexsational, third sex' – and even the word 'sex' itself, unless used to denote gender.

It was in the middle of this highly combustible situation, in March 1965, that the flashpoint occurred. The prostitute in *The Pawnbroker* exposed her bare breasts.

* * *

By giving *The Pawnbroker* a Code seal nonetheless, the Motion Picture Association of America was doing more than making an aesthetic judgment about what had hitherto been regarded as a straight moral issue. It was also tacitly admitting the breakdown of the Production Code. The Code had failed in its first aim, to protect the movie industry from the outrage and coercive power of pressure groups. Most producers were now undermining or bypassing it. The postures they frequently had to adopt to do so simply made their offence more vulgar without making censorship any easier. Producers of integrity were heavily handicapped by the Code if they attempted to observe it. At the same time, present-day standards of morality were laxer than those which the Code had been created to uphold – as *Newsweek* magazine remarked, 'If Hollywood is a fallen woman, it can blame the modern world for its downfall.' But whereas Hollywood had had to reform its delinquent ways in 1930 lest the State did a more painful job of house-cleaning, in 1965 the Courts were actually emboldening Hollywood by the verdicts they handed down. For all these reasons the M.P.A.A. embarked on an overhaul of the Production Code almost immediately after *The Pawnbroker* affair and the clash with the Legion of Decency. Instead of evaluating the moral compensations in a screenplay and seeing if they balanced the characters' sins, the censors in future would be able to take the film's overall tone and artistry into account. By October, 1965, Hollywood was considering a proposed set of 'production standards' totalling fewer than 200 words, as against the Code's 3,000. 'Brutality, illicit sex, indecent exposure, vulgar or profane words and gestures, and offensive treatment of religion and racial or national groups are noted as subjects for restraint, but interpretation in all cases, including the recently debated matter of nudity, is left to the discretion of the new administrators.'*

The Legion of Decency also began the work of extracting itself with dignity from the untenable situation into which its hair-splitting morality had led it. It is true that it gave *The Pawnbroker* a 'Condemned' rating 'for the sole reason that nudity has been used in its treatment'. But it added, with astonishing mildness, that '*nudity is not in itself objectionable and it might even have an artistic function in a film of quality* . . .' (Italics mine). It did not escape notice that the Legion had waited until the critics' reviews of *The Pawnbroker* appeared before issuing this toned down condemnation. The reviews were generally favourable. For the remainder of 1965, the Legion's policy appears to have been marked by unwonted caution. It did not hang a 'Condemned' rating round the neck of *What's New, Pussycat?* (1965), although the sex jokes and ribald innuendoes in this free-style comedy were pricklier protuberances than those in *Kiss Me Stupid.* Instead, the film got a 'B' rating – morally objectionable in part for all – which placed it out of bounds to everyone who had taken a Legion pledge but meant that cinemas which refused to play 'Condemned' films could screen it with a good conscience – and, as it turned out, bumper takings. Even so, the Legion felt constrained to state that 'the film avoids condemnation only because it is unbelievably dull and witless'. This remarkable judgment explains, better than any other, why the Legion's influence on Hollywood's artistic growth has been so negative.

By the end of 1965 the Legion had changed its name. Henceforth it was to be known as the National Catholic Office for Motion Pictures, thus shedding at last its titular claim to protect moviegoers against moral contagion. This more sophisticated attitude, the Legion declared, was in line with Pope John XXIII's policy of updating Catholic thought. It was also attributed, with rather an appearance of delay, to Pope Pius XII's 1957 encyclical, *Miranda Prorsus* (The Remarkable Inventions), which declared that 'the plain truth does not arouse disordered passions or impulses, at

* Ronald Gold, *Variety*, October 20, 1965.

least in mature persons'. In the light of this, the Legion was embarrassed to discover it had no category for what Mgr Little called 'legitimate mature films'. Subsequently Legion extremists were rebuked for expecting the Church 'to discourage serious film-making and to deprive mature viewers of legitimate fare.' And lest serious film-makers somehow felt that their efforts in this direction had not been sufficiently appreciated in the past, a series of awards was instituted early in 1966. One of them went to the film *Darling*, another to Fellini's *Juliet of the Spirits* (1965), a third to a picture about the sex pangs of teenage lovers. As if to stress the new outlook, there were no prizes for *The Greatest Story Ever Told* (1965).

Nevertheless the search for the aesthetic vision did not soften the keen eyesight with which the Legion still continued to appraise films before the public got a chance to see them. Shortly after the prizegiving, it was reported that the Legion had objected to shots in Sidney Lumet's film version of the Mary McCarthy novel, *The Group*. The shots included one of a man's hand on a girl's bosom: the distributors replaced it with substitute material. Not everything had changed since *The Pawnbroker*. Breasts, apparently, were still not 'necessary'.

How Hollywood will depict the sexual areas of life over the next few years depends on several developments which are not yet clear. One is the adoption and administration of a new Production Code which will not inhibit film-makers in search of realism: 'realism' being defined as a film's sureness in knowing who its characters are and where they belong in a setting that is recognisably that of life, but life understood and assimilated. The other development is a willingness on the part of the Legion of Decency in its new updated guise as the National Catholic Office for Motion Pictures to recognise that while it has the right to guide its members and sympathisers, it has no right to a say in what the entire American public shall see, or not see, on the cinema screen. If the Legion still hankers after wider jurisdiction, it would be wise to divert its energies from the moral welfare of adults to the protection of children. This will certainly be necessary if Hollywood's talents do prove equal to the 'new realism' of a revised Code. Ensuring that children do not see unsuitable films – or see them only in the company of appropri-

Life with a sex symbol: Clark Gable, pictured without his familiar moustache, confidently asserts his he-man appeal over Jean Harlow in *Red Dust*.

Life with a nature symbol: Almost 30 years later in *The Misfits*, his last film, Gable bends his back over the lettuce bed while Marilyn Monroe communes with the environment.

ate guardians – is the basis of the British system of film classification which has cleared the screen for many adult movies. But 'classification' is a dirtier word than 'censorship' in Hollywood – indeed it is what industry chiefs frequently mean when they say 'censorship' – because it would cut down the audiences for films which might be judged unsuitable for children. At present the responsibility lies with parents to decide which films their children shall see; and the Motion Picture Association of America has always opposed any transfer of this responsibility to itself.

If this is where the next censorship battle is fought, the 'morality crisis' of 1964–65 will have played a vital part in precipitating it.

Part Three
THE VICTIMS

'Before a man gets married, he's
like a tree in the forest. He
stands there, independent, an entity
unto himself. And then he's chopped
down. His branches are cut off – he's
stripped of his bark – and he's
thrown into the river with the rest
of the logs. Then this tree is taken
to the mill – and when it comes out
it's no longer a tree. It's the
vanity table, the breakfast nook,
the baby crib, and the newspaper that
lines the family garbage can.'

– Rock Hudson in *Pillow Talk*

CHAPTER TEN

IMPERFECT LOVER: MASTROIANNI

'(She) usually manages things in a subtle, almost imperceptible way: she assuages his (her husband's) feelings; she avoids open contests but generally has the last unspoken word. She keeps her place, of course. She would obviously lose her ascendancy if she forgot it.' Thus one eminent social critic on the place of women in his native land. Anyone familiar with Hollywood sex comedies will have no difficulty recognising the Doris Day type of manageress-wife, married to a considerate house-trained fellow who will remember her anniversary, leave her in peace during the day to get on with the tomato bottling but rush home to share the plumbing with her if it goes wrong, be polite to her parents and only insist on exercising his marital rights when the wolf at the neighbourhood country club needs a restraining punch on the jaw. But the writer continues: 'Her place may be in the kitchen (for lower income families), the drawing-room or boudoir (for the more affluent), and, for all, the double-bed at night; but wherever it is, it is a position of great power.' And now a doubt creeps into one's mind that it may not be quite the screen's usual half-acre of Scarsdale or Westchester that the writer has in mind. But he goes on: 'Men run the country, but women run men.' And immediately one's doubt dies down at this statement of the basic principles of the Hollywood sex comedy – even those that throw a conciliatory wink at the male sex in the last reel and imply that it is a woman's world only *because* there are men in it.

But the author of this quotation is no American, nor is he writing about America, still less Hollywood. Luigi Barzini concludes, 'Italy is, in reality, a cryptomatriarchy.'*

The next chapter examines the folklore of the Hollywood sex

* *The Italians*, by Luigi Barzini (Hamish Hamilton), p. 202.

comedy and the emasculating effect that an open matriarchy like that which prevails in the United States has had upon the sexual status of the sex comedy hero. This chapter chronicles an analogous tragedy: the downfall of the Italian lover in a society that, to employ the phrase Dr Barzini used in his stabbingly perceptive study, *The Italians*, is a cryptomatriarchy. As will be seen, the two trends touch; and the more Americanised the Italian sex comedy becomes, the more closely the hero's frustrations and comeuppance approximate to those of his Hollywood counterpart. Nowhere is the screen hero of either country more ruthlessly shown up as the beleaguered sex than in this genre of film. Sex comedies show him as anxious, frustrated, weak and made insecure to the point of impotence by the encroachment of the female on his self-esteem and virility. It was, of course, always characteristic of sex comedies that they made the boy labour mightily to get the girl. And after all the snubs and degradations she made him suffer while getting her, some cynics may have felt at the final fade-out that his victory was a Pyrrhic one. But times have got even rougher. And nowadays the male's confidence in his own masculinity is so badly shaken by the women he is matched against that it is arguable at the end of the film whether the poor sap is capable of enjoying even a priapic victory.

The view of the woman as the predominant, though not the most conspicuous character in Italian life is solidly sustained by Dr Barzini's study of his countrymen. What keeps her in power, he maintains, is being boss of the family, that sacred nucleus of Italian life, and all matters connected with it. The family's stability and reputation depend far more on the Italian wife's faithfulness than on her husband's – a fact incorporated in the Roman adultery laws, which are more severe on women than men. At the sametime, she is exalted and given a kind of sacred existence by many features outside the family. One sees evidence of this in the Roman Church's predilection for placing the Virgin 'on an almost equal footing' with her Son in ecclesiastical ritual and imagery. Even the fact that 'Mamma mia!' is the commonest exclamation is significant. It is in this sense, Dr Barzini concludes, that Italy is a cryptomatriarchy, with women ruling inside the family circle and acquiring a liking for domination and power over their menfolk.

But the Italian woman has a profane side to her too. She displays her enjoyment of being a woman in a way that is more defiant and pagan than her American counterpart. The latter has freed herself of the economic and religious servitude which the married Italian woman has still to accommodate herself to. But until marriage forces family obligations on her, it is the physical flirtatious side of being a woman that the Italian girl relishes. Such ambivalence has a frustrating effect on the Italian male. Preoccupied from an early age with proving his manhood to himself, he nevertheless finds he lives in a society which looks on adultery, and even the passing *avventura* with official disfavour. He is supposed to enjoy his sex life only where his Church prescribes: inside the circle of his family, and with parenthood not pleasure as the aim. And he has no hope of divorce as a remedy if things go wrong, or as a social amenity that he can make use of in order to enjoy fresh experience. In one part of his life he has to cope with the same kind of female assertiveness as the American family man; in the other part he lacks several of the defensive weapons that combatants in the American battle of the sexes handle so adroitly. His plight is reflected in his films.

* * *

The very words 'sex comedy' suggest something indigenously American, a form of entertainment like the Western on which Hollywood holds the parent patent. What the Italian cinema makes are, rather, social comedies about sex. The best of them can be effortlessly patrician or working-class, whereas the proletarian sex comedy is unknown in Hollywood. This is partly because sexual fantasy and not social realism is the departure point for the Hollywood films – fantasies generally tend to be set in a higher income bracket than the one the fantasist normally occupies. But it is also because the places and problems featured in Hollywood sex comedies are the ones that are familiar to the people who make them – the stars, producers, directors and especially the writers. The settings are also those they know personally: bachelor apartments, executive suites, ad agencies, TV studios, motels (which have taken over from hotels as the morals of the characters in the comedies have got less and less inhibited), divorce courts and psychiatrists' consulting rooms. The battle of the sexes is fought more tenaciously and openly in Hollywood, since the American woman's economic independence has enabled her to challenge the man's sexual supremacy on almost equal terms. Women in the Italian comedies tend to threaten the man's status indirectly and use the accumulated pressure of the Church, social custom, public opinion and especially the family group to curb his sexual freedom. The sex war in Hollywood is highly ritualised: the best comedies are those which permutate the few available plots most adroitly and give an appearance of novelty to the standard conundrum of will she, won't she, should she, shouldn't she? The characters have to keep donning or doffing the attitudes that camouflage their real intentions towards each other like quick-change artists: every suit of wolf's clothing is reversible sheepskin.

The characters in American sex comedies are not so much developed as programmed for action. In Italian films, on the other hand, the battle of the sexes springs from the very individualism of the characters. Italian stars do not type themselves so rigidly into archetypes like the bachelor playboy or the All-American virgin. They personalise the particular aspect of Italian manners or morals that the film is mocking and the comedy comes from the way the characters evolve quite naturalistically in the social setting of the story. But whatever their differences in tempo, style and depth of characterisation, the Italian and Hollywood sex comedies have one thing in common. In both, the male's place is highly precarious. And for the most striking single example of the fallen male one has to turn to Italy. Whereupon one discovers a startling paradox. For the Italian star who excels at portraying the comic and tragic sides of the congenitally weak male is the very same one who is commonly regarded as the most complete masculine sex symbol on the international screen today – Marcello Mastroianni.

The popular view of Mastroianni accounts for a large part of this paradox. It has slotted him firmly, though mistakenly, into the Latin tradition established, particularly in the Anglo-Saxon imagination, by two Italians: Casanova and Valentino.

Giacomo Casanova set the historical pattern of a love life where desire is perfectly consummated in performance and absolutely without fastidiousness in the choice of bedmates. It is acutely summed up by Dr Barzini: 'He pleased women at first sight, women of all ages and conditions, and usually succeeded in rendering them helpless and defenceless in front of his pressing entreaties. His physical capacity to satisfy the most exacting mistress by renewing his homages to her a practically unlimited number of times through the night and following day, with only short *entr'actes* between the exertions, is not as surprising as his feat of psychological endurance: he was never bored, never embittered by experience, sincerely admired one woman after another, and slipped into bed at a moment's notice . . . always admirably animated, till very late in life, by the same schoolboyish eagerness.'*

Superhuman attributes like these found their screen equivalent in Valentino, though it is perhaps significant that for him they were incarnated in characters who are not Italian by nationality. Perhaps he recognised that the world of *The Sheik* (1921) had more exciting connotations of polygamy for the women who were his mass public. In private life, Valentino seems to have sought out, or fallen victim to, women who were stronger characters than himself: his second wife, Natasha Rambova, alleged in her divorce suit that he was 'too domesticated and fond of home life'. If so, he certainly compensated for it in the *droit de seigneur* dynamism he brought to the pursuit of women on the screen. Even his physical defects worked for him there. One of his eyelids had a dead nerve in it and drooped slightly when his face was in repose: but this only intensified his air of connoisseurship as he looked the lovely victims over. He wasted little time on wooing women, but swept them off their feet. Nor did he do much explaining. To the abducted heroine who asked 'Why have you brought me here?' he returned the answer, 'Are you not woman enough to know?' Invariably, she was. The Valentino persona focused the new attitude of sexual permissiveness in the 1920s. His pop-eyed *homme fatal* looks laughable now. But in its time it sanctioned the fantasy of many women that it might be physically stimulating to be abducted by such a man and not feel guilty about it afterwards.

* Ibid., p. 93.

What the Valentino screen hero conformed to – possibly the only thing – was Casanova's rule of life: that masculine domination is the right relationship between the sexes.

It is all too easy to believe that Marcello Mastroianni is part of the same tradition. A popular image has been created to support it. 'The greatest screen lover since Valentino', says one writer in the international Press; 'a Latin idol to women filmgoers in the 1960s', states another; while a third pronounces him to be 'the closest thing to a masculine sex symbol the cinema has ever had'. The international magazine *Newsweek* carries the following report: ' "Please put it in capitals," pleaded Pamela Tiffin, 23. "I am the FIRST American actress to play opposite him, and I'm very proud of it." By "him", she meant Marcello Mastroianni, 41, Italy's matinee idol *numero uno* . . . "He's really a hunk of man," Pamela raved. "He's romantic, he's elegant, he's sensual, he's a Latin lover and yet he's a Teddy bear, too. There's something cuddly about him. And that voice of his! It makes your bones vibrate." '* The image of an irresistible male surrounded by available sex, and availing himself of it freely, is further enhanced by publicity, advertising, and even cinema posters like the one for his film *The Organiser* (1963). In this ruthlessly unglamorous film he appeared almost unrecognisably made up as a shabby, short-sighted, bearded, virginally timid *professore* of syndicalist sympathies who helps unionise the underpaid factory workers of nineteenth-century Italy. But the film distributors, in Britain at least, clapped a stock glamour picture of him on to the advertising for *The Organiser*. Mastroianni in a beard and pince-nez might have been too much for filmgoers, or even film actresses, conditioned to see him as a romantic, elegant, sensual, bone-vibrating Latin lover.

* * *

The fact is that almost every role Mastroianni has played contradicts this image of him. The most telling example is *Il Bell' Antonio* (1960), because this tragi-comedy directed by Mauro Bolognini is set in Sicily, where a man's virility and his social status are delicately

* *Newsweek*, November 29, 1965.

dependent on each other. Mastroianni plays a young man who has everything, except that most desirable Sicilian attribute, potency. His good looks, true love and desire for posterity are of no help when he marries a girl whose excessive purity literally unmans him – not till he gets the servant girl pregnant is his family's good name restored and his personal honour vindicated. It is true that Antonio is not completely impotent: this might have been too much for Mastroianni fans. The film nevertheless turns upside down the commonest ruse of Casanova, which was to feign impotence while professing love in order to enjoy sex. Antonio can have sex, but he is struck impotent when he wants to enjoy love. It is also true that the threat to his manhood comes from an idealised woman (Claudia Cardinale); and in a society where potency and virginity are male and female imperatives, it rather looks as if the film is rigging its hero's predicament in order to satirise the contradictions of public life there.

A later film, *Yesterday Today and Tomorrow* (1965), is open to the same objection, at least in the first of its three stories directed by Vittorio De Sica. But it is relevant to Mastroianni's popular image, because his underendowment in *Il Bell' Antonio* here becomes overendowment, but brings him no more peace of mind. Rather less, in fact. He plays a Neapolitan working man whose wife (Sophia Loren) is threatened with a prison sentence until she learns that under Italian law pregnant women cannot be sent to jail. To save herself from one kind of confinement, she resorts to another kind; and she keeps right on doing so, waving a doctor's certificate every time the police call until her complaisant but wilting husband collapses from exhaustion. As the prison van finally collects, she snarls at the prostrate Mastroianni, 'You fairy!'

Such a comedy can only work in a country which places a high premium on motherhood, if not family planning, and the film subverts this ideal inventively, at least until the fun of Miss Loren's repeated pregnancies begins to pall. (She is a comedienne whose charms are located slightly higher up than the womb.) But the built-in logic of the situation reduces the male to being simply an impregnating machine – a not very reliable one, either. Perhaps this is putting too solemn a gloss on a bit of broad social satire; but it will be as well to remember at least the social humour of it when considering the streak of heartless misogyny in the Hollywood sex comedy which reduces the female to being simply a breeding machine. 'Keep her pregnant all the time,' Charles Boyer urges his prospective son-in-law in one Hollywood sex comedy. 'But I don't love her,' Rock Hudson protests. 'That,' smirks Boyer, 'is part of the revenge.' Italian sex comedies humiliate and embarrass the male, but rarely carry the same charge of misogyny as their Hollywood counterparts.

No exception to the rule is *Divorce – Italian Style* (1961). Directed by Pietro Germi, and set again in Sicily where honour is as vital to life as oxygen, its comedy is based on the proposition that a man has to suffer, and be seen to suffer, sexual humiliation by his wife before the Law consents to take a mild view of his murdering her. Again the sex comedy evolves from the social hypocrisies. Mastroianni is a vain, lazy Italian nobleman whose effeteness and narcissism exemplified by his hair nets and limp moustache, set up a marvellously witty dissonance with the Latin lover he fancies himself to be – and that Mastroianni's fans, incidentally, fancy *him* to be. Encouraged by the Law's moderation towards provoked husbands, he plans a gunshot divorce to rid himself of a wife with a braying laugh and a tiny moustache of her own. This involves making a public cuckold of himself, parading his wife in hip-hugging dresses down the main street to test her appeal and tempt any likely taker; and then, when this fails, seeking to compromise her with a dismayingly weedy-looking old flame while the husband bureaucratically files away poison-pen letters that he has written to himself.

Everything in this very clever comedy emphasises the ridiculous posture of the male. It has the shrewdness, too, to let the Q.E.D. of the proposition rebound on Mastroianni – so that when he kills his wife, serves a token prison term and weds his pretty cousin, he actually *is* cuckolded by her. Everything is again tipped against Mastroianni's mythical image of the perfect lover. Note, however, that the aim of his plot is simply to be free to marry a more sexually attractive woman whereas the aim of the plot concocted by the married man in a corresponding Hollywood sex comedy, *How to*

Murder Your Wife (1965), is simply to get back to being a bachelor again. The message of the latter film is that women are a menace to any man rash enough to have more than a sleeping relationship with them. At least the Italian hero operates inside the social institution of marriage, or with a mistress whose relationship to him is virtually that of a wife. The American sex comedy hero is the victim of his psychological fears, the Italian of his marriage vows.

Marriage – Italian Style (1964), directed by Vittorio De Sica, is again based on the social realities that regulate the sex life of its hero. The Roman Catholic Church's views on divorce are so inflexible that, according to the film, many an Italian male acts on the principle, 'Pay her, don't marry her.' (The notion of a kept woman is alien to the Hollywood sex comedy in which women are either girl-friends who come and go, or else business girls who earn enough to keep themselves. The one major American sex comedy – it is really more than that – which revolves around a kept girl is *The Apartment* (1960); but its director was Billy Wilder, a notable nonconformist, and its kept heroine was an elevator girl who needed the money.) Mastroianni in *Marriage – Italian Style* plays a prosperous café owner who has been keeping Sophia Loren from the time they met in a war-time brothel to the time she graduates to running his business and then his household for him – leaving him free to run after his girl cashier. There is nothing in the least romantic in Mastroianni's calculation of his relationship to her. Since his aged mother is shown in one early scene as incapable of looking after him, he has simply made his mistress into a second mother, but without giving her a wife's status. The comedy springs from her erosion of his reluctance to marry her. First of all, she pretends to die: the presumption is that a death-bed marriage is the only one that can be faced with equanimity by an Italian male prudent about remaining unattached. This failing, she then reveals she has mothered three sons, one of them by him, and tortures his curiosity, pride and desire for posterity till he gives in and marries her. (Note how her bargaining power is loaded by the film: she has brought forth male children only.) The legitimising of his family is thus deployed by the woman as a weapon for curbing the male's sexual independence.

Again and again in his comedy roles, Mastroianni leads a sex life subjected to continual harassments, from physical impotence to domestic tyranny, and the weight of Church and State is mobilised by a strong-willed woman to bring him into line. Even when he incites the sleeping satyr in him to come out fighting, the result is only a hilarious bout of shadow-boxing: as in the last episode of *Yesterday, Today and Tomorrow* when his would-be boudoir Tarzan ('I'm a volcano!') lopes around the call girl's apartment thinking up kinky delights ('Do a strip-tease with just the refrigerator light on.') and winnowing his way through packs of paper hankies as he sweats in anticipation of the show that, of course, never comes.

Mastroianni comes out of the same comic mould as Jack Lemmon, Tom Ewell or Tony Randall in the Hollywood sex comedies. Day-dreaming and sexual fantasy, as in *Divorce – Italian Style*, are his escape routes, like theirs. But where Randall, Lemmon and Ewell are innocents in the matter of sex, Mastroianni puts on a spivvish competence that a commentator like Dr Barzini would connect with the ingrained love of 'show' in the Italian character. He excels at the type of self-centred lover, always glancing at himself in the mirror after kissing his mistress to ensure his tie is straight. He gives one the feeling that hair nets are adjuncts to the all-male safety-razor in his bathroom cabinet. It is a kind of con game he plays in films like the two on divorce and marriage, except that sexual vanity, not monetary gain, is his aim; and ultimately he takes himself in, so that the unmasking of him as an imperfect man touches off both the comedy and pathos of his situation. One senses this tone at its most concentrated in his quietest comedy performance, in the central story of *Yesterday, Today and Tomorrow*, which is the one adapted from Moravia. In it he is the bourgeois lover of a rich society bitch (Sophia Loren) who keeps telling him how little the world's goods mean to her. Too late he learns otherwise when he timidly takes the wheel of her Rolls-Royce, runs into a road sign and tries to smother a smoking tyre with her mink-lined rain-coat. Snappishly she reverts to the values of her class; and her lover is left in the lurch on the roadside, smarting with knowledge of his presumptuousness, incompetence and ignorance of rich women, not to say luxury automobiles.

* * *

Before he began filming *La Dolce Vita* (1959), Fellini offered the leading part to Mastroianni who was not then a star inside Italy and was unknown outside. The offer shows great perceptiveness on Fellini's part. 'What kind of role is it?' Mastroianni is said to have asked. 'A weak man,' answered Fellini. Rather touchingly came the reply, 'How did you guess?' The 'weak man' is the part Mastroianni has specialised in ever since, even in films with no comedy overtones. In a moment of resigned candour, he once admitted, 'The characters are connected by cowardice. They don't do to life, life does to them.' As the journalist in *La Dolce Vita*, he drifts through society, living life at second hand, jaded less by a surfeit of experience than by the effort it would cost him to taste experience at first hand. He is not even successful given the opulent parties, available women and permissive morals which surround him in his professional life. His sex life is ineffectual. His wife attempts suicide, his mistress's pleasure in copulation with him has to be pepped up by taking place on a prostitute's bed, and a Hollywood sex symbol leads him an elusive dance into the paddling fountain. 'He is like a mantis who has lost faith in the efficacy of prayer,' wrote a critic in *Time* magazine; and one might add '. . . and is wary of sex,' bearing in mind that it is during the sex act that the female mantis devours her mate.

The whole of the film he made for Fellini three years later, 8½ (1962), analyses the spiritual and mental anxiety of a man who has lost faith in the efficacy of *everything*. The plot is a self-indulgent fantasy if ever there was one; and one must record one's own impression that under a brilliant surface complexity, 8½ often seems hardly deeper than a finger nail. Given a good analyst and a mite of insight, one would expect to find out more about one's emotional blocs in fifty minutes than Fellini's hero discovers in two hours. Mastroianni plays a film director, rather like Fellini in appearance and attitude, who cannot begin to shoot his new picture until he 'finds himself'. As the American critic Pauline Kael pointed out, this is more like the fantasy of someone who dreams about being a film director than any real problem that a director of a film with a script, budget, sets and writers has ever run up against. Yet Mastroianni settles himself prehensilely round the role and seems close enough to the paralysed will-power of Fellini's hero to make one imagine that he, Mastroianni, is doing 8½ out of his need for similar therapy. In fact he strikes one as an actor who is continually finding out about himself by acting in films: a more generally beneficial activity than 'finding himself' by sitting around and not acting at all. (Which is what 8½ would presumably be all about if an actor, not a director, were its hero.)

This film's advertising again reflected Mastroianni's popular image with the public, not the actual kind of role he played. The scene selected for the British advertisements showed him cracking a bull whip to muster a bevy of harem beauties. This was simply a moment of wish fulfilment in the film. On the posters it looked the real thing and reinforced the public image of the actor as a masterful type who makes women shape up.

It was Mastroianni's gift for displaying precisely the opposite characteristic on the screen that commended him to Antonioni when he cast him as the palely loitering hero in *La Notte* (1961). 'I see the actor (generally) as part of the composition,' Antonioni said. 'I do not want the actor to become his own director. I never explain to the actors the characters they are playing. I want them to be passive.' Mastroianni was certainly a passive case in *La Notte*: an intellectual writer who is no intellectual and is never seen writing, a husband (for Jeanne Moreau) who yet is no husband since they cannot communicate with each other, a man who is impotent in relation to society and probably sexually impotent as well. Incidents abound in the film to suggest that sex as well as love has seeped out of their marriage. He puts up no resistance when a nymphomaniac in a hospital suite tries to assault him; nor can he work up any sexual excitement when he dutifully tries to make love to his wife at the end. Their attempt at copulation takes place beside a golf bunker – an apposite touch. They are dead even when they lie down.

Elio Petri's *L'Assassino* (1961) confirmed that Mastroianni is at his best when weakest. He played a pampered antique dealer running his business ineffectually but supporting himself luxuriously by cheques from woman friends, one of whom he is accused of killing. Whereupon the circumstantial evidence convinces him that he is at least morally guilty of the charge. The same director pursued his theme of accumulating menace in *The Tenth Victim* (1965) and projected Mastroianni into the twenty-first century where the sex war has been State-nationalised as a lethal sport with men and women licensed to kill each other, if they can, in order to bring back the old excitement into the game. (Significantly perhaps, this Italian vision of tomorrow retains religion, but depicts it as still so oppressive in the matter of obtaining a twenty-first-century divorce that most people do not bother to get married.) 'This year, killing women is the In thing to do,' says someone. But the film tilts the odds against the men; and Mastroianni, perfectly implying the low-charged batteries of male potency, is the intended tenth victim of Ursula Andress who has just notched up her ninth by shooting him through a bullet-firing double-barrelled brassière and then collecting his tie as a trophy – a barely concealed token castration.

If the approximation of the sex life to a blood sport is still half a century away, Mario Monicelli's *Casanova* 70 (1965) furnishes up-to-date references for the Latin lover of today. And what it reveals is his most precarious relationship with women. As Mastroianni's films get screened more widely abroad and especially in the United States, and as American finance is guaranteed to them, the sexual dilemma of the hero gets increasingly acute and Americanised. *Casanova* 70 is a sex comedy about impotence with none of the inherent pathos of *Il Bell' Antonio*. Its premise that the sexual emancipation of women has gone too far to make for a satisfactory relationship with them is surely a theme that connects more joltingly with the funny bone of Hollywood than Italy. Mastroianni plays an Italian major attached to Nato; and just as Nato functions best when danger threatens, Mastroianni needs a sense of danger in his pursuit of women if he is to function at all. The 'schoolboyish eagerness' of history's Casanova is too weak to animate him in an age when women's sexual freedom has robbed physical conquest of its thrills. An air hostess whom he entices to a hotel clinically swallows a pill, books an alarm call with the switchboard for exactly forty-eight minutes later, and announces she is ready. He is not. To cure his impotence, he decides to live dangerously, seeks passion with a lady lion-tamer in her cage, goes housebreaking in the delirious hope that his ladylove will mistake him for a burglar and shoot at him, and seduces a Sicilian girl by posing as a doctor while her bloodthirsty kinsfolk are waiting next door to learn if she is 'pure'.

Whereas his ancestor attacked chastity and marked up a victory when the woman yielded herself, the film's Casanova has his desire killed the minute a protesting virgin gives in. Like the Hollywood sex comedies, *Casanova 70* shows a clear misogynist bias by arguing that modern woman has made herself too available. Instead of acting on sexual impulse, the male has now got to engineer fetishist set-ups. The bias is plainest in a scene satirising a psychiatrist who hates women. Analysts are figures of malicious fun in Hollywood sex comedies, but much rarer in Italian films, which for obvious reasons, prefer the priesthood as the target for social satire. The ending of *Casanova 70*, with Mastroianni trying to get himself acquitted of a murder charge by swinging the court's sympathy round to the harassed male sex, is coincidentally similar to the ending of *How to Murder Your Wife* (1965). In the latter film the putative victim was Jack Lemmon's emasculating Italian wife played by Virna Lisi: in *Casanova 70* the same Virna Lisi plays the virgin who strikes Mastroianni impotent by abruptly surrendering to him. Each film did good business in the other's country – and no wonder. For in them the sexual dilemmas of the characters in the Hollywood and Italian comedies have become virtually interchangeable.

* * *

Valentino operated in a film world where the characters were not controlled by their neuroses and where the only requirement for the enjoyment of sex was abundant energy. Mastroianni is the product of a more anxious age in which men have less confidence in themselves – are even less sure of their own sex. He is certainly well aware of this in the parts he plays. His tremendous popularity gives him the economic power to demand and accept parts that fit the image he has of himself. His physical looks give the image variety. He has one of those no-faces, like Sir Alec Guinness's or Peter Sellers's, whose proportions and planes can be scrambled at will to let him take on new identities – often by as little as a flake of make-up, occasionally by a complete transformation like his *professore* in *The Organiser*. Inside him, less explicably, whirs the gyroscope of what one must inadequately call 'screen presence' – the force that one senses without seeing in the great film actors, that holds a performance perfectly in balance however rocky the rest of the film. It is a quite different thing from 'star quality', which is an emanation beamed outwards and often unconnected with a performance. When the two are present in the same artist, then one can speak of a great actor being also a great star. One can say that with certainty of Mastroianni.

But the paradox remains. Considering the drifting, faithless, hunted, tired, insecure and neurotic characters he has created in his own image, why should he still be revered as a sex symbol? It can surely only be because the type of male hero he plays is one that makes the strongest appeal to women today. It is a type that is much more likely to outlast its antithesis: which is James Bond, the bold, decisive, callous man of action. Bond is the product of male compensation, or, rather, over-compensation in every department, above and below the belt. Even at the peak of his superhuman feats, Bond was being overtaken by the bold, decisive, callous woman in the shape of Ursula Andress (*The Tenth Victim* (1965)) and Monica Vitti (*Modesty Blaise* (1966)). Mastroianni's ever-worried eyes may be secretly envying Bond: his publicity may have built up a misleading image of him as a virility symbol. It does not seem to matter to his popularity. What makes women filmgoers find him fascinating is the very fact of his weakness. Because he invariably plays imperfect men who are incapable of sharing the feelings that the women in his films have for him, he seems to strengthen the confidence of the women who go to his films that if they were only given the same chance all his problems would be solved. They would be the ones to make him feel love and return it. To have such a man to care for and cure is intensely gratifying to the female ego. It awakens a protective response akin to the feelings which Marilyn Monroe's child-like helplessness aroused in men.

But his need for therapy is only half the appeal he makes. Mastroianni's looks and mannerisms also manage to suggest to women what life with him would be like after treatment. The airs and graces that he gives himself in the sex comedies are weak, vain, funny – but also flattering to his female audience. They are those of a ladies' man who gets a narcissistic satisfaction out of making a fuss over women in a conspicuous and somewhat old-fashioned way. Mastroianni panting to get into bed with the call-girl in *Yesterday, Today and Tomorrow* is wildly funny; so is the speedometer effect that he creates in *Casanova 70* every time he is jerked from an enervated standstill to quivering satyriasis as he sniffs the chance of a perilous bout of love-making. But moments like these are almost wilfully out of character, which is partly why they are so funny. For his style is decidedly not that of an accelerating amorist. His preference is for slow motion. This is why his subtlest stretch of sustained comedy is to be found in *Divorce – Italian Style*, where all his Machiavellian pondering on how to do away with his wife has to synchronise itself with the unhurrying tempo of small-town life in Sicily. No man can droop to riper effect from post-coital fatigue than he does in *Yesterday, Today and Tomorrow* after keeping his wife out of prison by repeated pregnancies. No one can laze more repletely than he does in the domestic set-up of *Marriage – Italian Style* with a mistress imported into the house to do the chores and mother him, while he flirts with the girl at his café.

A certain lethargy is always detectable under the skin of every performance he gives. It is a highly seductive part of his image for women. For although a man who has to be dragged to bed is not going to cut a heroic figure in the sex war, nevertheless his very indolence can add to the anticipation he excites. The supposition is that one who takes his time in everything else he does, is not going to hurry unduly when it comes to his sex life – or fail to give his partner a sense of full accomplishment. This part of Mastroianni's appeal is not contradicted by the fact that he is continually playing men who are handicapped in just such expertise. What makes up for his deficiency is the wishful thinking of his mass public, in the main female and romantic, which is attracted by the sight of him as a suitable case for their care and at the same time aroused by the thought of him with all his powers restored. Screen roles and private fantasies complement each other. Mastroianni is certainly a victim of the sex war: he is also a sex symbol in spite of himself.

CHAPTER ELEVEN

THE LAST AMERICAN MASSACRE: ROCK HUDSON & CO.

'Films are the last place in America where men can still outwit women. Close the movie-houses and the game would come to an end.' The speaker may be allowed a certain amount of exaggeration, since he has a vested interest in seeing the game continuing, not to mention the movie-houses staying open. Stanley Shapiro is a writer-producer and one of the most consistently successful practitioners in the Hollywood sex comedy: the co-author of such films as *Pillow Talk* (1959, with Martin Richlin), *Lover Come Back* (1961, with Martin Melcher), *That Touch of Mink* (1962, with Martin Melcher) and *A Very Special Favour* (1965, with Nate Monaster). He is a man to whom attention should be paid. Sex comedies are a form of American folk culture that may never command the serious respect accorded to the Kinsey Reports (Male and Female), though the conclusions Dr Kinsey came to are still a stand-by source of inspiration for sex-comedy scenarists. There are possibly more verifiable, though not necessarily more veracious, indications of the relations between the sexes than sex comedies: the marriage and divorce statistics, for instance, equal employment laws, voting rights, Playboy Club subscriptions, male fashions designed for female wear, and so on. Nevertheless the Hollywood sex comedy is a mine of information about contemporary American attitudes to sex: a mine that never seems to get worked out, and never will be so long as changing social attitudes to sex and sex practices enable the writers to open up new seams at even deeper levels.

The sex comedy is predominantly a writers' cinema. It works by situation and especially by dialogue, if it works at all. The very nature of the sex relationships it deals in precludes a large number of players. But the same fact encourages inventiveness in manipulating the two or three archetypal Hollywood players for whom the roles are written. The stars associated with these roles are practically interchangeable. The writer's own inventiveness may give a character some of the distinctive touches of Rock Hudson, Cary Grant, Jack Lemmon or Tony Curtis. But too much individuality only destroys the stylised features of the hero, or the hero's pal (Tony Randall or Gig Young) or the heroine (Doris Day, Natalie Wood or Debbie Reynolds) and makes it that much more difficult to manipulate the sex-comedy formulae in new permutations. If they are rounder characters, a film with a much thicker social texture may emerge, and be a funnier comedy and a better film – such as Billy Wilder's *The Apartment*. But then it will hardly be what one means by a sex comedy.

The way in which the true sex comedy likes to use only a small, but custom-built, range of stars is proved whenever one of the archetypes is in short supply. Without a Judy Holliday or a Marilyn Monroe to personify good-natured dumbness or voluptuous innocence respectively, sex comedies constructed round these characteristics languished, or misfired, until Virna Lisi, an Italian sex symbol who resembled or was made to resemble Marilyn Monroe, was imported to play the bubble-brained beauty queen who turns Jack Lemmon's bachelor bliss into wedded hell in *How to Murder Your Wife*.

Nor are sex comedies a directors' cinema. Among directors who have successfully specialised in them are Richard Quine (*Sex and the Single Girl*, *How to Murder Your Wife*), Michael Gordon (*Pillow Talk*, *Move Over, Darling* (1963), *A Very Special Favour*), Norman Jewison (*The Thrill of It All* (1963), *Send Me No Flowers* (1964), and Delbert Mann (*That Touch of Mink*, *Lover Come Back*). Others like Billy Wilder (*The Seven Year Itch*, *Some Like It Hot*, *Kiss Me, Stupid*), Mark Robson (*Phffft* (1954)), Daniel Mann (*Who's Been Sleeping in My Bed?* (1963)) and Vincente Minnelli (*Goodbye Charlie* (1964)) are what could be called contributing directors, men with reputations already acquired in other genres. But the directors of sex comedies have to face the risk that any distinctive style they evolve may be so thickly overlaid by the house style of the studio they work for as to be almost undetectable. This is particularly true of films made by Gordon, Jewison and Delbert Mann for Universal, a studio which has specialised most successfully in sex comedies and romantic dramas coated with an impasto of production gloss.

There is another risk too. In many sex comedies the direction is subordinate to the work of the art designer. The decor and set dressing are made to add to the air of stylised realism that envelops a sex comedy: it is the same look that one sees, raised to its highest power, in TV commercials where everything not adding to the desired effect has been screened out in advance. Sex-comedy decor can also be used, as will be seen, to make manifest the sexual fantasies that the characters enjoy, or the sexual conflicts that make up the plot – so that in a film like *How to Murder Your Wife* it is the bachelor's home which is used literally to introduce the character played by Jack Lemmon and tell us what kind of man he is. A sex-comedy director must always be prepared to direct the scenery.

* * *

Ultimately it is the writer who is master of the revels. This is confirmed by the recent rise of two of the most inventive sex-comedy writers to be their own producers: George Axelrod and Stanley Shapiro. And what distinguishes the Hollywood sex comedies from the comedies involving sex which are made elsewhere in the world is precisely the angle at which the writer stands to society and sex. He is a sophisticate whose best scripts make their comments on sex and society inside a fairly rigorously prescribed comedy formula – just as the strip cartoons of Al Capp pack all kinds of contemporary observations into the churning *status quo* of Dogpatch. There are traces of a frustrated misogynist in the Hollywood sex-comedy writer. His sympathies lie with his own sex, but the sympathies of the box-office he serves are already rigged in favour of the women. It is surely significant that no woman has ever written a really stinging sex comedy. Claire Booth Luce wrote *The Women*, of course, but this scarcely qualifies, since it had no men in the cast – an opposite-sex comedy, perhaps. Metro-Goldwyn-Mayer who filmed it as written in 1939 later made good the absence of men in a 1956 remake entilted ambiguously *The*

Opposite Sex: it was not a success.

Above all, the Hollywood sex-comedy writer has a good working knowledge of psychiatry. Some screenplays sound as if they had been written by the scenarist in collaboration with his analyst. And in a sense, some of them have. For this kind of film, an analyst's couch is a most inspiring work-place. It is the very opposite of the mythical Procrustes bed. Instead of the person lying on it being cut down to the size that fits its dimensions, it has the capacity to accommodate any area of sexual experience that the writer wishes to explore with his analyst. There is this additional advantage: somehow life that seems a tragedy when one is upright becomes a comedy the moment one is lying down. Thus the material of the sex comedy comes from just those sexual problems which many Americans turn to their analysts for help in solving – impotence, frigidity, psychosomatic disorders, homosexuality, late pregnancy and change of sex, to mention a few. From these subjects are derived the tactics, grand strategy and very ammunition of the screen's sex war. This explains and dismisses the charge of 'bad taste' frequently levelled against the Hollywood sex comedy, since psychiatric consultants do not go out of their way to cater for taste, good or bad. 'Taste' is something one is supposed to leave in the anteroom and resume again on the way out. It is really irrelevant to the success or failure of a sex comedy.

The commonplaces of psychiatry leave contrail vapours across the conversation in any place where Americans gather to relax and talk; and this helps explain why the Hollywood film censors are far more tolerant of situations, innuendoes and lines of dialogue in sex comedies which they would not consider passing in more 'serious' films. (It also helps explain why, in a society less fliply oriented towards popular psychiatry, the British film censor views such comedies with more concern than they sometimes warrant.) A notorious example of this permissiveness on the part of the Hollywood censors occurs in the Shapiro-Monaster screenplay of *A Very Special Favour* when bachelor Rock Hudson gazes dreamily after the girl who is leaving his apartment with a skillet clasped to her bosom after cooking his breakfast, and rhapsodises, 'She says my eggs will touch no pan but hers.'

It is also easy to understand why analysts and analysis are the butt of malicious jokes in so many sex comedies. Either the writer has no personal experience of analysis and lets his mockery assert his healthy disrespect for it; or else he has been in analysis and feels the widespread human need to show his scars and regale his audience with the humours of the operation. The medieval painter of religious subjects used to place his patron in miniature among the saints; with less piety the Hollywood writer of sex comedies puts his analyst into the supporting cast.

* * *

Sex comedies can be divided into two classes. One can call them Sex and the Single Man comedies and Sex and the Married Man comedies. In both classes the protagonists are never fewer than two, rarely more than four, and most frequently, just three. In the first class they comprise the playboy, the bachelor girl and the hero's best pal: in the second class they comprise the husband, the wife and the other woman or the other man. The first is about seduction, the second about marriage. In the seduction comedies the male is trying to get the female where she belongs, which is in his bed: in the marriage comedies, the female is trying to get the male where he belongs, which is under her thumb. In both cases, the female wins. That is to say, she only allows herself to be seduced after marriage in the Single Man comedies, while in the Married Man comedies she only allows the man who is already her husband to seduce her. Every male in a sex comedy thinks that women exist for sex: that is his mistake. Every female in a sex comedy knows that she exists for marriage: that is her strength. The reasoning behind this is made clearer from the way that intercourse is regarded in all sex comedies emanating from Hollywood. As a character in *A Very Special Favour* puts it, 'In America they don't have sex: they commit it.' Sometimes even, when the wife is played by Doris Day whose screen image is that of a wholesome All-American girl, female filmgoers must be allowed to keep their illusion that she has never had intercourse at all, before or after marriage, the presence of small children notwithstanding. These, then, are the ground rules: now for the game and players.

Comedies of the Sex and the Single Man class begin by striking a defiant posture in favour of bachelorhood. 'As long as one of them's running around free, no woman is safe,' says one of the wives in *How to Murder Your Wife*. And what she means is not a maniac with a meat axe, but a red-blooded bachelor. The playboy hero seems really to justify the warning. From the composite picture provided by Rock Hudson, Frank Sinatra, Cary Grant and Tony Curtis at one time or another, he is handsome, oversexed, promiscuous and sophisticated, able to telephone two girls simultaneously and woo each with the same amorous monologue, and adept not only at taking a girl for a ride but also encouraging her to pay for the gas and leaving her feeling it was a privilege. In full male enjoyment of the double standard of morality, he lays siege to female chastity, sometimes resorting for assistance to push-button warfare in the shape of an automated apartment where the door locks itself, mood music comes in on cue and the settee flips out into a double-bed complete with turned-down sheets. Even the furnishings are an extension of his lechery. True to his origins in adolescent fantasies, the sex-comedy hero holds down only a narrow range of jobs, all with significant fantasy aspects, in ad agencies, paperback publishing, song writing, TV soap-opera, comic-strip illustration ... His only fear is a castrating apprehension of marriage, the tender trap.

The sex-comedy heroine is also anti-marriage at the start – or, rather anti-sex. Either she has never tried it – which is usually Doris Day's role – or else she is a demi-virgin, which means that she tried it once and didn't like it. Either way, she is wedded to her career. She dresses chicly, but is getting spinsterish round the edges. What bothers her is that holding down a man's job is making her less of a woman. When her job is that of a marriage counsellor, like Natalie Wood in *Sex and the Single Girl*, or a psychiatrist, like Leslie Caron in *A Very Special Favour*, the screenplay writers are able to score a double hit – once off women who have unfitted themselves to be wives, and again off advisers who teach others about sex and marriage but are scared of it themselves.

Third in the sex comedy's cast is the hero's best pal, and he is the most emotionally disturbed of the lot. Usually he is rich, idle, Ivy

League – and Tony Randall, when he is not Gig Young. If the playboy arouses the envy of male moviegoers, his buddy is there to make them feel superior again. For in everything to do with sex, this bland jellybaby is amiably incompetent or just plain cowardly. He is frequently undergoing analysis, and he is the patient every analyst dreams about having. 'Those poor people,' Randall says smugly in *Lover Come Back*, throwing a pitying glance at his office employees, 'they go through life convinced they're happy. They never realise how sick they are.' Either he has mother problems and keeps getting married to one girl after another in order to consummate his rebellion against his mother; or else he has father problems, has been frightened off sex and keeps on trying to re-assert his masculinity. In *Lover Come Back*, Randall makes his entry looking ostentatiously masterful and proceeds to prod the late-rising playboy (Rock Hudson) out of his bed with a walking stick given him by his analyst as a confidence-booster. Sleepily Rock grabs the phallic prop, breaks it in two, and Randall slumps into his usual traumatic jelly. Potency is not so easily mocked in sex comedies: either you've got it, or you haven't.

Sometimes the heroine has a girl-friend of her own who stands as an awful warning of what she will turn into if she misses out on marriage: a sharp-tongued, harsh-voiced, poker-faced, man-wary chaperone who may have a ring in her purse as a vestigial token of her availability still. She is an elder brother in skirts, the way the hero's best pal is a weak sister in trousers.

In fact, these supporting players personify the main aim of the sex comedy's principal sparring partners in the battle which is now ready to commence: it is to make each other neurotically unsure of their gender, their sex appeal and their potency. Round One in this contest is usually a clever bit of shaping-up to each other, though some sneaky jabs are landed on the female's sexual identity while her guard is down. With Rock Hudson monopolising the party line in *Pillow Talk* with his girl-talk, Doris Day's career girl applies for a telephone of her own – and finds that she only qualifies for one if she is pregnant. Beginning of inadequacy fears. In *Lover Come Back* the same two stars work for rival ad agencies. But while Doris burns the midnight oil preparing lay-outs, Rock oils prospective clients by laying on show girls. 'I don't use sex to steal an account,' she fumes. 'When do you use it?' he asks snidely. 'I don't,' jumps out of her mouth involuntarily. Freudian slips are common in the preliminary footwork, though this one is more felicitous than Natalie Wood's declaration in *Sex and the Single Girl* that she is 'going to teach the unmarried women of America to stop behaving like mice and start behaving like men' – which sounds like a slip followed by a crash.

In Round Two the scriptwriter's misogynist fist inside the male glove fairly rains blows down on the female until, thoroughly alarmed about her ingrown virginity, she is ready to fall into his arms, and so to bed. But to get thus far, the playboy must invariably adopt the most astonishing ploy in the entire sex-comedy game – he has to conceal his virility from the girl, sometimes to the point of unmanning himself. This stratagem gets more and more uninhibited in films between 1958 and 1965. It seems related to the loosening up of public reluctance to discuss 'embarrassing' problems like impotence; but it may also reflect the growing tolerance towards homosexuality in various areas of American life and the arts. *Pillow Talk* shows Rock Hudson masquerading as a Texan who squires Doris Day about town with the most gentlemanly display of manners; while at the same time Rock the playboy is planting doubts by telephone in her mind about her escort – and by implication herself. Yes, he *is* the perfect gentleman, but is that really flattering to her as a woman? When he refrains from kissing her, is it just because he respects her or is she really not his type? Of course, he *looks* virile enough, but can one be quite sure? Maybe he dotes on his mother and collects cook-book recipes. And sure enough, Rock's *alter ego* acts as cissily as predicted, and Doris gets panicky. After making men keep their distance for so long, has she now fallen for one with no urge to come hither?

Lover Come Back, the sequel to *Pillow Talk*, stretches her on the same old-maid's rack while Rock swaps his ad man's grey-flannels for rustic tweeds and a porcupine beard, poses as a country bumpkin, a kind of Adam before the apple, and makes her take him round town and show him what sophisticated folk do. This involves a visit to a strip show which makes her blush – not so much for her sex, one feels, as at sex itself. *A Very Special Favour* tortures the repressed career woman with the same fear of unrepressed sexuality when the playboy – Rock Hudson again – confides in Leslie Caron's frigid psychiatrist that women simply will not leave him alone ('What I'd give to have a body nobody wants') and then makes her believe that too much champagne turns her into a rampant nymphomaniac like the others. Discovering his trick, she hits back at his most vulnerable area by pretending to take on a prodigiously endowed lover with whom he is too poorly equipped to compete. He ripostes by pretending that her indifference has turned him homosexual. No longer is this trick just a matter of *Pillow Talk*'s oblique suggestiveness, of mother, cook-book recipes and drinking tea with the little finger raised. Rock openly dresses up a girl-friend in boy's clothes – 'I always wanted to be part of a triangle,' she says, 'but I never thought I'd be the other man' – and moves into a motel with the 'young fellow' to wait for Leslie Caron to come rushing round to rescue him with kisses and psychotherapy. This is possibly the first time that inversion appears, at star level, anyhow, in post-war Hollywood comedy. (The stars of *Some Like It Hot* are not inverts, but involuntary female impersonators.) Short of feigning a sex change, the sex comedy hero has now gone about as far as he can go in getting his girl by self-emasculation – if he still wants to be able to enjoy the prize, that is.

* * *

Pretending to be impotent was the rake's classic trick for getting the bed-sheets opened to him; but recent sex comedies employ it more clinically than in the days when Marilyn Monroe, with not an impure suspicion in her head, sportingly offered to help Tony Curtis overcome this disability in *Some Like It Hot*. Five years later, in *Sex and the Single Girl*, clinical psychiatry has set its brand rawly on the altruistic innocence of the same situation. Now it is the woman who has to be sexually stimulated. And the same actor, Tony Curtis, faking the same affliction – called 'acute shyness' in Hollywoodese – solicits the sympathy of Natalie Wood's marriage counsellor so effectively that simply itemising the erogenous areas of the body for him acts as an aphrodisiac on her.

But the sex comedy employs some other stock stimulants and tranquillisers. The commonest are alcohol and immersion, either partial (as in a rain shower) or total (as in a river or lake). Approved by the Hollywood censors, these plot ploys apparently are the only permissible ways in which adult people in sex comedies who are not wedded to each other can get on intimate terms. Before clothes are discarded, for example, they first have to be wet. Hence the high incidence of couples getting caught in cloudbursts over Manhattan, or falling in the Hudson river, and having to repair to one of their respective apartments to dry off. The logic is that couples who shed dry clothes have only one thing on their minds, whereas couples who strip off wet clothes have two, the other being pneumonia. Sex in this case is officially deemed to be a side-effect of avoiding one's death of cold. It is unglamorous, but practical. Similarly couples who are shown waking up in bed together, to their mutual surprise, are invariably found to have gone to bed drunk. Somewhat later they usually recall enough of the night before to discover that they got married anyway: so the film has it both ways. The world protrayed in the Hollywood sex comedy is one where sex, illicit or marital, is hardly able to be achieved sober. The career girl who decides to give in to the playboy fortifies her resolution till it is 70% proof; the frigid type who has to be thawed out in one night is fed champagne and then tall storiesabout her liberated libido till she believes she is a man-eater; even the young newly-weds with 'bedroom problems' in *Never Too Late* (1965) sneak off to a motel in mid-afternoon with a *vin blanc* for a last try at inducing a pregnancy – as if they were plotting a guilty assignation, not planning a family.

Liquor has a double advantage for a scriptwriter: a little of it goes to the heroine's head and puts her virtue titillatingly in danger, while too much of it lays her out flat but insensible and puts her purity beyond jeopardy. (An unspoken assumption of sex comedies is that no man ever takes advantage of an incapable woman.) This may not be wildly inventive, but at least it is a more sightly prophylactic than the psychosomatic rash that Doris Day develops in *That Touch of Mink* to keep Cary Grant outside her bedroom door when they have flown to Bermuda together. (At the end of the film, the tables are turned: it is the husband whom the fear of marriage brings out in spots.)

The sex comedy's last round is a short, but active one; and the fight which up to then has gone the man's way ends with a knock-out or a points decision for the female. The reason for this is brutally simple: 80% of the audiences for sex comedies are married women. So male pride and potency have to get hurt in order to flatter the female vanity and self-assurance. Arousing jealousy is the heroine's standard strategy, exemplified by Doris Day checking into a motel with a willing man-friend in *That Touch of Mink* so as to make Cary Grant green-eyed. *Pillow Talk* is hardly less rough on Rock Hudson. 'At least my bedroom problems can be solved in one bedroom,' Doris Day flings at him, 'you couldn't solve yours in a thousand bedrooms.' And to rub in her meaning she re-decorates his mechanised seduction pad as a flashy brothel, all bead curtains and bulbous Cupids, with an African fertility symbol jeering superciliously at him.

One American phenomenon that has caused the Single Man class of sex comedy to throw out a sub-group has been the enormous success of the Playboy clubs and magazine, founded by Hugh Hefner, from the mid-1950s on, as a highly profitable enterprise with a proselytising philosophy for the unattached but available male. Hefner has propagated a hedonistic view of sex which is Hollywood fantasy made manifest. He has shown the same artfulness as the sex comedy in giving the sensation of sex, but none of the satisfaction. Hefner's handmaidens are the Playboy bunnies who staff the clubs: but the chief characteristic of the rabbit, which is its fertility, is the one never referred to in any discussion of these scantily-clad, cotton-tailed Playmates. They are strictly for show, sex symbols who flatter the male ego. Hefner's real invention, as Tom Wolfe remarked, is living in a self-controlled environment created for man's pleasure. In other words, being able to rule over a harem. The 'harem' is in fact localised in the Playboy Mansion, Chicago, which is the commercial capital of the organisation, but also the play centre of its lord and master who keeps open house twenty-four hours a day, resides in bachelor splendour under a floor and a half of bunnies' dormitories, and toils over the so-called

Playboy 'philosophy' from a cross-legged position on an eight and a half foot circular, motor-driven, rotatable, vibratable bed.

Now the harem theme in films goes back at least as far as Cecil B. de Mille's Babylonian tableaux. But Hollywood comedies from the mid-1950s on – from the time of *The Tender Trap* (1955), that is – tend increasingly to emulate the peculiarly self-centred and adolescent, though admittedly intriguing, Playboy environment in which boy does not meet girl any longer, but has girls there all the time. The films cluster thickly round the 1960s, when the Playboy idea was in seed. Rock Hudson in *Come September* (1961) finds himself landed with a *palazzo* of co-eds when he sneaks off to Europe to enjoy his fall vacation with Gina Lollobrigida. Dean Martin in *Who's Been Sleeping in My Bed?* plays a TV soap opera idol harassed for sympathy by his neighbours' sex-starved wives. Tony Curtis and Jerry Lewis in *Boeing Boeing* (1966) are found maintaining a between-flights roosting place for airline stewardesses. But the most symptomatic of all those films is surely *Under the Yum-Yum Tree* (1963), in which the usually innocent Jack Lemmon plays the lecherous landlord of Centaur Apartments which he rents only to young women, retains a key for every front door and has his own guest room papered in blood red, furnished with a double bed the size of a small yacht and equipped with automated violins. 'All this exotic decor has an overpoweringly romantic effect on girls who've never been in the house before,' is not a line of dialogue from *Under the Yum-Yum Tree*, though it might well be one. It is simply a Hefner executive on the monochromatic spell cast over its guests by the Red Room apartments in the Playboy Mansion. Those who urge Hugh Hefner to turn film producer miss the point: Hollywood's dream factory has scarcely improved on his make of dream, from which the sex comedies increasingly borrow.

* * *

If Stanley Shapiro is the most distinctive champion of the ruttish bachelor, George Axelrod is a one-man defence league for the cowed husband. There is no more inventive specialist in comedies of the Sex and the Married Man class. The most celebrated of them is, of course, *The Seven Year Itch*, which dealt with the American husband's urge to change wives every seven years. Ten years after writing it, Axelrod produced a film about the American husband's urge to kill his wife almost daily. Plainly he is a man who does not let his thinking stand still. But to chart the course of such a progressive artist is to realise how little room marriage comedies leave for sexual manoeuvring, compared with bachelor free-for-alls – if only because the hero of the former starts the film where the hero of the latter ends it, on the wrong side of the bars. The inventiveness lies in the break-out he stages.

His situation is usually dire. No matter how desirable or glamorous his wife is, she has reduced him to a state of dependence. If the couple have children, be sure they have been brainwashed into disrespect for the nominal head of the house by a game of matriarchal make-believe – e.g., 'Let's make believe Daddy's smart, even if we know he's an idiot.' Every neighbourhood, be it ever so law-abiding, has a flourishing Mafia run by local wives and their married girl-friends and aimed at keeping down their menfolk in particular and man in general. Evidence of this is bloodcurdingly plentiful. 'I heard what you said!' Claire Trevor barks at her baffled mate in Axelrod's *How to Murder Your Wife*, even though the poor sap has been in the next room at the time and she could have heard nothing. 'Need to control him,' she explains to another wife a moment later. 'Simply a matter of keeping him off balance. Men are always as guilty as hell about something.' It is true that Leslie Caron is not married to Dick Shawn in *A Very Special Favour* when she says, 'You're not using that dandruff brush I bought you.' But from this remark, who could tell? Its blend of solicitude, rebuke and humiliation is the authentic marriage song of the Hollywood housewife. Any bachelor in this branch of comedy is, as already stated, regarded with as much suspicion as a homicidal maniac. No woman considers herself safe till he has been married off. But no husband need imagine that his wife's marriage vows mean anything more than that, having made them, she can now consider herself truly independent 'to enjoy the good things of life . . . spend money and have little affairs and still be taken care of.'

Axelrod's most characteristic screenplays all chronicle the revolt of the serfs. And the fact that although they are anti-marriage they end up accepting it in order to gratify female filmgoers does not blunt the main attack. His screenplay for *Phfft* was very underrated at the time, 1954, perhaps because of the film's absurd title. *Phfft* is the sound made by an expiring marriage, in this case that of Jack Lemmon and Judy Holliday who have been married for the ominous seven years and now agree on a friendly separation – after first quarrelling fiercely about who thought of the idea. Directed by Mark Robson, *Phfft* first of all attacks marriage by sanctifying divorce. It transfers all the woozy platitudes people utter at weddings to every part of the un-wedding at Reno. 'Oh, what a beautiful divorce,' sobs their lawyer. 'They hated each other, and that's all that matters.' Even the sacred institution of the First Anniversary telegram is venomously traduced by Lemmon's cable, 'REMEMBER WHAT DAY IT IS?' sent on the eve of the final decree.

Once freed from his wife, the ex-husband goes into a kind of recuperation and is nursed back to virility and the full life by a bachelor buddy with such remedial hobbies as painting, dancing, girls, fast cars and moustache-growing. But on hearing his lecherous pal is making a play for his ex-wife, Lemmon dashes to the rescue; and reconciliation follows. The ostensible box-office moral is that even divorce enhances the value of marriage; and it is one that will go down big in Upper Sandusky, the home of the small-town virtues from which Doris Day so often comes in screen life. But the real moral that Axelrod implies is much more worldly and cynical: it is that even when divorced, the American male cannot shake himself free of the woman he stays mentally hitched to. His instincts tell him to head for the prairies, all his reflexes take him back to the corral.

Film censorship frustrated Axelrod's next screenplay, *The Seven Year Itch*, in using the stage situation of the meek and mild husband, played by Tom Ewell, actually having an affair with the upstairs blonde. Now he only sins in fantasy. This is a pity. For while the timid soul's imagination soars to the heights of adulterous fantasy, his body remains at ground level. His fastest pass is the one he makes while they memorably pick out Chopsticks on the piano; and he immediately repents of it. There is a lot that is comic in the film, nothing at all that is carnal. Conventional marriage values are upheld in the end and it would be straining for irony to conclude that *The Seven Year Itch* shows how an understanding mistress makes a man into a better husband. For the film's enforced aura of fantasy keeps Marilyn Monroe not just a platonic sex symbol, but practically an ectoplasmic one. The real, cruel moments in the film's view of marriage are the early ones that catch Tom Ewell alone, emerging from his hen-pecked state now that his hen has been packed off to the country for the summer months with the family. Cautiously he begins to utter the crows of a summer bachelor – but what weak ones they are! Not to have to come home and smell the vegetables cooking. Not to have a hard day at the office and then be quizzed about it over dinner. Happiness for this life-time husband is not a release on parole, but simply an improvement in prison conditions.

One could have imagined from *The Seven Year Itch* that life with a wife is sheer hell simply because she is not Marilyn Monroe. Axelrod might have written his bitterest screenplay so far expressly to disabuse one of this notion. For Virna Lisi, the Italian star whom an inebriated Jack Lemmon marries in *How to Murder Your Wife* when she jumps out of a cake at a stag supper, is as near Monroe's double as could be found in a month's casting. But life with her is cruel disillusionment.

Up to then Lemmon's existence has been a work of art. His Manhattan house is such a living example of bachelor luxury that it is almost a character in the movie. To nurse him, he has the perfect manservant, always at hand to see the morning shower precisely matches his master's body temperature and the evening Martini has just the right chill on it. Women come and go, of course, but are always gone before he wakes up. He enjoys a vicarious virility, too, since before drawing his fabulously successful strip, 'Bash Brannigan, Secret Agent', he acts out the adventures in the streets of New York. Marriage brings this Paradise crashing down round him. The film is a heartless catalogue of all the ways that women erode a man's spirit. Underneath the meticulously sophisticated surface comedy one feels there exists a bottomless reservoir of misogynist savagery. His new wife looks everything that a man can desire carnally. But she behaves like a malign poltergeist threatening his male self-sufficiency. She drives out his manservant, turns his home into a chintzy horror, hangs her nylons like suffragette banners over his bath-tub and a sign saying 'DANGER – MEN DRINKING' over the bar which could become the flashpoint of marital revolt. She spoils his man-about-town figure by over-feeding him, and she even emasculates his strip cartoon into a soggy family serial called 'The Brannigans'.

If the film had been made in the best of all possible worlds for screenplay writers – i.e., one with no box-office to appease – one feels Lemmon's wife would not have been reprieved from the death penalty promised by the title. As it is, the murder plan he roughs out never gets off the drawing board, though it lands him on a charge of suspected homicide. But his murderous indictment of feminist domination – 'Marriage is not a basic form of nature, it's an invention . . . it exists only because the women say so' – wins him an acquittal from the all-male jury and speaks more violently than the act itself. And this time Axelrod's fantasy does not pull the sting out of his wife-baiting. The happy – i.e., pro-feminist – ending is there all right for those who need it and will see no other: husband and wife are united at the fade-out, and her Italian mother is imported to keep the manservant happy in his work. But the urge that drives Lemmon back into his wife's arms is fairly basic, mainly biological and in all likelihood of short duration. Man cannot live without women, the film is saying, but he cannot live married to one, either.

* * *

This sour, defiant comedy may mark an upturn in the steadily falling graph of male supremacy as measured by the Hollywood marriage comedies over the last ten years. Marriage is the female's revenge for all she has to suffer in the seduction comedies; and there is hardly another marriage comedy which does not show her enjoying it. Her husband's role is generally that of a compliant stooge right from the fade-in. *Send Me No Flowers* bases its morbidly funny script, by Julius Epstein, on the notion of casting a he-man like Rock Hudson as a chronic hypochondriac who believes he is not long for this world and, being a well-broken-in husband, resolves to leave it with the minimum inconvenience to his wife, Doris Day – even to the extent of lining up a new mate for her to marry 'after what her Bridge club decides is a decent interval'. In *The Thrill of It All*, the husband is a professionally promising gynaecologist who has to take a back seat when his wife, Doris Day again, becomes the object of national adulation for doing TV commercials for 'Happy Soap'. It is only pregnancy, the male's last weapon, which restores the balance of that marriage. Still greater power devolves on Polly Bergen in *Kisses for My President* (1964) in which she is elected the first woman President of the United States, making America a matriarchy in name as well as fact. Significantly there is no place under the Constitution for the husband of the Chief Executive. And again it is only pregnancy that prematurely terminates her term of office: her husband, it would seem, has to arrange a political abortion as the last hope of regaining his marital rights.

The matriarchal pattern in Hollywood sex comedies duplicates the steady inroads that women have made into the male's political, economic and sexual rights in America at large. In all the sex comedies, whether about seduction or marriage, the man gets weaker and more febrile or impotent, while the woman gets more masculine and dominant. The apotheosis of the trend is visible in Axelrod's screenplay for *Goodbye Charlie* in which Tony Curtis's lecherous buddy Charlie is shot by a jealous husband just before the film opens and comes back reincarnated in the shape of Debbie Reynolds – a male spirit in a female body, arousing all kinds of libidinous attraction and guilty recoil on the part of Curtis. Even the minor sex jokes in the sex comedies tend to display the sexual ambiguousness of the man's role. Rock Hudson in *Pillow Talk* makes a running joke out of hiding from Doris Day in the office of an obstetrician, in circumstances that make the doctor think that parthenogenesis has arrived and a man is going to have a baby. The same joke is repeated, as a result of garbled radio-cab messages, in *Strange Bedfellows* (1963).

At the same time as the hero's sexual identity is getting blurred on the screen, the American male is losing his sexual status in society. The latter development is simply the real-life extension of the former into the sphere of employment. Since the Voting Rights Act came into force, in mid-1965, it has been an offence in America to discriminate against the applicant for a job on the grounds of race, colour, creed – *or sex*. This wholly new provision, affecting all U.S. employers of 100 or more workers (and soon to be reduced to twenty-five or more), makes it unlawful, for example, to treat jobs as specifically men's or women's work unless the sex of the employee is an essential part of the requirements. It makes it illegal to forbid the hiring of married women unless the same rule applies to married men. Nor is it lawful to publish separate male and female lists of help-wanted advertisements without a disclaimer that the law prohibits sex bias. The plot complications that such a law as this offers the writers of sex comedies can easily be imagined. At the end of 1965, for example, two prostitutes had appealed against their convictions, alleging they were the victims of sex bias because their male clients had not been charged along with them. It is a made-to-order situation for Billy Wilder and his long-time collaborator, I. A. L. Diamond. And what opportunities for misogynist ridicule, female *hubris* and male *angst* will Shapiro or Axelrod squeeze out of a law like this when they run it through their comic wringers?

The satisfying awareness it gives women of being in control of their menfolk is thus one reason why the Hollywood sex comedy appeals to large female audiences, while the menfolk can relish vicariously the sexiness of the jokes and basic situations. But there is another reason why women are attracted to sex comedies. It is connected with their own sexual insecurity. For many years the most popular sex comedy star in America has been Doris Day. Many of her films were made in collaboration with her producer-writer husband, Martin Melcher, and her image has been as astutely manufactured for its market as many a desirable consumer product. What she sells is female virtue, the idea that wholesomeness pays off handsomely. She is kept deliberately low on sex appeal. Even at forty, she has a boyish figure and face and no mammary expansion beyond the normal. Women therefore do not see her as a threat to themselves or their menfolk, as they might see Virna Lisi or Natalie Wood. Indeed Doris Day's appeal is not at all localised: she is liked by many women in all age groups, and by not a few men. And this is at a time when sexual permissiveness in society is running at such a pitch that many women are reported to feel themselves inadequate to make the response they believe that men expect from them. To such women, Doris Day must be infinitely reassuring.

She is no loose-liver on the screen: that is certain. But neither is she a prig. Whenever she does act with undue prudishness, like averting her eyes at the strip show in *Lover Come Back*, one suspects that this touch, as well as being put in for its humour, can only make certain types of women filmgoers feel complacently aware of their own broad-mindedness. Doris Day has sex without being sexy. Her screen wardrobe is calculated to counter Rock Hudson's calumny of old-maidishness by endowing her with the kind of chic simplicity that looks as if it could be bought on Main Street – until one tries to buy it. Above all, she gets her man without the strain of being sexually over-eager; and this is much more compatible with the normal woman's aptitude and talents before and after marriage.

Yet the Doris Day character has another little twist to her that completes her endearing image for women. She *can* be a bully, she *does* show her claws, she *will* release her aggressiveness – but always against the man who has tried to do her wrong. And the revenge she exacts by forcing him into humiliation, remorse and finally marriage is the sweetest part of the satisfaction she gives her sex. Rock Hudson, Cary Grant, Jack Lemmon, Tony Curtis and the rest. They stand there, each of them, in all their glorious manhood before marriage – 'like a tree in the forest . . . independent, an entity unto himself.' Yet they are doomed from the start, the victims of the sex comedies, perhaps to be permitted one last request before they are chopped down. If they are wise, it will be: 'Don't bury me next to a woman.'

ACKNOWLEDGMENTS: PERSONAL AND GENERAL

I owe thanks for their suggestions, advice, and help in obtaining illustrations and viewing films to: Margot, Lady Davson, Signor Ricardo Aragno, Dr S. H. Lucas, Sir Anthony Glyn, Bart, Mr Eric Hiscock, Mr James Card (Vice-Director, George Eastman House), Mr Christer Frunck (Head of Information, Swedish Film Institute), Mr Philip Jenkinson, Mr Kevin Brownlow, Miss Vivienne Richardson, Mr Cleland Rimmer, Mr William Gilbert (BBC TV), Mr Rowland Elzea (Curator of Collections, The Wilmington Society of Fine Arts), Mr Ernest Lindgren (Curator, National Film Archive), Mr Leslie Hardcastle (General Manager, National Film Theatre), Miss Mary Herscott (Director of Publicity, Gala Films), Mr Gerald Lewis (Director of Publicity, Paramount Film Service), Mr Leonard Samson (Director of Publicity, Warner-Pathé Distributors), Mr Charles Young and Mr Geoffrey Watkins (Director of Publicity and Press Officer respectively, Rank Film Distributors, U.K. Division), Mr Edward A. Patman (Director of Publicity, Metro-Goldwyn-Mayer Pictures), Mr William Chalmers (Managing Director, Planet Films), Mr Louis Blaine (Director of Publicity, Universal Studios, Hollywood), and to the research staffs at the Tate Gallery, Westminster Public Reference Library, New York Public Library and the recently closed and much missed United States Information Services Library, London.

I must express a particularly heavy debt of gratitude to Mr Stanley Read, the Director, and his staff at the British Film Institute, especially for the help I received from the Archive Cataloguing Department, the Book, Information and Stills Libraries, and the National Film Archive who, with Studio Corot, prepared frame enlargements from many of the films viewed.

Permission to quote from the following works is gratefully acknowledged:

The Autobiography of Cecil B. de Mille (W. H. Allen & Co.).

Elinor Glyn by Anthony Glyn (Hutchinson).

Elizabeth Taylor by Ruth Waterbury (Robert Hale).

The Face on the Cutting Room Floor by Murray Schumach (William Morrow & Co.). Copyright 1964 by Murray Schumach.

The Films of Greta Garbo compiled by Michael Conway, Don McGregor and Mark Ricci, with an introduction by Parker Tyler (Citadel Press).

Fun in a Chinese Laundry by Josef von Sternberg (The Macmillan Co. of New York and Secker & Warburg Ltd).

Garbo by John Bainbridge (Frederick Muller Ltd).

Garbo by Fritiof Billquist (Arthur Barker).

Goodness Had Nothing To Do With It: The Autobiography of Mae West (W. H. Allen & Co.).

Harlow: An Intimate Biography by Irving Shulman (Mayflower/Dell), by permission of the author and Scott Meredith Literary Agency.

The Italians by Luigi Barzini (Hamish Hamilton Ltd)

Judgment at Nuremburg by Abby Mann (Cassell & Co. Ltd).

Lolita by Vladimir Nabokov (Weidenfeld & Nicolson Ltd).

Marilyn Monroe by Maurice Zolotow (W. H. Allen & Co.).

A Million and One Nights by Terry Ramsaye (3rd imp. 1964, Simon & Schuster, Inc., New York; Frank Cass & Co. Ltd, London).

The Public Is Never Wrong by Adolph Zukor (G. P. Putnam's Sons). Copyright 1953 by Adolph Zukor.

The Real and the Unreal by Bill Davidson (Harper & Row, Inc.).

The Rise of the American Film by Lewis Jacob (Harcourt Brace & Co.).

Romantic Adventure by Elinor Glyn (Ivor Nicholson and Watson Ltd).

The Stars by Edgar Morin (Transatlantic Book Services).

Sunshine and Shadow: The Autobiography of Mary Pickford (William Heinemann Ltd).

Upton Sinclair Presents William Fox (published by the author).
When the Movies Were Young by Linda Arvidson [Mrs D. W. Griffith] (E. P. Dutton & Co. Inc.).
The first stanza of Rudyard Kipling's poem, *The Vampire*, is reproduced by permission of Mrs George Bambridge, Methuen & Co. Ltd, and The Macmillan Co. of Canada.

Gratitude is expressed to the Editors and Proprietors of the following newspapers and periodicals for quotations acknowledged in the text: *Evening Standard*, *The Sunday Times*, *The Daily Telegraph*, *The Stage*, *Variety*, *Pictureshow*, *Picturegoer*, *Films in Review*, *Image*, *Photoplay*, *Sight and Sound*, *Films and Filming*, *Newsweek*.

Acknowledgment is made to the following film distribution companies for the use of illustrations: Gala Films, Metro-Goldwyn-Mayer, Paramount, Planet Films, Rank-Universal, Twentieth Century-Fox, United Artists, Warner-Pathé.

Elinor Glyn's illustration for the frontispiece of *Three Weeks* is reproduced by the kindness of Margot, Lady Davson.
The photograph of the author on the jacket is by Peter Sellers.

INDEX